ASSET PEDAGOGIES IN LATINO YOUTH IDENTITY AND ACHIEVEMENT

Asset Pedagogies in Latino Youth Identity and Achievement explores the theory, research, and application of asset-based pedagogies to counter approaches that fail to challenge deficit views of youth. Presenting details on the role of teachers' knowledge about students' language and culture as strengths as opposed to deficiencies, Francesca A. López connects classroom practices to positive outcomes, preparing teachers to use asset pedagogies to promote academic achievement and implement asset-based teaching practices. Making thorough use of examples from research both in and out of the classroom and concluding with concrete applications from experienced educators, this book provides future teachers with a critical understanding of how to support Latino youth.

Francesca A. López is Associate Professor of Education Policy Studies & Practice at the University of Arizona, USA.

ASSET PEDAGOGIES IN LATINO YOUTH IDENTITY AND ACHIEVEMENT

Nurturing Confianza

Francesca A. López

Routledge
Taylor & Francis Group

NEW YORK AND LONDON

First published 2018
by Routledge
711 Third Avenue, New York, NY 10017

and by Routledge
2 Park Square, Milton Park, Abingdon, Oxon, OX14 4RN

Routledge is an imprint of the Taylor & Francis Group, an informa business

Library of Congress Cataloging-in-Publication Data
A catalog record for this book has been requested

ISBN: 978-1-138-91141-3 (hbk)
ISBN: 978-1-138-91142-0 (pbk)
ISBN: 978-1-315-69271-5 (ebk)

Typeset in Bembo
by Deanta Global Publishing Services, Chennai, India

CONTENTS

CONTRIBUTORS

Mictlani González has served Tucson Unified School District (TUSD) for twenty-three years as a bilingual teacher, minority student recruitment specialist for gifted and talented education programs, curriculum specialist in the Mexican American/Raza Studies Department, Interim Director of the Mexican American/Raza Studies Department, Cultural and Multicultural Integrationist, and Program Coordinator for Culturally Relevant Pedagogy and Instruction. In Chapter 7, she describes the components of her Indigenous epistemology–informed methodology that she terms Culturally Humanizing Pedagogy, which nurtures student academic and cultural identity.

José Alberto González, a former TUSD Mexican American Studies teacher, presents his asset-based pedagogical approach to education, which at its core is centered on a pedagogy of love that centralizes the lived experiences of his barrio students. In Chapter 8, he intertwines critical race theory and critical pedagogy with aims to foster students' critical awareness with the intent to empower his students to navigate, challenge, and assert their humanity in a schooling apparatus rife with social practices, formation, and discursive oppression. In his chapter, he explains the role of Critical Race Theory on his pedagogy, which centralizes the experiences of his students and informs all classroom interactions (curricular and interpersonal).

Isabel Kelsey is an experienced elementary teacher of more than twenty years. She has taught kindergarten through fifth grade students in mainstream, bilingual and English Language Developmental (ELD) settings. In Chapter 9, she describes her experiences and educational background that influenced her Culturally Responsive Practices in K–5 classrooms.

Julie Elvick was born and has lived her entire life in Tucson, Arizona. After attending Tucson Unified School District schools and the University of Arizona, Julie began teaching in the Tucson Unified School District, and has done so for nearly three decades. Currently, she teaches fifth grade. In Chapter 10, she details her continuing journey toward developing a pedagogy of teaching and learning centered on Indigenous philosophy and Reggio-Emilia asset-based pedagogy as a teacher who works with children from ethnic and socio-cultural backgrounds different from her own.

Alexandro "Salo" Escamilla has served TUSD for sixteen years as a teacher of reading, writing and social studies at the middle and high school levels; project specialist for the Mexican American/Raza Studies Department; and an itinerant teacher for Culturally Relevant Pedagogy and Instruction. In Chapter 11, he describes the components for culturally relevant curriculum and culturally responsive pedagogy based the ideals of Chicanismo and carnalismo that were established during el movimiento ("the movement").

ACKNOWLEDGMENTS

My journey conducting the research highlighted in this book would never have happened if it were not for the numerous individuals who opened doors for me along the way. In my academic journey, mentors who guided me in developing skills and critically examining issues made the possibility for the research to develop. All the errors and omissions, however, remain my own. Among the great minds who so graciously shared of their expertise in ways they may never really know are Ruben Donato, Kathy Escamilla, Jessica Decuir-Gunby, Susan Faircloth, Patricia Gándara, Gene García, Gene Glass, Norma Gónzalez, Kris Gutiérrez, Etta Kralovec, Carol Lee, Robert Lowe, Amado Padilla, Darrell Sabers, Geoffrey Saxe, Paul Schutz, Deborah Stipek, Angela Valenzuela, and Guadalupe Valdés. Thank you for being amazing scholars who give so much of yourselves to others. I am proud to carry out my work on the shoulders of giants.

I am also grateful for the funding that allowed me to undertake an otherwise seemingly impossible task. The National Academy of Education/Spencer Postdoctoral Fellowship, as well as the University of Arizona College of Education Erasmus Fellowship, made it possible for me to carry out the research in ways that would have been impossibly prohibitive without the funding.

Upon arriving in Tucson, Arizona, with a funded study but no relationships with schools, it was Ron Marx—then Dean of the College of Education at the University of Arizona—who opened the doors to the Tucson Unified School District. Without his leadership and commitment to public education, I know I would have had a much more difficult time being able to carry out the research I had proposed. Ron introduced me to Augustin (Auggie) Romero, then Director of Multicultural Curriculum, to whom I am eternally thankful for literally walking me to potential school sites. Auggie introduced me to school principals so that I could explain my study, with the hope that they would see the merit in the additional time I would be asking of their teachers. Luckily for me, I met some of the most caring and giving individuals who are part of the reason I now call Tucson "home." C.C., M.C., I.K., L.D., and R.O.—schools were more like home with their leadership. In fact, I do not exaggerate when I say I often felt more like I was visiting my own tías, tíos, primas, and primos when I visited school sites. I am also grateful to Heliodoro T. Sanchez and Dynah Oviedo, who each played instrumental roles in my ability to carry out the research.

Balancing the multiple demands of the academy at times feels like walking on a tightrope, but not when there are colleagues and friends who are like family. I am indebted to Carol Brochin, Nolan Cabrera, Regina Deil-Amen, Kevin Lawrence Henry, Jr., Jill Koyama, Andrea Romero, and Sara Tolbert for their support and friendship. A special thank you to Regina for comments (and encouragement) on earlier versions of this book.

I was lucky enough to have a group of incredible burgeoning scholars who provided meticulous research support in a variety of capacities: Charlene Bruce, Benjamin Caldera, Angela Champion, Mitzy Ocegueda González, Amy Olson, Veronica Romo, Ruby Vega, and Marylyn Valencia. I am indebted to them for their tireless efforts and persistence.

Before I was an academic, I was a bilingual elementary teacher. Luis, Sarahi, David, Ana Rosa, Oscar, Ricardo, Jaime, Jacqueline, Itzel, Antonio, Maura … you made me want to be better. You transformed my life's purpose, wherever you might be.

I am also indebted to Norma González, José González, and Lorenzo López, doctoral students at the University of Arizona. Their commitment to youth in the Tucson Unified School District, and their extraordinary depth of knowledge— which they graciously share—was transformational for me. You exemplify courage in the face of adversity, and truly represent the Mexican proverb, *They tried to bury us. They didn't know we were seeds.* I know I am blessed to have been able to work with each of you.

Although they are no longer with us, I would not be the person I am (or care so deeply about the research in this book) had it not been for my mother, Marta Iglesias, and my grandparents, Pedro Quintana and Adelisa Lucero. Adelisa had the gift of making me feel truly welcome each and every time I visited; Pedro made *everyone* feel like they were the most important person in the world. I treasure these qualities for what they gave me growing up, and what I try to emulate because of them. My childhood memories are snapshots of love: lunches where many of us gathered (my mother was one of eight children—so there were *many* of us when cousins were included) to savor not only the meal, but each other's company. I long for the days that are now but memories. The last time I had the opportunity to speak with my grandmother was after my mother's death, where we both struggled to find words. She had lost her eldest daughter (and passed away just six months later), and I had lost my mother. We both knew the deep sorrow we each felt, and it only made the sadness that much more painful. I have tried to live with their spirit guiding me in the most difficult of times. To Marta, I owe the aspiration to be as courageous, loving, and strong as she was. There is not a day that goes by that I do not think of her—she is in many ways a huge part of this book.

It is true what they say—that we don't accomplish anything on our own. It was my husband, Javier, whose encouragement and partnership helped me endure the most seemingly impossible of endeavors. We juggled a difficult balance of work and children along our careers, which took us far from our extended network of support. There is no one in this world whom I know I can rely on as much as him. He has risked quite a bit to allow me to pursue my academic goals, and I am eternally grateful for his belief in me. I would not be who I am without him or our children, Javiercito, Diego, and Anni. They forced me to keep a firm grounding on what truly matters in this life. Javiercito, my intellectual deliberator, helps me see our world though his (now) adolescent eyes. Diego, who was nicknamed "Mr. Contreras" by my cousin because he will argue the "contrary" of whatever is being said, has given me the gift of seeing things in more than one way. Anni's sense of justice has been a salient marker in her personality from her toddler years. I can't help but see so much of my mother in her. And it is for her, as well as Diego and Javier, that I so firmly believe that the work represented in this book—not just my own, but the giants whose work informed my own work—must transform classrooms for our youth.

FOREWORD

> ...the most viable multicultural teacher education programs combine moral convictions and courage, critical analyses, and political activism with high-quality curriculum and instruction in advocacy and in responding to opposition.
>
> *(Gay, 2005, p. 224)*

Responding to the urgent and pressing need for teacher education programs that can bring together critical analyses with high quality curriculum, Francesca A. López offers conclusive policy recommendations that could and should be heeded by stakeholders at levels. *Asset Pedagogies in Latino Youth Identity and Achievement: Nurturing Confianza* is an open invitation to reconsider and resolutely address how Latino youth, especially emergent bilinguals, have been inequitably disenfranchised historically and persistently.

This book hits all the right notes in the carefully detailed background of politics and policies that have impacted Latino youth in Arizona. However, the incisive analysis and documentation of one particular school district, Tucson Unified (TUSD) propels this book into the 'must-read' list of teacher educators, policy makers and parents. López, in a keen and penetrating analysis of a four-decade-old desegregation case, captures the nuanced profile of TUSD (and other majority-minority urban districts), and argues persuasively that desegregation orders can run counter to the spirit of *Brown vs. Board of Education*. By defining successful integration as the "absence of a concentration of Latinos in schools", successful schools have been obliged to turn away the very students the desegregation order is supposed to protect due to racial balance concerns. This has the effect of reducing the number of Latino students who have access to these high achieving schools and as a result, "integration has come at a cost for Latino youth in TUSD."

Adding to the contentious amalgam of policy regarding integration and de-facto segregation are the ill-considered language policies implemented in Arizona under the Arizona Department of Education. Emergent Bilinguals (also known as English Learners) are grouped homogenously to the extent possible based on English proficiency as they receive explicit English instruction in four-hour blocks (Arizona Department of Education, 2008). As López points out, emergent bilinguals are segregated from students with differing levels of English proficiency as well as from academic content that is covered while they attend the four-hour block of English instruction. This has the effect of undermining the playing field in ways that are disadvantageous for students who are learning English as they do not receive the same content knowledge in math, science, social studies, etc. as their peers due to their assignment to the four-hour block

Given this backdrop of systematic marginalization for students of color, López makes the case for Asset Based Pedagogies as a necessary part of the skill set that teachers bring to the classroom. Although there is abundant literature on approaches that can fall under the rubric of Asset Based Pedagogies (culturally relevant pedagogy, culturally responsive pedagogy, funds of knowledge, culturally sustaining pedagogy, cultural modeling, cultural wealth, etc.), López addresses the gap in the literature that explicitly links teachers' ABP beliefs and behaviors to student outcomes. While recognizing the validity and depth of studies that are ethnographic and qualitative in nature, López argues that quantitative studies can augment and support existing evidence in order to more fully inform policy. It is to that end that she capably applies quantitative methods to more effectively comprehend how Asset Based Pedagogies can be linked to student outcomes. In an unusual departure from traditional frameworks, López applied a *race-reimaged perspective* as a lens for examining teacher' beliefs and behaviors and how they influence students' identity and achievement. This analytic optic, which implies a serious revision to the traditional teacher expectations framework, is utilized by López to contrast 'direct' and 'signal' influences imbricated in student outcomes. López describes the subtle, yet often normalized ways in which signal influences can subvert student learning. She argues that since traditional approaches consider only direct influences, they will fail to capture ideologies and practices that can reduce signal influences. Because López situates the study that is the basis for this book as an examination of how teachers' expectations and critical awareness relate to student achievement, she points to inherent flaws in the assumptions about teacher expectations that fail to consider the historical contexts, which are often the backdrop of signal influences, of minoritized students. To address these flaws and oversights, she examines how Asset Based Pedagogies, which assume a level of critical awareness, relate to Latino students' identity and achievement.

In her first analysis, she found that teacher expectations were not a signifi-cant predictor of student achievement, but critical awareness *was* related to students' spring reading and mathematics achievement after controlling for fall achievement in each content area. This is a significant and in some ways surprising finding, since teacher expectations did not predict achievement after controlling for students' prior scores, as it contradicts seemingly robust relationships between students' prior achievement and teacher expectations. Because prior research has demonstrated that teachers can hold biases that are detrimental to students of color, her conclusion points to an unexpected finding that critical awareness predicted higher achievement above and beyond teacher expectations alone.

In light of this finding, López set out to more deeply examine the role of critical awareness, attempting to uncover whether critical awareness might play a role in the relationship between teachers' expectations and student achievement.

Because I myself have been a member of the "Asset Based Pedagogy" circle of scholars, I have had a long term investment in investigating exactly these types of questions. López is correct, that the evidence for ABP is long-term and deeply transformative. However, her quantitative analyses on these issues sheds a new light on how ABP is not only part of a humanizing pedagogy, but is also validated as an outcome driven practice. Collectively, her findings suggest that high expectations are certainly important, but without critical awareness, "high expectations are susceptible to biases that impede teachers' ability to behave in ways consistent with high expectations." For example, López' findings demonstrate that students with teachers who have high levels of both expectations and critical awareness perform approximately ½ SD higher in student reading and mathematics achievement over the course of one academic year. This is a finding that should be front and center for every school district as they engage with student learning outcomes.

While we can talk about Asset Based Pedagogies as effective curriculum, without teachers who can implement these within a caring and engaged learning environment, ABP can be reduced to a superficial topography of "cultural" traits. The chapters authored by classroom teachers offer a rich palette of classroom-grounded and student-centered practices that draw in learners. The heartfelt and passionate narratives of the last chapters illustrate the power and transcendence of Asset Based Pedagogies. Whether drawing from their own painful educational experiences, or reaching deep inside their own critical awareness, the teachers who wrote for this book are an example of the committed, dedicated and insightful teachers who will always make a difference. Their profound commitment to their students, to their own critical awareness, and to sustaining and nurturing their students is a testament to how ABP can lead to a critical reflexivity toward both teaching and learning. Their centering of the valued ways of both their students and of the communities in which they teach makes their teaching acts of both love and resistance. One cannot read their words and not come away hoping that these are teachers who will persist against all odds. Their long term engagement with communities is evident as they anchor their pedagogy within historical and social memories and knowledges that strengthen a mutually educative weaving of pedagogy, theory and practice.

The promise of Asset Based Pedagogies has yet to be fully realized as we live in a historical moment when neoliberal logics foster a market-driven approach to the teaching and learning of the upcoming generation. Yet we can continue to be hopeful that the power of recognizing and sustaining, rather than erasing and invisibilizing, the strengths of youth and communities can be a continually evolving paradigm for envisioning and opening community-rooted pedagogies within which learners can thrive.

Norma González
Professor Emerita
Teaching, Learning, and Sociocultural Studies
College of Education
University of Arizona

FOREWORD

This book is proof of an exciting new wave of critical work by young scholar–researchers that are emerging to challenge old ideas about such things as the existence of and reasons for an achievement gap between Latino and White students. At the forefront of these younger scholar–researchers is Professor Francesca A. López who, armed with a broad range of educational and social science theory and research skills, focuses on the Tucson Unified School District as her laboratory to study how Latino students in the district have fared academically. She is intent on showing that the achievement gap is only symptomatic of a deeper problem having to do with how Latino students are instructed in the classroom.

The approach that López takes is multifaceted, empirically sophisticated, and insightful because as a Latina researcher she possesses the dual perspective of being a university researcher using the tools of her profession while also using the lens of a cultural insider. She can offer insights into why traditional pedagogies might be ineffective with Latino students who are astute enough to see how such pedagogies do not address the reality of their minority status that is increasingly under attack in subtle and not so subtle ways by both local and national leaders and educational policy makers. For instance, Latino students in Arizona are very aware that some politicians and educators are intent on weakening educational equity for Latino students by enforcing policies that disparage Latino culture through the dismantling of Mexican American ethnic studies classes and bilingual programs. These actions do not go unnoticed by even elementary school age students, and it is a tribute to López that she is willing to dedicate her intellectual skills and professional energy to improve education for future generations of Latino students.

There is a saying that "to the victor go the spoils," and it is well known that the victor also writes history in his favor. However, Francesca A. López like other young Latina scholars is not accepting of an ascribed marginalized status, but is challenging time-worn beliefs about the achievement gap between Latino and White students. Through this book she is re-writing the story of why the achievement gap persists and doing so with empirical data, not rhetoric about genetic or cultural deficits, as did many of her non-Hispanic predecessors. López is using the same empirical methods and tools used by established researchers before her to offer empirically based reasons for why there are gaps on standardized tests of achievement between majority and Latino students.

With a researcher's finesse López shows that teachers who are not prepared to instruct Latino children in culturally appropriate ways are doing a disservice to Latino students. However, make no mistake, this book is not about teacher bashing. It is a research-based treatise on how to unite the school culture with the culture that students bring to the school by recognizing the home culture as an asset that can have a powerful effect in teaching and learning.

This is not a new approach, advocating for educational reform and accompanying teacher preparation, However, because of Professor López's insider status as a Latina, she is able to dig deeper into Latino culture and language to understand the root causes of educational inequity and underachievement of Latino students. For example, she rejects a deficit approach and advances a culture asset-based approach to theorizing about Latino student school achievement. Fundamental to this approach is understanding that emerging English bilingualism (in this case Spanish and English) is not a deficit and a hindrance to learning. Rather, bilingualism is a linguistic asset in a twenty-first century global world. Similarly, Latino students don't arrive at school as empty vessels to be filled with knowledge by an assimilation-oriented teacher. Rather, they come from homes that are rich in cultural knowledge, and, if seen as a pedagogical asset, this can go a long way in making students feel welcomed and prepared to learn.

López expands her audience's thinking by discarding the traditional teacher expectations framework and replacing it with a race-reimaged framework that is research based, and which takes into account how students envision their ethnic identity and how they receive and interpret disparaging and racist messages from teachers and non-ethnic peers. This theoretical approach is complex because it focuses on subtle contextual behaviors between teachers and students that signal whether students are valued as individuals for the assets they bring to the classroom. This is not "pie in the sky" theory for the sake of theory, as so often university researchers are accused of, but in the hands of a master such as López shows how the theory and data can work hand-in-hand to transform teaching into what she calls "asset-based pedagogy." López offers an important theoretical framework that is supported by empirical data and from which policy recommendations follow that will be invaluable for classroom teachers, university-based teacher-educators, school administrators, educational researchers, and policy makers.

Important, too, is that Professor López tackles some very thorny and complicated educational issues; she situates her research in Tucson, a hotbed of anti-immigrant policies and legislation that has eliminated bilingual programs and ethnic studies classes for Mexican heritage students in the state, while at the same time witnessing a dramatic shift in student demographics from a largely White school district to one that is now heavily Latino. An interesting contextual overlay too is a court-ordered school desegregation mandate for the Tucson Unified School District that may no longer have the consequence for which it was originally intended more than thirty years ago because of demographic shifts due to immigration, the rise in charter schools in the Tucson area, an increase in a student population, many of whom reject the idea of identifying with a single ethnic group, and the possible antiquated ideas of what constitutes school desegregation in the twenty-first century.

Amado M. Padilla
Professor and Chair
Developmental and Psychological Sciences
Graduate School of Education
Stanford University

1

INTRODUCTION

Francesca A. López

> By casting Latino students as bearers of valuable assets—language and cultural knowledge—we may find that they have as much or more to offer as students who have traditionally garnered success in US schools. Perhaps we could even "relabel" Latino students in a way that also allows them to believe in their own potential.
>
> *(Patricia Gándara, 2015, p. 460)*

The United States has a long, lamentable history of marginalizing Latino[1] youth. Even with numerous education reform efforts ostensibly aimed at aggressively addressing achievement disparities, Latino students continue to be underrepresented in a vast array of achievement outcomes. Whether we are examining data on K–12 achievement trends, high school graduation rates, college matriculation, or any other criterion, we seem to have failed in making any progress in closing the so-called "gap" for Latino students. In other words, disparities between Latino and higher achieving White students remain, and, unfortunately, this enduring gap is often interpreted as evidence that Latino achievement has not improved at all. Yet, contrary to the discourse that suggests there has been no improvement in educational outcomes among Latino students, there *have* been substantial real gains across various metrics over the past several decades—with Latino student growth often surpassing that of White students (see Gándara, 2015). One example is Latino students' performance on the National Assessment of Educational Progress (NAEP) in reading and mathematics, which demonstrates that they have steadily increased performance across both grade levels and subjects (see Figures 1.1–1.4[2]). It is because White students have also made gains over the course of forty years, however, that disparities remain. So why is it that educational outcomes have improved over time, but not in ways that reduce disparities? The answer lies in the

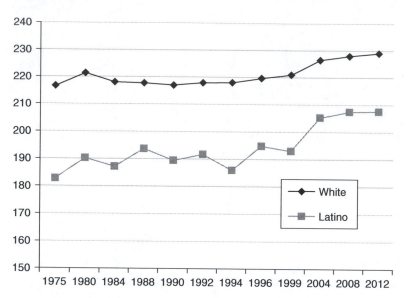

FIGURE 1.1 Average scale scores for reading, grade 4, National Assessment of Educational Progress.

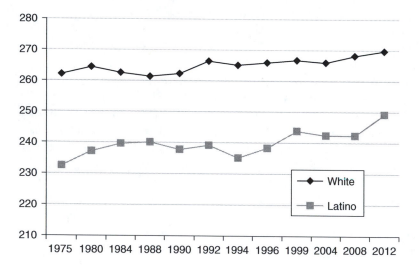

FIGURE 1.2 Average scale scores for reading, grade 8, National Assessment of Educational Progress.

fact that educational outcomes are not a product of educational rigor alone. While we may attribute some or much of the overall gains students of all backgrounds have experienced over the past several decades to more rigorous standards, higher standards alone cannot address disparities.

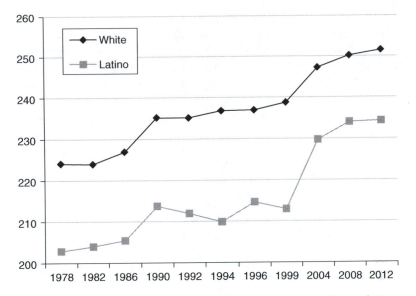

FIGURE 1.3 Average scale scores for mathematics, grade 4, National Assessment of Educational Progress.

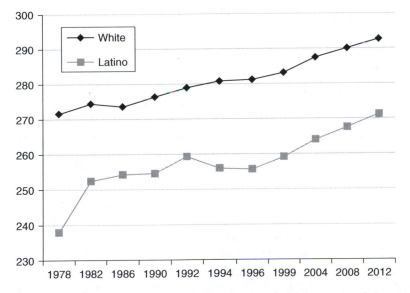

FIGURE 1.4 Average scale scores for mathematics, grade 8, National Assessment of Educational Progress.

Social Equity Theory

There are many theories that help explain why historically marginalized students remain underrepresented in gifted education, Advanced Placement courses, high school completion, college matriculation, and so on. Although there are various theories[3] that explain how stratification originated and has been maintained (e.g., the role of power, privilege, and access, and how these phenomena maintain the marginalization of some groups as they create more access for others), most are beyond the scope of this book. This is not to say the theories and knowledge undergirding them are irrelevant—quite the contrary, understanding the source of stratification and how it is maintained is the very kind of knowledge I am not alone in asserting that teachers must have to be successful (as explained in more detail in Chapter 4). But other scholars have already provided us with invaluable information in ways I would not attempt to match, much less surpass. I will leave it to readers to seek out the compelling work of David Berliner, Sam Bowles and Herb Gintis, Antonia Darder, Lisa Delpit, Patricia Gándara, Gene Glass, Norma Gonzalez, Jay Gould, Ian Haney Lopez, Douglass Massey, Jeannie Oakes, Guadalupe Valdés, Angela Valenzuela, and many others whom I am sure I have failed to name. Instead, I decided to describe a theory that I believe helps explain why disparities in achievement between historically marginalized and White youth persist despite multiple reform efforts to "close achievement gaps." The theory helps elucidate the kinds of dynamics that take place in classrooms that affect some students but not others—knowledge and behaviors that those of us who are teacher and leader educators have much more immediate, direct access to help transform—which are the essence of this book.

Social Equity Theory (SET; see McKown, 2013) rests on the premise that we are social beings who infer information from our surroundings, and that by inferring and internalizing socially transmitted messages, our performance is affected in a myriad of ways. These socially transmitted messages fall into two broad categories: those that affect everyone and anyone, regardless of background (known as *direct* influences), and those that affect individuals based on membership to a particular group (known as *signal* influences). By understanding these two types of socially transmitted messages, we can begin to see why we continue to see achievement disparities for Latino youth, as well as other historically marginalized youth (see Figure 1.5).

Direct influences. There are many kinds of direct influences that play a role in the academic trajectory of youth. Some of the direct influences that are beyond the scope of this book involve aspects of neighborhoods and parenting. It is likely to be no surprise that where children live (their home and neighborhood) as well as the resources available to caregivers (both in terms of materials and time) provide experiences that either hinder or support youth as they progress through school. While the issue of inequitable distribution of resources is of the utmost importance given the ever-increasing number of children who live in poverty, the focus of this book compels me to focus on the kinds of socially transmitted messages that take place in classrooms. And it turns out that there is an abundance of direct influences that transpire in classrooms; they involve "the quality of instruction and the quality of student–teacher relationships" (McKown, 2013, p. 1123),

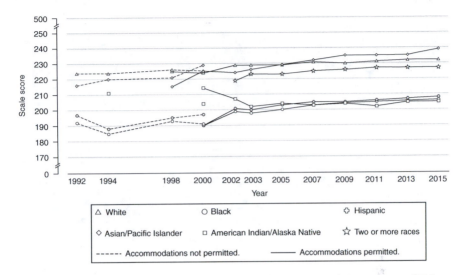

FIGURE 1.5 Average scale scores for reading, grade 4, National Assessment of Educational Progress (NAEP).

which have a robust history in education research (e.g., Brophy & Good, 1984; Good, 2014). To summarize this vast body of research (which is described in more detail in Chapter 4), we know that there is a link between *teachers' expectations* and how teachers reflect their beliefs in their behaviors (e.g., providing information, eliciting information, pacing of instruction), and we know that behaviors that reflect high quality of instruction are associated with students' academic identities and improved student achievement. The prominence of this research can be discerned from its presence in licensure standards for teacher preparation (e.g., Council of Chief State School Officers, 2011) and widely used teacher quality evaluation assessments (e.g., Danielson, 2013; Pianta, La Paro, & Hamre, 2008). In fact, this research is so very institutionalized in teacher preparation and evaluation that it is rare to find non-educators, let alone teachers, who have not heard of the "self-fulfilling prophecies" and the role they play in promoting or hindering student success.

It is important to acknowledge the role of direct influences in student achievement: quality of instruction, along with other direct influences, collectively explain all disparities—but only until around the time students are in second grade (see Figure 1.6). Let us recall that direct influences, including behaviors that reflect high quality instruction, are *not contingent on students' ethnicity*; the quality of the educational environment is a direct influence that affects all students. All students (albeit to varying degrees) will exhibit the consequences of ill-prepared teachers, just as all students' performance will improve if standards become more rigorous (including the curriculum and the extent to which teachers are prepared). This assertion is supported with evidence of the correlation

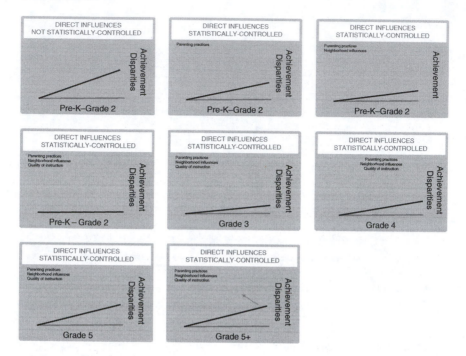

FIGURE 1.6 Visual representation of achievement disparities for historically marginalized students after controlling for "direct influences" across time.

between increased educational standards and the general improvement on NAEP for all student groups regardless of grade level or subject—but particularly for mathematics (as shown in Figures 1.1–1.4). Quality schools, quality teachers, and rigor, however, are less accessible to historically marginalized students (Oakes, 2005). This is the reason statistically controlling for these and other direct influences explains achievement disparities. But what happens after students are about eight years of age, when we see disparities once again increase even when controlling for various direct influences? Why does the combination of neighborhoods, parenting, and quality instruction explain all the disparities for children only until about third grade? The answer lies in signal influences.

Signal influences. There are socially transmitted messages that *are* contingent on ethnicity, known as *signal influences*. Whereas direct influences affect all students, signal influences affect historically marginalized youth with "social events that signal to members of negatively stereotyped groups that they are devalued because of their group membership" (McKown, 2013, p. 1125). Notably, children become keenly aware of stereotypes and biased behaviors by around the age of eight— the same time we begin to see disparities climb after statistically controlling for direct influences. In other words, we can statistically explain disparities due to direct influences until children are developmentally capable of perceiving and

Diversity in Children's Books 2015

Percentages of books depicting characters from diverse backgrounds. Based on the 2015 publishing statistics compiled by the **Cooperative Children's Book Center**, School of Education, University of Wisconsin-Madison. *ccbc.education.wisc.edu/books/pcstats.asp*

0.9%	2.4%	3.3%	7.6%	12.5%*	73.3%**
American Indians/ First Nations	Latinx	Asian Pacifics/ Asian Pacific Americans	African/ African Americans	Animals, Trucks, etc.	White

Illustration by David Huyck, in consultation with Sarah Park Dahlen & Molly Beth Griffin. Released under a Creative Commons BY-NC-SA license: https://creativecommons.org/licenses/by-nc-sa/4.0/

* About a quarter of the total children's books published in 2015 were picture books, and about half of those depict non-human characters, like animals & trucks.
** The remainder depict white characters.

FIGURE 1.7 Diversity of children's books. Illustration ©2016 David Huyck, in consultation with Sarah Park Dahlen and Molly Beth Griffin.

internalizing signal influences. The source of increasing disparities, then, is that historically marginalized youth discern signal influences that their White peers do not. Unfortunately, the insidiousness of signal influences is that they are abundant in classroom settings: they are transmitted through dynamics such as group composition (e.g., the paucity of student representation in accelerated, gifted, and/or advanced courses), curricular materials (see Figure 1.7), and teacher behaviors. Thus, whereas increased rigor, quality teachers, and quality schools provide direct influences[4] that affect all students but are less accessible to historically marginalized students (Oakes, 2005), signal influences accumulate in childhood and influence the identity and achievement of youth belonging to devalued groups. This is why no amount of direct influences in the form of rigor and quality schools and teachers has ameliorated disparities, even though achievement trends have improved overall (see Figures 1.1–1.5).

How do we begin to reduce signal influences in classrooms? Unfortunately, the traditional teacher expectations framework that has been institutionalized in teacher preparation, certification, and evaluation considers only direct influences (see Figure 1.8). As such, it fails to reflect the necessary beliefs and behaviors that can reduce signal influences, thus altering the trajectory of historically marginalized students. This knowledge requires a revision to the traditional teacher

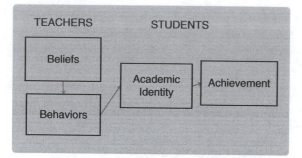

FIGURE 1.8 Visual representation traditional teacher expectations framework that reflects the body of research on teacher expectations, which has informed the ways we address direct influences in teacher preparation and practice (e.g., Good & Brophy, 2010; Rosenthal, 1991).

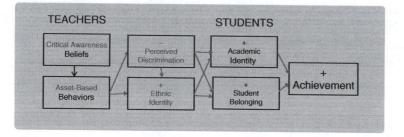

FIGURE 1.9 Visual representation race-reimaged teacher expectations framework that reflects the body of research on critical awareness, asset-based pedagogy, and racialized student identities (Decuir-Gunby & Schultz, 2014; López, 2017).

expectations framework. It is this vision I present in this book—a *race-reimaged perspective* (Decuir-Gunby & Schutz, 2014)—applied to teacher expectations (see Figure 1.9).

Why a Race-Reimaged Perspective?

Educational history reveals—particularly when we consider SET—that many policies and practices promulgated in the name of upward mobility actually promote stratification. The banning of bilingual classes in the guise of promoting English proficiency and the absence of equitable Latino representation in books are just two of the many educational policies and practices that produce signal influences and contribute to the marginalization of Latinos in the schooling process. These and other deficiency approaches to education—those that implicitly and explicitly require Latinos to abandon their cultural and linguistic backgrounds—reflect adherence to the belief that assimilation leads to success.

Those who hold such beliefs blame the lack of upward mobility among Latinos, from schooling to career, as a cultural deficit rather than a structural one (see, for example, Huntington, 2004). Achievement disparities (in spite of improvement of outcomes over time) are often used to substantiate this widely held belief. This circular argument obscures the reason behind disparities that are rooted in deficiency approaches in the education of Latino students (as well as other students who are not typically reflected in the curriculum).

Why Research on Asset-Based Pedagogy?

Many scholars have advocated against an assimilationist view of Latino youth. Instead, they argue that students' culture and language should be viewed as *assets* and incorporated into classroom practice. They assert that incorporating students' culture and language in school, what I collectively refer to as "asset-based pedagogy,"[5] provides a bridge that connects the dominant school culture to students' home and heritage culture, thus promoting academic achievement for historically marginalized students. Here, the focus on academic achievement requires a brief note of clarification. There are inherent issues with the use of achievement scores. Among them is a narrow view of the kind of student outcomes we should aspire all youth to develop (never mind that it is a statistical impossibility that all students reach "above average" given the very nature of how achievement scores are developed). Indeed, we should want more than high test scores for our youth given the detrimental consequences of such a narrow focus (e.g., Valenzuela, 2005). That said, I used achievement scores as outcomes (albeit not exclusively) in the research I describe in this book for two key reasons. One is to be consistent with scholars' assertions that there is a need to link asset-based pedagogy to achievement outcomes to more forcefully influence policy (Sleeter, 2004). The other is because ignoring the power of achievement scores denies marginalized students access to power (Delpit, 1988). After all, if achievement scores did not matter, it would be of no consequence that Latino youth continue to underperform compared to their White counterparts.

Among the numerous scholars who have dedicated their platforms to the promulgation of asset-based views, many lament that the research examining the role of asset-based practices in promoting achievement tends to be "overwhelmingly based on case study approaches and ethnographic or other qualitative methods" (Goldenberg, Rueda, & August, 2008, p.107). Although this body of research has provided us with detailed depictions of classroom experiences for historically marginalized students that can be overlooked by quantitative studies, much of it has not explicitly linked asset-based practices to achievement outcomes and, as such, has limited serious consideration among policymakers. Because of this, scholars have called attention to the need to make the link between asset-based pedagogy and student outcomes explicit with quantitative empirical work (Goldenberg et al., 2008; Sleeter, 2004)—and it was this call to action that led me on the path to carry out the research presented in this book.

The Study

Before detailing some of the characteristics of the teachers and students who participated in my research, it is essential to briefly situate the climate for teachers in the state of Arizona to gain an appreciation of just what was asked of the participants, and just how profound their contribution to our knowledge is. According to the Network for Public Education's (NPE) "50 State Report Card," Arizona earned an "F" due to its failure to use "research-based strategies to improve education and create equal opportunities for all children" (NPE, 2016, p. 2). Among Arizona's most embarrassing failures are teacher salaries, which are the second lowest in the nation after controlling for cost of living (NPE, 2016). Yet, low teacher salaries are just one of the many consequences of Arizona leading the nation in the reduction of funding to K–12 and higher education (CBPP, 2016). Another consequence of reduced education funding is that tuition for higher education has more than doubled over the past decade. This has created an egregious burden for local students who enroll (or would have enrolled) in teacher preparation programs and will not earn the necessary income to pay off student debt if they remain in Arizona (CBPP, 2016).

Higher tuition and insultingly low salaries for positions that require a college degree, coupled with the escalating attacks against the teaching profession in states like Arizona, have resulted in an extreme teacher shortage. Rather than remedy the detrimental context for teachers, Arizona Governor Doug Ducey responded to the teacher shortage by eliminating the state requirement for teacher certification in May of 2017—allowing school districts the discretion of deciding who meets criteria to teach. This legislation came on the heels of a controversy where the state of Arizona had been found guilty of illegally withholding school funding, only to partially reinstate the funding with a voter-approved amendment to the Arizona constitution.[6] Other funding-related and professionalization issues have a longer history (e.g., charter schools) and are described in more depth in Chapter 3—but it is not an understatement to say that the state of Arizona seems to be doing everything it can to deprofessionalize teaching.

I conducted the research highlighted in this book in the Tucson Unified School District (TUSD) in Tucson, Arizona, over a period of two years. In those years, and to the present, teachers are evaluated on a yearly basis with "value-added models"[7] that take into consideration other teachers' scores, their prior scores (with a completely different set of students), and the school's overall performance,[8] among other factors that are completely out of teachers' control. This gives pause for thought: teachers are rated according to circumstances over which they have no control, and have that label of performance attached to their worth along with the numerous other events contributing to the deprofessionalization of teaching. This is the context of the teachers who voluntarily agreed[9] to participate in my study.

The research questions that guided my work, which are visually represented in Figure 1.9, focused on examining how teachers' beliefs were related to their behaviors, and how teacher behaviors were in turn related to students' identity and achievement outcomes. Despite the assault on the teaching profession, thirty-six teachers agreed to participate in my study knowing that I would be asking them about their beliefs and practices, and that I would be examining how their beliefs and practices were related to students' perceptions of ability, ethnic identity, and their academic outcomes. These teachers are experienced (Table 1.1), have stayed in the classroom in spite of policies that push so many teachers out, and were willing (sometimes eager) to help inform research. Without them, this book could not have been written.

Who are the teachers? As presented in Table 1.1 and consistent with national trends, around 86% of the participating teachers identified as women. Inconsistent with national trends, however, a majority of the participating teachers identified as Latina/o. Moreover, more than half held a bilingual endorsement (64%) in a state that eliminated bilingual education in 2001 (a topic I elaborate on in Chapters 2, 3 and 4); the remaining teachers had a Structured English Endorsement to comply with state requirements. Although these were the characteristics of the teachers who participated in the study, I would be remiss not to point out that they are not representative of the district or state. The teachers who volunteered (in contrast to those who were recruited but who decided not to participate) were more likely to share the participating students' ethnicity, more likely to have had at least five years of teaching experience, and more likely to have been lifelong Tucsonans. This is speculation on my part, but it seems that the teachers willing to put themselves on the line (with more work and with an evaluation of how their beliefs and behaviors related to students' achievement) were those with a particularly strong vested interest in the students and community.

Who were the students? Across the six schools where the thirty-six teachers had agreed to participate in my study, there were a total of 568 Latino students in grades 3, 4, and 5 whose parents or guardians allowed participation (see Table 1.1), representing about 64% of the students I recruited to participate. In the years the study took place, TUSD was close to 65% Latino, with an overwhelming majority of the Latino population identifying as Mexican American, not unlike the demographics of many Southwestern cities. Also like most large districts that are located in the heart of large cities, almost half (46%) of the Latino student population in the district qualifies for free or reduced lunch. Although close to 5% of Latino students in the district are classified as emergent bilinguals[10] (EBs) because their parents report Spanish as the language spoken at home, this percentage is strikingly low given the context and history of Tucson. The depressed estimate

TABLE 1.1 School-Level Demographic Information

ABP Level	Magnet	% Teachers Latino	% Certified Bilingual	3rd Grade Teachers N	4th Grade Teachers N	5th Grade Teachers N	Average Years Teaching	Students N
High	Yes Bilingual	75	100	3	2	3	20	158
High	Yes Bilingual	83	100	2	2	2	11	63
Mid	No Bilingual	75	38	3	3	2	12	82
Mid	No Bilingual	83	50	3	2	1	11	76
Low	Yes Technology	71	43	3	2	2	12	175
Low	No	100	0	1	0	0	10	14
Total		**78**	**64**	**15**	**11**	**10**	**13**	**568**

is an artifact of inconsistencies in how the home language has been determined in Arizona, which was found to be in violation of Title VI of the Civil Rights Act (Goldenberg & Rutherford-Quach, 2010). Detailed information about the changing EB demographics is discussed in Chapter 3.

The schools. Of the six schools that participated in the study, three schools are magnet schools with a focus designed to attract families throughout the district to comply with desegregation oversight (a topic I discuss in much more detail in Chapter 2). Two of the magnet schools offer a bilingual curriculum (Spanish/English) and one emphasizes technology. In addition to an emphasis on bilingualism, the two bilingual magnet schools offer cultural extracurricular activities (e.g., mariachi[11] and folklórico[12]). Moreover, one school self-identifies as having a focus on multicultural education and social justice. Of the three non-magnet schools, two offer bilingual[13] classes. Although the mode of delivery of Spanish is distinct across the bilingual schools, they share the goals of bilingualism and biliteracy. I selected the participating schools for my research because of their varying curricular approaches and the lack of substantial variation in academic achievement (i.e., none of the participating schools had been considered by the district as schools in need of remediation).

Overview

For many readers, Tucson, Arizona, may be familiar due to the controversies that have made national headlines. The most recent involves House Bill 2281, which was created in 2010 to target the TUSD's Mexican American Studies program. One of the prohibitions delineated is any course "designed primarily for pupils of a particular ethnic group" (HB2281, 2010, p. 1). The history of Arizona's restrictive and discriminatory policies, however, extends far beyond the law that in 2012 forced the TUSD to eliminate Mexican American Studies. Accordingly, to contextualize the research I present here, I provide a macro-to-micro overview of the context for Latino youth in this book in Part I. I begin by discussing the national landscape for Latinos (and in particular, Mexican Americans, given the location and demographics of the study), as well Arizona's discriminatory policy milieu in Chapter 2. The contextualization of the demographic shifts in the United States, along with historical treatment of Mexican and Mexican heritage students, highlights the historical roots of assimilative strategies that contribute to signal influences in schools today. In Chapter 3, I provide a discussion of the TUSD's history with a specific focus on the constraints they face as a school district still under court oversight for desegregation, which is complicated by educational policies that also produce signal influences that extend beyond those described in Chapter 2.

In Part II of this book, I present a review of the extant research that informs the framework of my research. I begin with the teacher expectation research that has such a robust history that it has made its way to teacher certification.

It is the reason educators, particularly those certified through university-based programs, know about high expectations and the self-fulfilling prophecy. I also, however, point out inconsistencies and limitations in this work that are more fully addressed by a *race-reimaged perspective* (Decuir-Gunby & Schutz, 2014) that considers the assets historically marginalized students possess. Part II, then, is a discussion of theories focused on teacher beliefs and behaviors—both theories that ignore signal influences related to race and ethnicity and those that explicitly focus on it—along with the findings of my study (Chapter 4). Part II also includes a discussion of how teacher beliefs and behaviors influence students' identity and achievement (Chapter 5). The findings presented in Chapters 4 and 5 inform the discrete policy recommendations that I present in Chapter 6.

It was my expectation when conceptualizing this book that readers would be provided with both the theories undergirding the importance of asset-based practices and detailed accounts of how these practices are expressed for various teachers. To that end, my journey conducting the research highlighted in this book led me not only to confirm answers about how teachers' beliefs and behaviors can promote Latino students' identity and achievement outcomes—which I expected given the extant body of literature focused on asset-based practices—but also, albeit unexpectedly, to have the privilege of getting to know teachers whose expertise and pedagogy exemplify asset-based pedagogy in every sense of the word. Although they are not necessarily teachers who participated in the research highlighted in this book, the research I carried out and my visits to schools led to district-wide work that ultimately led me to the individuals who share their expertise here. It was unknown to me when I first met them, but the fact that some were bilingually certified and had taught in Tucson schools prior to Proposition 203, and others were former Mexican American Studies teachers, explained why they possessed such profound knowledge about Latino students' historical contexts and engaged heavily in asset-based practices. It is an honor to be able to highlight their work in Part III of this book.

Nurturing Confianza

I called this book *Asset Pedagogies in Latino Youth Identity and Achievement: Nurturing Confianza* because the word *"confianza,"* as is the case with many words in Spanish, has multiple meanings that capture the essence of the extant scholarship and my research findings. *Confianza* can be translated as confidence, trust, and hope. For teachers to nurture *confidence* in Latino students' own abilities—one of the strongest predictors of achievement—teachers must understand the historical context that contributes to the disparities evident today. They must also, however, foment students' beliefs in the assets they possess, which in turn helps develop students' positive identities and awareness as members of historically marginalized groups in discriminatory contexts. One need only briefly examine the terminology often used in education to describe Latino, as well as other historically marginalized students, to find words such as *at risk, English learner* (or worse, *Limited English Proficient*), *disadvantaged*, and several others that reflect deficit views of youth. By instead focusing on assets (e.g., students who are emergent bilinguals), we can transform beliefs to consider the assets every student possesses. Accordingly, *confianza* also exemplifies that there must be *trust* between teachers and students for students' identities to develop in positive ways in the contexts of schools. In engaging in asset-based practices, teachers and students are part of the *hope* of equitable access to the multiple forms of capital that can eliminate disparities and the maintenance of stratification.

Notes

1 Although I focus on Mexican American students in this book, the issues with accurate disaggregation (see Nieto, 1999) prevent me from using "Mexican American" instead of the more general category of "Latino" throughout.
2 Source: US Department of Education, Institute of Education Sciences, National Center for Education Statistics.
3 Here, I am referring to the accumulation of ideas with empirical support.
4 Direct influences can be found both within schools, where different tracks (gifted and talented; Advanced Placement) are differentially accessible to historically marginalized students, as well as between schools, where the tendency is to find higher quality schools and instruction in more privileged settings (see Oakes, 2005).
5 To capture the breadth of asset-based educational practices, I use the term "*asset-based pedagogy*" but retain authors' terminology when quoting their work.
6 Proposition 123, which passed with a margin of less than 2%, increases education funding with money that includes principal from state land trust funds. Prior to the amendment, only interest generated by state land trust funds could be used to ensure the education funding of Arizona students indefinitely.
7 For a detailed account of the issues related to the use of value-added models for teacher evaluations, see Haertel (2013).
8 The scores reflect student performance on the Arizona statewide assessment for English and mathematics (AzMERIT) and the Arizona Instrument to Measure Standards in science (AIMS).
9 The research had Institutional Review Board approval for both the district and the University of Arizona.
10 Consistent with Garica, Kleifgen, and Falchi's (2008) assertion that students who are acquiring English as a second language "are in fact *emergent bilinguals*" (p. 6), I use the term EB instead of the more frequently used "*English learners.*"
11 Music that is "the primary musical representation of Mexican nationalism in Mexico, a representation sustained and elaborated when Mexicans migrated to the United States" (Clark, 2005, p. 227).
12 Dance that "[stands] as public symbols of Mexican culture" (Ramírez, 1989, p. 15).
13 Although magnet schools that offer Spanish collectively refer to their approach as "bilingual," they must navigate the state policies that limit instruction in language other than English to students who are identified as proficient in English or are at least ten years of age.

References

Brophy, J., & Good, T. L. (1984). *Teacher behavior and student achievement.* Occasional Paper No. 73. Retrieved from http://eric.edu.gov/?id=ED251422

Center on Budget and Policy Priorities (CBPP). (2016). Cuts to Arizona's higher education system jeopardize our economic future. Retrieved at http://www.cbpp.org/sites/default/files/atoms/files/sfp_highered_az.pdf

Clark, S. (2005). Mariachi music as a symbol of Mexican culture in the United States. *International Journal of Music Education, 23*, 227–237

Council of Chief State School Officers. (2011). InTASC model core teaching standards: A resource for state dialogue. Retrieved from http://www.ccsso.org/documents/2011/intasc_model_core_teaching_standards_2011.pdf

Danielson, C. (2013). *The framework for teaching: Evaluation instrument.* Princeton, NJ: Danielson Group.

Darder, A. (2012). *Culture and power in the classroom: A critical foundation for the education of bicultural students* (2nd ed.). Boulder, CO: Paradigm Press.

Decuir-Gunby, J., & Schutz, P. (2014). Researching race within educational psychology contexts. *Educational Psychologist, 49*, 244–260.

Delpit, L. (1988). The silenced dialogue: Power and pedagogy in educating other people's children. *Harvard Educational Review, 58*, 280–299.

Gándara, P. (2015). With the future on the line: Why studying Latino education is so urgent. *American Journal of Education, 121*, 451–463.

García, O., Kleifgen, J. A., & Falchi, L. (2008). From English Language learners to emergent bilinguals. *Equity Matters. Research Review No. 1.* Campaign for Educational Equity, Teachers College, Columbia University.

Goldenberg, C., & Rutherford Quach, S. (2010). The Arizona home language survey and the identification of students for ELL services. Civil Rights Project/Proyecto Derechos Civiles. Retrieved at http://escholarship.org/uc/item/6gb926q1#page–3.

Goldenberg, C., Rueda, R. S., & August, D. (2008). Sociocultural contexts and literacy development. In D. August & T. Shanahan (Eds.), *Developing reading and writing in second language learners: Lessons from the Report of the National Literacy Panel on Language Minority Children and Youth* (pp. 95–130). Washington, DC: Center for Applied Linguistics and Newark, DE: International Reading Association.

Good, T. (2014). What do we know about how teachers influence student performance on standardized tests: And why do we know so little about other student outcomes? *Teachers College Record, 116*, 1–23.

Haertel, E. (2013). Reliability and validity of inferences about teachers based on student test scores. Educational Testing Service William H. Angoff Memorial Lecture Series. Retrieved at https://www.ets.org/Media/Research/pdf/PICANG14.pdf.

Huntington, S. P. (2004). The Hispanic challenge. *Foreign Policy, 141*, 30–45.

Huyck, D., Park Dahlen, S., & Griffin, M. B. (2016). Diversity in Children's Books 2015 infographic. sarahpark.com blog. Retrieved from https://readingspark.wordpress.com/2016/09/14/picture–this–reflecting–diversity–in–childrens–book–publishing/. Statistics compiled by the Cooperative Children's Book Center, School of Education, University of Wisconsin–Madison: http://ccbc.education.wisc.edu/books/pcstats.asp. Released for non–commercial use under a Creative Commons BY–NC–SA 4.0 license.

McKown, C. (2013). Social equity theory and racial–ethnic achievement gaps. *Child Development, 84*, 1120–1136.

Network for Public Education. (2016). *Valuing Public Education: A 50 State Report Card.* Retrieved at https://networkforpubliceducation.org/wp–content/uploads/2016/01/NPE–Report–Card–Smaller.pdf.

Nieto, S. (1999). *The light in their eyes: Creating multicultural learning communities.* New York, NY: Teachers College Press.

Oakes, J. (2005). *Keeping track*. New Haven, CT: Yale University Press.

Pianta, R. C., La Paro, K. M., & Hamre, B. K. (2008). *Classroom assessment scoring system (CLASS) manual, K–3*. Baltimore, MD: Paul H. Brookes Publishing Company.

Ramírez, O. N. (1989). Social and political dimensions of folklórico dance: The binational dialectic of residual and emergent culture. *Western Folklore, 48,* 15–32.

Sleeter, C. (2004). Context-conscious portraits and context-blind policy. *Anthropology and Education Quarterly, 35,* 132–136.

Valenzuela, A. (2005). *Leaving children behind: How "Texas-style" accountability fails Latino youth.* Albany, NY: Suny Press.

PART I

A Macro-to-Micro Overview of the Context for Latino Youth

2

CONTEXT FOR LATINO YOUTH

Francesca A. López

> *According to the ideology of the American Dream, America is the land of limitless*
> *opportunity in which individuals can go as far as their own merit takes them. According*
> *to this ideology, you get out of the system what you put into it. Getting ahead is*
> *ostensibly based on individual merit, which is generally viewed as a combination of*
> *factors including innate abilities, working hard, having the right attitude, and having*
> *high moral character and integrity. Americans not only tend to think that is how the*
> *system should work, but most Americans also think that is how the system does work.*
> *(McNamee & Miller, 2004)*

Education is believed to be the conduit to social mobility. After all, higher levels of education are correlated with higher levels of employment and a widely held belief is that the pursuit of education is at the discretion of the individual (see McNamee & Miller, 2004). What historical trends show us, however, is that educational and career trajectories are largely a function of resources—and those who have resources most often beget more resources (e.g., Bowles & Gintis, 1976, 2002). This remains true despite more than half a century of education reform efforts purportedly aimed at eliminating achievement disparities associated with poverty.

The Elementary and Secondary Education Act (ESEA) was the first legislation that provided special funding for children in poverty with compensatory programs (Title I). One of Lyndon B. Johnson's 1965 "War on Poverty" initiatives, the ESEA is viewed as the catalyst to "other movements toward equality of educational opportunity" (Halperin, 1975, p. 6). Among them are bilingual education programs, which reflected "awareness of the suffering of children forced to speak one language at home and another in the schools" (Halperin, p. 6). Despite several reauthorizations of the ESEA, however, the *Statistical Portrait of Hispanics in the United States*[1] (Stepler & Brown, 2016) provides a salient illustration of ways stratification has been maintained in the United States for Latinos. In terms of education, for example, the proportion of Latino students who drop out of school is twice (6%) that of White students (3%), and Latinos who have earned at least a bachelor's degree represent less than half (14%) that of Whites (34%). The same kinds of disparities can be found in terms of employment: the unemployment rate for Latinos is close to 9%, compared to 6% of Whites, and the median earnings of Latinos is only about 70% of the median earnings of Whites. The situation may seem insurmountable, given that more than twice the proportion of Latinos below the age of 18 live in poverty (32%) compared to White (13%) children. These statistics, among many others, highlight the insidious cycle of poverty that is inherently linked to ethnicity and race. If education really is the great equalizer, why is stratification so impermeable?

Some may point to these data trends to argue that there are inherent deficiencies in Latinos that contribute to their underrepresentation in achievement and employment outcomes. There is an abundance of documentation, however, that details the various ways stratification has been maintained in spite of the effort and perseverance of historically marginalized groups, with schools found to be *sources* of stratification rather than remedies (e.g., Apple, 2004; Bowles & Gintis, 1976; Darder, 2012; Oakes, 2005; Valenzuela, 1999). With this knowledge as a backdrop, many asset-based practices address the needs of all historically marginalized students who share higher rates of poverty and lower rates of success in school (see Gay, 2010), which I detail in Chapter 4. Despite sharing unfavorable outcomes rooted in poverty and inequitable schooling experiences, however, there are marked historical differences that contextualize the genesis of the need for asset-based practices for Latino youth. Although a "cultural–historical approach can help researchers and practitioners characterize the commonalities of experience of people who share cultural backgrounds," it is important to avoid "'locating' the commonalities within individuals" (Gutiérrez & Rogoff, 2003, p. 21). Thus, to provide background while avoiding the essentialization that has been critiqued by many scholars, we must consider both historical and present-day contexts within Latinos' "dynamic cultural communities" (Gutiérrez & Rogoff, 2003, p. 21).

In 1965 (the same year the ESEA passed), Congress passed the Immigration and Nationality Act that replaced a national origins quota system (although disclaimers were still included) (Public Law 89–236). Since then, the proportion of the U.S. population that is non-U.S.-born has steadily grown, reaching 13% in 2010—a proportion that had not been reached since the 1920s (Krogstad & Keenan, 2014). Notably, 50% of immigrants since 1965 are from Latin American countries (Krogstad & Keenan, 2014). Latinos now make up about 17% of the United States population, with those of Mexican descent representing close to 64% of all Latinos (Stepler & Brown, 2016).[2] Although close to half of Latino adults in the United States were born in Mexico, the U.S.-born Latino population has "continued to grow at a faster rate than the immigrant population" (Krogstad & Lopez, 2014). Thus, a rapidly growing segment of the U.S. population includes U.S.-born, Latino children of Mexican descent.

For many Latinos in the United States who have Mexican lineage, history includes colonization, assimilation, segregation, and inferior schooling. In a review of the historically focused literature on the educational experiences of Latinos in the United States, Nieto and Irizarry (2012) found that they "have been characterized, among other realities, by segregated classrooms and schools, limited access to qualified teachers, corporal punishment, and 'sink or swim' approaches to language learning" (p. 17). Despite many similarities in the educational experiences of Latino students, however, there are marked differences in the histories of different Latino groups in the United States that have often been ignored and as such, contribute to the essentialization of asset-based practices. To attenuate this issue in this book, what follows provides a history for one of the most representative groups in the United States and the overwhelming majority of students in the research presented in this book: students of Mexican descent. Given that the conquest of Mexico in 1848 (Klein, 1996) "is largely unknown to teachers and the general public" (Nieto, 1999, p. 133), what follows is a brief review of the earlier schooling experiences of Mexican-descent youth. The account presented here is by necessity not highly detailed, but other scholars have already provided this much-needed nuance in understanding the history of Mexican presence in U.S. schools (see San Miguel & Valencia, 1998). By summarizing some of the salient historical markers for Mexican-descent students, however, the relevance of asset-based practices can be better understood.

Mexican-Descent Students

The Treaty of Guadalupe Hidalgo in 1848 "signaled the beginning of decades of persistent, pervasive prejudice and discrimination against people of Mexican origin who reside in the United States" (San Miguel & Valencia, p. 353). The treaty ended the Mexican American War and annexed almost 530,000 miles of once-Mexican territory that included "present-day Arizona, California, western Colorado, Nevada, New Mexico, Texas, and Utah" (San Miguel & Valencia, 1998, p. 354). Many of those who lived in the conquered territories, despite having been promised full rights to their property, had land claims "that were not recognized by the United States" (Klein, 1996, p. 209).

For colonized Mexican children, schooling transformed from "an accommodative public school system in the Southwest into an essentially American institution" (San Miguel & Valencia, 1998, p. 360). By the 1870s, "Spanish was prohibited in the public schools" and "school officials eliminated Mexican culture from the public school curriculum by removing classes pertaining to ... Mexican history" (San Miguel & Valencia, 1998, p. 362)—a chilling historical marker that has been repeated, despite multiple attempts to infuse the curriculum with Mexican history, to the present day (HB 2281, 2010).[3] In place of the accommodative curriculum was a Eurocentric curriculum that was particularly evident in history textbooks, which "contained only disparaging comments about the Mexican presence in the Southwest" (San Miguel & Valencia, 1998, p. 363). This, too, has been repeated in the present day as evidenced by the Texas social studies text that was up for adoption by the Texas State Board of Education, which included the following description:

> In contrast, Mexican laborers were not reared to put in a full day's work so vigorously. There was a cultural attitude of "mañana," or "tomorrow," when it came to high-gear production. It was also traditional to skip work on Mondays, and drinking on the job could be a problem.
>
> *(Isensee, 2016)*

The book was rejected by the Texas State Board of Education, in large part because of educators and community activists; however, the efforts to impair the activists' efforts are documented (Latimer, 2016).

By the 1890s, dramatic changes in the Mexican American population took place that included increased social differentiation. Nevertheless, as a group, Mexican Americans continued to be "politically powerless, economically impoverished, and socially alienated" (p. 364). Mexican-descent children also had increased access to schools, but inferior schools and segregation expanded significantly, with "culture and class [becoming] crucial in maintaining and extending this practice over time" (San Miguel & Valencia, 1998, p. 365). Not all Mexican Americans had access to school, however, with agricultural migrants and secondary school-age students among those who were excluded from public education altogether (San Miguel & Valencia, 1998).

Although protests against segregation were evident in 1910, it was not until 1954, notably the same year *Brown v. Board of Education* overturned *de jure* segregation, that the U.S. Supreme Court decided that Mexican Americans were protected by the 14th Amendment in *Hernandez v. Texas* (1954). The plaintiffs claimed that although they were classified as White, there was clear evidence of their treatment as a subordinate class given the systematic exclusion of jurors of Mexican descent. Despite this decision, a deficiency-orientation toward Mexican-descent children has been a historical marker of their educational experiences since the annexation of the Southwestern states that were once Mexico. For example, a 1933 study summarized findings by stating:

> In general, the type of Mexican child taken into the Arizona school tends to be backward in rate of mental development, lags a year behind other pupils, shows a heavy failure percentage, and an early elimination in school.
>
> *(as cited in San Miguel & Valencia, 1998, p. 372)*

This same study, sponsored by the Office of Education of the U.S. Department of the Interior, also found pervasive segregation, inadequate and inappropriate teaching materials, and ill-equipped teachers (San Miguel & Valencia, 1998). Notably,

FIGURE 2.1 Librotraficantes (Banned Books), by Tanya Alvarez. Used with permission.

although it has been more than eighty years since the findings were disseminated, these issues persist (Gándara & Orfield, 2012)—as do the deficiency orientations implicit in descriptions such as *at-risk* and *English language learner* (García, Kleifgen, & Falchi, 2008). As this overview of some of the salient historical markers for Mexican-descent youth highlights, schooling as colonization replaced accommodative cultural and linguistic practices, and yet it is the students who are described as deficient rather than the schooling practices they endure. Restoring cultural practices, with a more explicit and purposeful asset-based perspective, has been sought after for over 160 years. The fact that assimilative approaches under the guise of educational reform have failed to improve academic outcomes for many Latino students underscores one of the reasons scholars have looked to asset-based practices to counter this trend.

History of Federal Mandates to Meet the Needs of EBs[4]

Although 26% of the Latino population speaks only English at home, 74% of Latinos report speaking Spanish at home (and half of these households report speaking both Spanish and English) (Krogstad & Keenan, 2014). Rather than building on the assets of bilingualism that so many of our Latino youth possess, over four decades of shifting legislation, focused on the rights of non-English speaking students that stems from the Supreme Court decision in *Lau v. Nichols* (1974), have contributed to persistent achievement disparities between Latino emergent bilinguals (EBs) and their peers, regardless of grade level or subject area (see Figures 2.2 and 2.3).[5]

The political landscape of the United States has shaped the ebb and flow of language policies. Early in our history, ideologies were purported to "justify the exploitation of enslaved African peoples" (Wiley & Wright, 2004, p. 146) as well as to "expedite deculturation and pacification" among Indigenous populations (p. 146). In 1906, Congress enacted an English language requirement for citizenship "undoubtedly in reaction to an all-time high level of immigration" (Linton, 2004, p. 282).

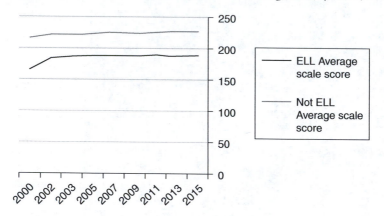

FIGURE 2.2 Reading 4th grade, NAEP.

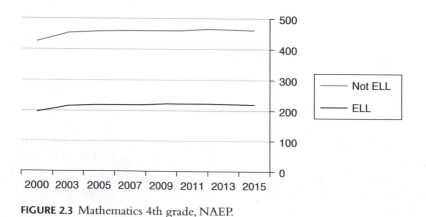

FIGURE 2.3 Mathematics 4th grade, NAEP.

Despite numerous bilingual schools prior to World War I, the use of German and other foreign languages became restricted in schools "until Grades 6 to 8, when it was less likely that children would draw on their native languages" (Wiley & Wright, 2004, p. 147). In more recent times, the anti-bilingual climate that tends to target Spanish speaking populations has increased commensurately with the growing Latino population (Wiley & Wright, 2004) that is attributable in part to legislation "to open the nation's borders" passed by Congress in 1965 (Krogstad & Keegan, 2014).

As mentioned earlier, scholars consider the ESEA as the stimulus that facilitated efforts aimed at educational equity. In 1968, the ESEA included the first legislation in our recent history that focused on the rights of EB students with Title VII, known as the "Bilingual Education Act" (for a historical account of the law, see Lyons, 1990). Title VII was optional, providing competitive funding to school districts for research on approaches to language acquisition. Two events in 1974, however, prompted a change in the optional nature of Title VII. One was the Supreme Court's decision in *Lau v. Nichols* (1974), which determined that the failure to provide students who do not speak English with "adequate instructional procedures" (para. 1) was a violation of the 1964 Civil Rights Act. The second was the Equal Educational Opportunity Act (EEOA), which

> requires state educational agencies and school districts to take action to overcome language barriers that impede English Language Learner students from participating equally in school districts' educational programs.
>
> *(US Department of Justice, n. d., para. 6)*

The 1974 amendments to the Bilingual Education Act included explicit reference to bilingual education programs that "provided instruction in English and in the native language of the student to allow the student to progress effectively through the educational system" (Stewner-Manzanares, 1988, p. 3). Amendments also included "capacity-building efforts" that included the expansion of curricula, research, and staffing so that "school districts could develop enough expertise to operate bilingual education programs without federal assistance" (p. 3).

Between 1978 and 1988, successive reauthorizations of the Bilingual Education Act changed the language of the law from mandating exclusively bilingual education strategies to including immersion strategies (see Gándara & Rumberger, 2009; Ramirez et al., 1991). Capacity-building was also altered, so that program funding was reduced to support school districts for only one to three years (Stewner-Manzanares 1988). With No Child Left Behind (NCLB) in 2001, Title VII became Title III and eliminated all references to biliteracy, bilingualism, and bilingual education (Gándara & Rumberger, 2009). The notion of capacity-building has remained, although it is limited to the following description:

> Each recipient of a grant under this subpart shall use the grant in ways that will build such recipient's capacity to continue to offer high-quality

language instruction educational programs and special alternative instruction programs to limited English proficient children after Federal assistance is reduced or eliminated.

(NCLB 2001, Sec. 3215)

To ensure compliance with the Equal Education Opportunity Act of 1974, which "prohibited instructional programs that in effect excluded English language learners" (Moran 2011, 408), three criteria were outlined by the Fifth Circuit Court of Appeals in the *Castañeda v. Pickard* (1981) decision. The criteria were 1) that language acquisition instructional programs must be supported by experts in the field, 2) school districts must provide adequate resources and personnel to carry out the instructional program, and 3) the program must be evaluated and inform necessary adjustments (see Moran, 2011).

The first of the *Castañeda* criteria has a vast body of research spanning several decades. Reviews of empirical studies have favored approaches that incorporate students' native language (August & Shannahan 2008; Rolstad, Mahoney, & Glass, 2005; Slavin & Cheung 2005)—approaches considered to be *additive* (Lambert, 1985). Nevertheless, in the late 1990s and early 2000s, California, Arizona, and Massachusetts replaced bilingual education with Structured/Sheltered English Immersion[5] (SEI) after proponents of SEI promulgated its superiority to effectively transition EBs to English fluency (e.g., Crawford 1997; Rossell 2002). Although one of the pervasive limitations cited in reviews examining the effectiveness of different language acquisition instructional programs is the absence of randomized studies, researchers utilizing random assignment have found that bilingual approaches do not hinder English proficiency development (Slavin, Madden, Calderón, Chamberlain, & Hennessy, 2010; Tong et al., 2008).

Despite evidence that bilingual approaches do not impede English acquisition (Slavin et al. 2010) and are also associated with better achievement outcomes than English only approaches (Valentino & Reardon, 2015), Arizona, California, and Massachusetts replaced earlier mandates favoring bilingual approaches with SEI, a term that had not been "in current use in the language education profession but is a confusing combination of terms" (Krashen, 1997). Indeed, the confusion with terminology was equally unclear to the teachers charged with its implementation in classrooms (Wright & Pu, 2005).

The lack of appropriate funding, the second criteria in *Castañeda v. Pickard,* has resulted in lawsuits in almost every state (Horsford & Sampson, 2013). Although the replacement of bilingual education with SEI began in California, Arizona is among the most visible in facing challenges rooted in accountability to the second criteria, described in more detail in the subsequent section. The third criteria, which is closely tied to the first, reflects the matter of *how* to ensure equitable educational opportunities for Latino EBs in the United States, and it persists as "one of the most volatile questions in American education" (Cummins, 1992, 91). Namely, the experts that support the program are chosen more often based on ideology than evidence.

To illustrate, proponents of SEI have misrepresented the sentiments of noted language acquisition scholars to create an image of support for SEI, and thus be in compliance with the first criteria outlined by *Castañeda v. Pickard*. A research summary presented by the Arizona Department of Education asserts that August and Hakuta (1997) "concluded that little scientific research had been conducted with school-age EBs and expressed their concern about how 'politics have constrained the development of sound practice and research in this field.'" The politics August and Hakuta referenced, however, were the very ones that have maintained SEI in Arizona. Indeed, in a declaration to the State of California, Hakuta (1998) explicitly states that citations of his and other scholars' work "misrepresent its main findings." He further asserts that "there is no defensible theory base to the programs prescribed by Proposition 227" and "outcomes for students placed in programs similar to those proposed by Proposition 227 are alarmingly poor, hardly worthy of state-wide prescription, and harmful to students." Despite Hakuta's declaration, SEI continues to be implemented in Arizona, with his work cited by the Arizona Department of Education as *support* for SEI.

Latino EBs in Arizona[6]

Arizona policies reflect numerous efforts to eliminate Latino cultural and linguistic heritage in schools (see Jiménez-Castellanos, Combs, Martínez, & Gómez, 2013). Prior to the language restrictions that resulted from Proposition 203 (2000), a voter-approved amendment to the Arizona Constitution declared, "all political subdivisions of this State shall act in English and no other language" (*Yniquez v. Arizonans for Official English,* 1995). The amendment, however, was found to be in violation of the First Amendment of the U.S. Constitution. In the Court's opinion, the amendment's impact fell "almost entirely upon Hispanics … since language is a close and meaningful proxy for national origin, restrictions on the use of language may mask discrimination against specific national origin groups" (*Yniquez v. Arizonans for Official English*, 1995).

Many of the legislative efforts that have persistently failed to meet the needs of EBs—the overwhelming majority of whom are Latino (see Gándara & Orfield, 2012; Thompson, 2013)—have been promulgated with the guise of meeting their needs (see Jiménez-Castellanos et al., 2013). In response to the federal district court decision that "had begun fining Arizona $500,000 a day for failing to respond to court orders to increase funding for EB education in a way that reflected the actual needs of the students" (Gándara & Orfield, 2012, p. 10), Arizona House Bill 2064 (2006) created a task force charged with implementing a program that had explicit guidance in contrast to the nebulous formulation of SEI that had existed up to that time. As a result, since 2006, Arizona policy has expressly required the segregation of EBs given its self-appointed status as an "English first" state.

The more recent SEI model used in Arizona requires that EBs are grouped homogenously to the extent possible based on English proficiency, and that they receive explicit English instruction in four-hour blocks (ADE, 2008). Thus, EBs are typically segregated from students with different English proficiency levels as well as from academic content that is covered while they attend the four-hour block of English instruction. In a review using various sources of evidence to determine the extent to which Arizona's SEI implementation was addressing the needs of EBs, Martinez-Wenzl, Perez, and Gándara (2012) found that

> SEI as implemented in Arizona carries serious negative consequences for EB students stemming from the excessive amount of time dedicated to a sole focus on English instruction, the de-emphasis on grade level academic curriculum, the discrete skills approach it employs, and the segregation of EB students from mainstream peers.
>
> *(para. 4)*

In contrast to SEI, the evidence favoring dual language approaches is overwhelming (see Thompson, 2013). One reason dual language programs are considered the solution to traditional methods of providing equitable learning opportunities to EBs is because they are viewed as assets to their peers (Collier & Thomas, 2004). As Thompson (2013) explains:

> Dual-language programs hold appeal for another important reason, as well. Some critics of attempts to equalize opportunities within education via compensatory programs, such as temporary English as a Second Language pull-out programs, charge that these programs are inadequate because they do not capitalize on or develop the unique abilities of marginalized students. In the case of linguistic minority students, such compensatory programs leave the status quo, in this case the monolingual English norm, unchallenged, while ignoring the valuable bilingual skills that linguistic minority students bring to school.
>
> *(p. 1267)*

Although a review of the extant research on dual language approaches reveals a focus on the benefits to EBs, the potential of these programs to address the needs of Latino, English-proficient youth has been long ignored. Indeed, considering work by scholars who assert that English-proficient Latinos are also pervasively underserved in schools (Valenzuela, 1999) as well as evidence that language is key in informing students' identity and achievement (e.g., González, 2001; Ovando, 2003), examining the ways dual language may ameliorate disparate achievement outcomes for *all* Latino youth is salient. An additional consideration is that the matter of examining language and achievement trajectories is not simply a conceptualization of EB and non-EB. As described by García (2009):

> In cases when bilingualism is developed after the language practices of a community have been suppressed, the development of the community's

mother tongue is not a simple addition that starts from a monolingual point … Therefore, bilingualism is not simply additive, but recursive.

(p. 52)

In Arizona, all teachers[7] must meet the requirements for SEI endorsement, which ranges from "three semester hours of courses related to the teaching of the English Language Learner Proficiency Standards," "completion of 45 clock hours of professional development in the teaching of the English Language Learner Proficiency Standards," or "a passing score on the Structured English Immersion portion of the Arizona Teacher Proficiency Assessment." These highly disparate requirements reflect policies that were adopted in Arizona in 2008.

Indeed, in a review of teachers' perception of SEI, Rios-Aguilar et al. (2012) found that SEI strategies restricted EBs' access to academic content and inclusion among peers. Regardless of Arizona's state policy, teachers acknowledge that they are both content and language teachers, and as such, require the training that can better prepare them to meet the needs of their students (Cruze, Cota, & López, 2017) and can explain why the graduation rate among EBs has become dismal, dropping from 44% in 2006–2007 to 18% in 2013–2014 (NCELA, n.d.).

Standards for teacher preparation are particularly urgent in Arizona, where researchers have documented notable differences among teachers with varying certifications. Lillie, Markos, Arias, and Wiley (2012), for example, found that

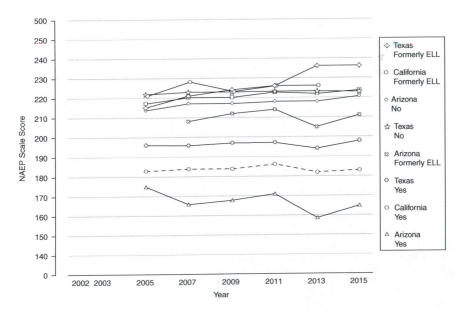

FIGURE 2.4 4th grade reading performance of EBs, Former-EBs, and Never-EBs in Arizona, California, and Texas.

whereas teachers invariably use English instruction to comply with state policy regardless of certification, teachers with bilingual/ESL certification

> drew on their past experiences teaching in ESL or bilingual classes, as well as their previous preparation for said endorsements, as means for negotiating what the state was asking them to do in the four-hour model and what they felt was best for their students.

> *(p. 13)*

Moreover, regardless of state policy, teachers acknowledge that they are both content and language teachers, and, as such, require the training that can better prepare them to meet the needs of their students (Cruze, Cota, & López, 2016). Thus, research and practitioners agree that more than is currently required is necessary, but the state remains woefully ineffectual. This claim is substantiated by the performance of EBs in Arizona, who underperform compared to their EB peers in both Texas and California even when they are no longer labeled EBs (see Figure 2.4).

As detailed in this chapter, deficiency views of Latino youth are a prominent part of U.S. history. Restricting knowledge (e.g., banning Mexican history and Spanish from schools), as well as promulgating pejorative descriptions of Mexicans, has been a reoccurring theme. Although education policies that hinder access to cultural and linguistic resources have remained ineffectual, these sociopolitical/sociohistorical contexts are further complicated by other policies specific to Arizona that I review in Chapter 3.

Notes

1 Although I focus on Mexican American students in this book, the issues with accurate disaggregation (see Nieto, 1998) prevent me from using "Mexican American" instead of the more general category of "Latino" throughout.
2 Numerous other countries are represented in the United States and include Costa Rica, Cuba, Dominican Republic, Guatemala, Honduras, Nicaragua, Panama, El Salvador, Argentina, Bolivia, Chile, Colombia, Ecuador, Paraguay, Uruguay, and Venezuela as countries of origin. Given the history of colonization that is unique to those of Mexican and Puerto Rican descent, I focus on these Latino groups in this review.
3 Judge Tashima found that there was racial animus in the creation and implementation of HB 2281 and deemed it a violation of students' First Amendment rights (*González v. Douglas*, 2017).
4 This section includes excerpts that originally appeared in López, McEneaney, and Nieswandt (2015).
5 Source: NAEP Data explorer.
6 This section includes excerpts that originally appeared in López (2016).
7 All teachers must have content-area certification and SEI endorsement.

References

Apple, M. W. (2004). *Ideology and curriculum* (3rd ed.). Boston, MA: Routledge.

Arizona Department of Education. (2008). Structured English Immersion EDL Models. Retrieved from http://www.azed.gov/wp-content/uploads/PDF/SEIModels05-14-08.pdf

August, D., & Hakuta, K. (Eds.). (1997). Improving schooling for language-minority children. Washington, DC: National Academy Press. Retrieved from http://www.nap.edu/ openbook.php?record_id=5286&page=R1

August, D., & Shanahan, T. (Eds.). (2008). *Developing reading and writing in second-language learners: Lessons from the report of the National Literacy Panel on language-minority children and youth*. New York, NY: Routledge.

Bowles, S., & Gintis, H. (1976). *Schooling in capitalist America* (Vol. 57). New York: Basic Books.

Bowles, S., & Gintis, H. (2002). Schooling in capitalist America revisited. *Sociology of Education, 75*, 1–18.

Collier, V. P., & Thomas, W. P. (2004). The astounding effectiveness of dual language education for all. *NABE Journal of Research and Practice, 2*, 1–20.

Crawford, J. (1997). The campaign against Proposition 227: A post mortem. *Bilingual Research Journal, 21*, 1–29.

Cruze, A., Cota, M., & López, F. (April, 2017). A decade after Arizona SEI: Teachers' perspectives on implementation of SEI and alternative approaches. Paper presented at the annual meetings of the American Educational Research Association, San Antonio, TX.

Cummins, J. (1992). Bilingual education and English immersion: The Ramirez Report in theoretical perspective. *Bilingual Research Journal, 16*, 91–104.

Darder, A. (2012). *Culture and power in the classroom: A critical foundation for the education of bicultural students* (2nd ed.). Boulder, CO: Paradigm Press.

Gándara, P., & Orfield, G. (2012). Segregating Arizona's English learners: A return to the "Mexican Room"? *Teachers College Record, 114*, 1–27.

Gándara, P., & Rumberger, R. (2009). Immigration, language, and education: How does language policy structure opportunity? *Teachers College Record 111*, 750–782.

García, O. (2009). *Bilingual education in the 21st century: A global perspective*. Malden, MA and Oxford: Basil/Blackwell.

García, O., Kleifgen, J. A., & Falchi, L. (2008). *From English learners to emergent bilinguals*. Equity Matters Research Review No. 1, Teachers College, Columbia University.

Gay, G. (2010). *Culturally responsive teaching: Theory, research, and practice* (2nd ed.). New York, NY: Teachers College Press.

González, N. (2001). *I am my language: Discourses of women and children in the borderlands*. Tucson, AZ: University of Arizona Press.

Gutiérrez, K. D., & Rogoff, B. (2003). Cultural ways of learning: Individual traits or repertoires of practice. *Educational researcher, 32*, 19–25.

Hakuta, K. (1998). Supplemental declaration to State of California. Retrieved from http://www.languagepolicy.net/archives/hakuta3.htm

Halperin, S. (1975). ESEA ten years later. *Educational Researcher, 4*, 5–9.

Horsford, S. D., & Sampson, C. (2013). High ELL-growth states: Expanding funding equity and opportunity for English language learners. *Voices in Urban Education, 37*, 47–54.

Isensee, L. (September 14, 2006). Texas textbook called out as "racist" against Mexican–Americans. National Public Radio. Retrieved at http://www.npr.org/sections/ed/2016/09/14/493766128/texas–textbook–called–out–as–racist–against–mexican–americans.

Jiménez–Castellanos, O., Combs, M. C., Martínez, D., & Gómez, L. (2013). English language learners: What's at stake for Arizona? Latino Public Policy Center, Morrison Institute for Public Policy, Arizona Indicators, Arizona State University. Retrieved from http://arizonaindicators.org/sites/default/files/content/publications/ELL_stake.pdf.

Klein, C. A. (1996). Treaties of conquest: Property rights, Indian treaties, and the Treaty of Guadalupe Hidalgo. *New Mexico Law Review, 26,* 201–255.

Krashen, S. D. (1997). A researcher's view of Unz. Retrieved from http://www.languagepolicy.net/archives/Krashen1.htm.

Krogstad, J. M., & Keegan, M. (2014). From Germany to Mexico: How America's source of immigrants has changed over a century. Washington, DC: Pew Research Center, http://www.pewresearch.org/fact–tank/2014/05/27/a–shift–from–germany–to–mexico–for–americas–immigrants/.

Lambert, W. E. (1985). Some cognitive and sociocultural consequences of being bilingual. In J. E. Alatis and J. J. Staczek (Eds.), *Perspectives on bilingualism and bilingual education: International dimensions of bilingual education.* Washington, DC: Georgetown University Press.

Lillie, K. E., Markos, A., Arias, M. B., & Wiley, T. G. (2012). Separate and not equal: The implementation of Structured English Immersion in Arizona's classrooms. *Teachers College Record, 114*(9), 1–33.

Linton, A. (2004). A critical mass model of bilingualism among US-born Hispanics. *Social Forces, 83,* 279–314.

López, F., McEneaney, E., & Nieswandt, M. (2015). Language instruction educational programs and academic achievement of Latino English learners: Considerations for states with changing demographics. *American Journal of Education, 121,* 417–450.

McNamee, S. J., & Miller, R. K. (2004). The meritocracy myth. *Sociation Today, 2.* Retrieved at http://www.ncsociology.org/sociationtoday/v21/merit.htm?wptouch_preview_theme=enabled.

Martinez–Wenzl, M., Perez, K., & Gándara, P. (2012). Is Arizona's approach to educating its ELs superior to other forms of instruction? *Teachers College Record, 114,* 1–32.

Moran, R. F. (2011). Equal liberties and English language learners: The special case of Structured Immersion initiatives. *Howard Law Journal, 54,* 397–424.

Nieto, S. (1999). *The light in their eyes: Creating multicultural learning communities.* New York: Teachers College Press.

Nieto, S., & Irizarry, J. G. (2012). Instructional practices and approaches. *Journal of the Association of Mexican American Educators, 6,* 17–21.

Oakes, J. (2005). *Keeping track.* New Haven, CT: Yale University Press.

Ovando, C. (2003). Bilingual education in the United States: Historical development and current issues. *Bilingual Research Journal, 27,* 1–25.

Ramirez, J. D, Yuen, S. D., Ramey, D. R., & Pasta, D. J. (1991). *Final report: Longitudinal study of Structured Immersion Strategy, early-exit, and late-exit transitional bilingual education programs for language-minority children.* San Mateo, CA: Aguirre International.

Rios–Aguilar, C., Canche, M. S. G., & Moll, L. C. (2012). Implementing structured English immersion in Arizona. *Teachers College Record, 114*(9), 1–18.

Rolstad, K., Mahoney, K., & Glass, G. V. (2005). The big picture: A meta–analysis of program effectiveness research on English language learners. *Educational Policy, 19,* 572–594.

Rossell, C. H. (2002). *Dismantling bilingual education implementing English immersion: The California initiative.* San Francisco: Public Policy Institute of California.

San Miguel, G., & Valencia, R. R. (1998). From the Treaty of Guadalupe Hidalgo to Hopwood: The educational plight and struggle of Mexican Americans in the Southwest. *Harvard Educational Review, 68*, 353–413.

Slavin, R. E., & Cheung, A. (2005). A synthesis of research on language of reading instruction for English language learners. *Review of Educational Research, 75*(2), 247–284.

Slavin, R. E., Madden, N., Calderón, M., Chamberlain, A., & Hennessy, M. (2011). Reading and language outcomes of a multiyear randomized evaluation of transitional bilingual education. *Educational Evaluation and Policy Analysis, 33*, 47–58.

Stepler, R., & Brown, A. (2016). *Statistical portrait of Hispanics in the United States.* Pew Research Hispanic Trends Project. Retrieved at http://www.pewhispanic.org/2016/04/19/statistical–portrait–of–hispanics–in–the–united–states/.

Stewner-Manzanares, G. (1988). The Bilingual Education Act: Twenty years later. *New Focus, Occasional Papers in Bilingual Education, 6*, 2–8.

Thompson, K. D. (2013). Is separate always unequal? A philosophical examination of ideas of equality in key cases regarding racial and linguistic minorities in education. *American Educational Research Journal, 50*, 1249–1278.

Tong, F., Lara-Alecio, R., Irby, B., Mathes, P., & Kwok, O. (2008). Accelerating early academic Oral English development in transitional bilingual and structured English immersion programs. *American Educational Research Journal 45*, 1011–44.

U.S. Census Bureau. (2010). The 2010 statistical abstract. Retrieved from http://www.census.gov. DC: US Department of Justice. Retrieved at http://www.justice.gov/crt/about/edu/types.php.

Valentino, R. A., & Reardon, S. F. (2015). Effectiveness of four instructional programs designed to serve English learners: Variation by ethnicity and initial English proficiency. *Educational Evaluation and Policy Analysis, 37*, 612–637.

Valenzuela, A. (1999). *Subtractive schooling: U.S. Mexican youth and the politics of caring.* Albany, NY: SUNY Press.

Wiley, T. G., & Wright, W. E. (2004). Against the undertow: Language minority education policy and politics in the "age of accountability." *Educational Policy, 18*, 142–68.

Wright, W. E., & Pu, C. (2005). Academic achievement of English language learners in post–Proposition 203 Arizona. Policy brief, Education Policy Studies Laboratory Language Policy Research Unit, Arizona State University, http://epsl.asu.edu/epru/documents/EPSL–0509–103–LPRU.pdf.

3

THE CONTEXT OF THE STUDY

TUSD Desegregation and Obstacles for Latinos[1]

Francesca A. López

In 1909, Tucson Unified School District (TUSD) decreed the separate-but-equal (*Plessy v. Ferguson* 1896) segregation of Black students in its schools (Cooper, 1967), subsequently opening Dunbar, a school for African American students (Brown, 2012). Three years prior to the reversal of segregative policies with the Supreme Court's decision in *Brown I*, however, TUSD became the first district in the state of Arizona to repeal mandatory segregation (Brousseau, 1993). As a result, Dunbar was renamed John Spring and students were reassigned to the neighboring schools, Roosevelt and University Heights (Brown, 2012; TUSD, 1978). Without a more fully defined desegregation plan, however, the Department of Health, Education, and Welfare (HEW) determined in 1973 that TUSD schools remained racially imbalanced and required more forceful action to be in compliance with the *Brown II* decision (Brousseau, 1993). Despite ceasing new school construction in areas of growth, modifying attendance lines, and initiating a voluntary "ethnic transfer policy to encourage student transfers to other schools when both schools would improve in ethnic balance," twenty-eight TUSD schools were still "racially identifiable" in 1974 (Brousseau, 1993, para. 7).

That same year, the National Association for the Advancement of Colored People (NAACP) and the Mexican American Legal Defense and Educational Fund (MALDEF) each filed a lawsuit against TUSD on the behalf of African American and Mexican American parents. The lawsuit charged the district with segregation and discrimination (*Fisher-Mendoza v. TUSD*, 1978). The cases were consolidated in 1975; Roy Fisher and Maria Mendoza "were certified as class representatives" for the students (*Mendoza v. United States*, 1980, para. 1). In its 1978 decision, the District Court found that TUSD had indeed failed to remedy vestiges of segregation and discrimination for African American students, but found no such dual school system had existed with respect to Mexican American students, nor did any continuing system-wide practice of intentional discrimination occur.

(Mendoza v. United States, 1980, para. 4)

Nevertheless, to remedy "current effects of the past intentionally segregative acts of the School District" (*Mendoza v United States*, 1980, para. 4), the District Court ordered the desegregation of nine schools. Of the six schools considered to be vestiges of prior segregation, John Spring, Roosevelt, and University Heights were closed in 1978 (Brousseau, 1993). The remaining three schools were considered to reflect past discriminatory acts that included the timing of construction and attendance boundaries, which resulted in a school that was predominantly White despite being situated in a predominantly Mexican American community. TUSD submitted a Settlement Agreement that went beyond the Court's order, delineating desegregation efforts in twenty-one schools by closing some schools and establishing magnet schools to promote voluntary desegregation. The Court approved TUSD's desegregation plans, establishing federal oversight of the district (*Mendoza v. United States*, 1980).

Among the twenty-eight schools deemed racially segregated by HEW in 1973 and the Court in 1978 were Borton, Carrillo, Davis Bilingual, and Holladay elementary schools (Brousseau, 1993). As outlined in the Settlement Agreement, these elementary schools became magnet schools in the late 1970s and early 1980s to address desegregation by attracting non-minority students from other areas of the district. Soon after their designation as magnet schools, all the schools were lauded as successful exemplars of integration, having met the court-ordered ethnic proportions that were not to exceed 50%[2] in any category (Brousseau, 1993; Grant, 1982). The Superintendent of TUSD at the time wrote:

> The Tucson Unified School District has avoided most of the negative and divisive results of desegregation. Credit is due largely to parent and community involvement, magnet programs that encouraged and produced voluntary transfers, and board support for and commitment to success rather than bare-bones compliance.

> *(Grant, 1982, p. 539)*

Although credit for meeting integration criteria is appropriately attributed to the appeal of magnet schools, there were other factors that abetted the increase of White student enrollment in previously majority–minority schools. One contributing factor was TUSD Board Policy 5090, which had been in place since 1969 to prevent students from transferring within the district unless the transfer improved the ethnic balance of both schools. District demographics also played a role, given that White students represented a numerical majority (65%) of district enrollment at the time. Together, these factors contributed to the appearance that integration was a success due to the voluntary nature of magnet schools.

Evidence that TUSD was compliant with the court-ordered ethnic proportions soon after the involvement of the courts notwithstanding (Brosseau, 1993; Grant, 1982), it was more than a quarter of a century before the District Court issued a *sua sponte* order in 2004, compelling TUSD to file a petition for unitary status—a "unitary, nonracial system" (*Green*, 1968, p. 391 U.S. 440)—that would terminate federal oversight. In response to TUSD's petition in 2005, the District Court determined that TUSD had not provided sufficient evidence that it had "eliminated the vestiges of de jure segregation to the extent practicable" (*Fisher v. United States*, 2007) and required TUSD to submit a "comprehensive report on its compliance efforts with regard to student assignments" ("Ninth Circuit," 2011). After a review of the compliance effort documentation, the District Court deemed TUSD unitary in 2009, despite its acknowledgement that the district had not monitored desegregation efforts to the extent required by the Court. Judge Bury asserted: "the Court finds that TUSD's lack of good faith is proven by the simple fact that these expert reports were only secured by the Defendant to belatedly support its Petition for Unitary Status" (*Fisher v. U.S.*, 2008). Nevertheless, in his decision deeming TUSD unitary, pending the district's submission of a post-unitary plan, Judge Bury stated:

> The Court finds that the ethnic and race ratios required under the Settlement Agreement desegregation plans were implemented and maintained for 5 years, and eliminated to the extent practicable the vestiges of de jure segregation.
>
> *(Fisher v. U.S., 2008)*

The plaintiffs, Fisher and Mendoza, appealed the decision; the Ninth Circuit Court reversed and remanded the District Court's decision (*Fisher-Mendoza v. TUSD*, 2011). In its decision, the Ninth Circuit Court considered the District Court's findings that TUSD had neither demonstrated good-faith compliance with the desegregation efforts outlined in the Settlement Agreement nor eliminated vestiges of past discrimination given its negligence in addressing *Green*[3] factors that included transportation and extracurricular activities. Accordingly, the Ninth Circuit Court decision pointed to Supreme Court precedent, which guides courts to grant unitary status only *after* good faith efforts are presented, and not when "a plan that merely promises future improvements is adopted" (*Fisher v. TUSD*, 2011, p. 9791). Given the complexities of the case, the District Court appointed Willis D. Hawley as Special Master in January 2012. Hawley's role, as an expert on desegregation issues, was to oversee the creation of a unitary status plan (USP) for TUSD.

Although the District Court had found evidence that TUSD had previously maintained appropriate ethnic ratios in magnet schools when it granted TUSD unitary status, the reversal of the decision required that TUSD evaluate the current state of integration in all magnet schools. In following the Court's orders, TUSD contracted Education Consulting Services (ECS) to review the magnet programs for integration. Among the agency's findings was that many of the magnet schools were racially identifiable and lacked the infrastructure that would enable the district to achieve court-ordered integration, which included central coordination and support; focus and strategy regarding diversity, outreach, and marketing; and recruitment efforts (TUSD, 2013a). It should be noted that the findings regarding TUSD's lack of integration in magnet schools after several years of meeting enrollment ratios came shortly after TUSD's Board Policy 5090, which had prevented students from transferring within the district unless the transfer improved the ethnic balance of both schools, was deemed unconstitutional by Judge Bury in 2007. Judge Bury based his decision on the Supreme Court's ruling in the consolidated cases of *Parents v. Seattle School District* and *Meredith v. Jefferson County Board of Education*,[4] which considered any use of race or ethnicity as a factor in voluntary desegregation student assignment plans unconstitutional (Davis, 2013, p. 7). The Supreme Court's decision, however, was based in part on the fact that the districts involved in the case were "not under a court-ordered desegregation decree" (Arizona State Senate, 2008, p. 3). As such, Judge Bury's error in eliminating Board Policy 5090 contributed in part to TUSD's inability to maintain the racial and ethnic balance across magnet schools that is essential to achieving unitary status.

Judge Bury directed Hawley to propose a magnet plan in collaboration with the plaintiffs and TUSD that would result in the most effective remediation of past segregation reflected by no more than 70% of students belonging to any one ethnic or racial group (*Fisher v. TUSD*, 2013)—a modification of the original 50% racial concentration threshold that considered the current district demographics. To wit, at the time of the Court's decision in 1978, TUSD's student enrollment was 65% White; by 2013, it was 65% Latino. After reviewing ECS's findings, Hawley, TUSD, and the plaintiffs outlined a magnet plan that included the elimination of magnet status for several schools located in the most Latino-dense areas of the district, whereas magnet status would be retained and potentially expanded in schools that were located in less Latino-dense areas. Thus, Borton and Holladay were labeled successful magnet[5] schools, whereas Carrillo and Davis Bilingual were considered non-compliant and were threatened with the loss of magnet status (TUSD 2013a; see Tables 3.1–3.4).

Although the schools deemed out of compliance are located in the most Latino-dense areas of the district, non-compliance due to ethnic and racial proportions is a relatively recent phenomenon. Carrillo's Latino enrollment did not surpass the threshold until the 2003–2004 school year, the same year White student enrollment in the district dropped to approximately 36% (see Figure 3.1). For Davis Bilingual, the pivotal year was 2000–2001 (see Tables 3.1 and 3.2), the year Arizona's Proposition 203 replaced bilingual education with Structured

TABLE 3.1 Carrillo Elementary, Magnet School Designated as Non-Compliant

		1996–97	1997–98	1998–99	1999–0	2000–1	2001–2	2002–3	2003–4	2004–5	2005–6	2006–7	2007–8	2008–9	2009–10	2010–11	2011–12	2012–13	2013–14	2014–15	2015–16	Overall change from 1996–2016
White	N	81	76	81	78	72	61	41	25	26	24	20	24	34	38	12	12	14	11	26	32	
	%	33.6	32.2	35.8	32.1	30	25.7	18.1	13.1	16	13.9	10.7	10.3	11	10.8	3.5	3.8	4.5	3.6	8.8	11.3	
% Change			-1.4	3.6	-3.7	-2.1	-4.3	-7.6	-5	2.9	-2.1	-3.2	-0.4	0.7	-0.2	-7.3	0.3	0.7	-0.9	5.2	2.5	-22.3
African American	N	6	6	4	10	7	6	10	6	4	5	12	28	21	14	18	11	10	12	12	8	
	%	2.5	2.5	1.8	4.1	2.9	2.5	4.4	3.1	2.5	2.9	6.4	12.1	6.8	4	5.3	3.5	3.2	3.9	4.1	2.8	
% Change			0	-0.7	2.3	-1.2	-0.4	1.9	-1.3	-0.6	0.4	3.5	5.7	-5.3	-2.8	1.3	-1.8	-0.3	0.7	0.2	-1.3	0.3
Hispanic	N	142	138	125	140	146	153	157	140	117	134	148	170	233	278	291	285	274	276	251	234	
	%	58.9	58.5	55.3	57.6	60.8	64.6	69.2	73.3	72.2	77.5	79.1	73.3	75.6	78.8	85.8	89.6	88.4	89.6	84.8	83	
% Change			-0.4	-3.2	2.3	3.2	3.8	4.6	4.1	-1.1	5.3	1.6	-5.8	2.3	3.2	7	1.2	-1.2	1.2	-4.8	-1.8	24.1
Native American	N	11	16	16	15	14	17	17	20	15	9	7	10	19	23	16	9	10	7	6	8	
	%	4.6	6.8	7.1	6.2	5.8	7.2	7.5	10.5	9.3	5.2	3.7	4.3	6.2	6.5	4.7	2.8	3.2	2.3	2	2.8	
% Change			2.2	0.3	-0.9	-0.4	1.4	0.3	3.0	-1.2	-4.1	-1.5	0.6	1.9	0.3	-1.8	-1.9	0.4	-0.9	-0.3		-1.8
Asian	N	1	0	0	1	1	2	0	0	1	1	0	0	1	0	0	1	1	0	0	0	
	%	0.4	0	0	0.4	0.4	0.9	0.9	0	0	0.6	0	0.3	0.3	0	0.3	0.3	0.3	0	0	0	
% Change			-0.4	0	0.4	0	-0.4	0.9	-0.9	0	0.6	-0.6	0	0.3	-0.3	0.3	0	0	-0.3	0		-0.4
Total	N	241	236	226	243	240	237	227	191	162	173	187	232	308	353	337	318	310	308	296	282	

TABLE 3.2 Davis Bilingual Elementary, Magnet School Designated as Non-Compliant

		1996–97	1997–98	1998–99	1999–00	2000–01	2001–02	2002–03	2003–04	2004–05	2005–06	2006–07	2007–08	2008–09	2009–10	2010–11	2011–12	2012–13	2013–14	2014–15	2015–16	Overall change from 1996–2016
White	N	58	51	52	47	53	54	54	50	46	49	53	63	62	55	29	33	33	37	39	44	
	%	26.4	22.8	23.2	21.7	23	21.1	21	19.6	17.9	19.4	20.1	23.2	22.1	19.8	9.6	10.5	10.3	10.6	11.3	13.2	
% Change			-3.6	0.4	-1.5	1.3	-1.9	-0.1	-1.4	-1.7	1.5	0.7	3.1	-1.1	-2.3	-10.2	0.9	-0.2	0.3	0.7	1.9	-13.2
African American	N	13	15	11	10	8	8	7	6	5	3	3	3	1	4	4	5	5	6	3	8	
	%	5.9	6.7	4.9	4.6	3.5	3.1	2.7	2.4	1.9	1.2	1.1	1.1	0.4	1.4	1.3	1.6	1.6	1.7	0.9	2.4	
% Change			0.8	-1.8	-0.3	-1.1	-0.4	-0.4	-0.3	-0.5	-0.7	-0.1	0	-0.7	1	-0.1	0.3	0	0.1	-0.8	1.5	-3.5
Hispanic	N	139	146	152	153	165	185	190	187	192	184	192	195	207	208	259	267	272	296	297	269	
	%	63.2	65.2	67.9	70.5	71.7	72.3	73.9	73.3	74.7	73	72.7	71.7	73.9	74.8	85.5	84.8	85.3	85.1	86.1	80.8	
% Change			2	2.7	2.6	1.2	0.6	1.6	-0.6	1.4	-1.7	-0.3	-1	2.2	0.9	10.7	-0.7	0.5	-0.2	1	-5.3	17.6
Native American	N	9	10	9	7	4	9	4	9	11	11	10	5	5	6	9	7	7	6	3	6	
	%	4.1	4.5	4	3.2	1.7	3.5	1.6	3.5	4.3	4.4	3.8	1.8	1.8	2.2	3	2.2	2.2	1.7	0.9	1.8	
% Change			0.4	-0.5	-0.8	-1.5	1.8	-1.9	1.9	0.8	0.1	-0.6	-2	0	0.4	0.8	-0.8	0	-0.5	-0.8	0.9	-2.3
Asian	N	1	2	0	0	0	0	2	3	3	5	6	6	5	5	1	2	0	0	0	2	
	%	0.5	0.9	0	0	0	0	0.8	1.2	1.2	2	2.3	2.2	1.8	1.8	0.3	0.6	0	0	0	0.6	
% Change			0.4	-0.9	0	0	0	0.8	0.4	0	0.8	0.3	-0.1	-0.4	0	-1.5	0.3	-0.6	0	0	0.6	0.1
Total	N	220	224	224	217	230	256	257	255	257	252	264	272	280	278	302	314	319	348	345	333	

TABLE 3.3 Borton Elementary, Magnet School Designated as successful

		1996-97	1997-98	1998-99	1999-00	2000-01	2001-02	2002-03	2003-04	2004-05	2005-06	2006-07	2007-08	2008-09	2009-10	2010-11	2011-12	2012-13	2013-14	2014-15	2015-16	Overall change from 1996-2016
White	N	100	110	112	112	117	118	114	105	109	117	120	138	138	123	91	101	120	91	95	93	
	%	44.8	50	50.7	51.1	54.2	51.8	47.5	42.3	44.5	45	45.1	47.4	40.5	35.3	26.6	27.4	28.5	22	20.7	21.4	-23.4
% Change			5.2	0.7	0.4	3.1	-2.4	-4.3	-5.2	2.2	0.5	0.2	2.3	-6.9	-5.2	-8.7	0.8	1.1	-6.5	-1.3	0.7	
African American	N	14	14	13	10	12	10	19	20	20	15	23	20	19	19	12	14	14	20	26	25	
	%	6.3	6.4	5.9	4.6	5.6	4.4	7.9	8.1	8.2	5.8	8.6	7.6	5.5	5.5	3.5	3.8	3.3	4.8	5.7	5.7	-0.6
% Change			0.1	-0.5	-1.3	1.0	-1.2	3.5	0.2	0.1	-2.4	2.8	-1.0	0.0	0.0	-2.0	0.3	-0.5	1.5	0.9	0.0	
Hispanic	N	105	91	91	91	79	91	95	109	106	122	118	120	154	178	201	216	248	259	293	283	
	%	47.1	41.4	41.2	41.6	36.6	39.6	39.6	44	43.3	46.9	44.4	41.2	45.2	51.1	58.8	58.7	58.9	62.6	64	65.1	18
% Change			-5.7	-0.2	0.4	-5	3	0	4.4	-0.7	3.6	-2.5	-3.2	4	5.9	7.7	-0.1	0.2	3.7	1.4	1.1	
Native American	N	1	3	4	5	7	8	8	7	6	4	5	12	17	11	11	12	14	9	7	7	
	%	0.4	1.4	1.8	2.3	3.2	3.5	3.3	2.8	2.4	1.5	1.9	4.1	5	3.2	3.2	3.3	3.3	2.2	1.5	1.6	1.2
% Change			1.0	0.4	0.5	0.9	0.3	-0.2	-0.5	-0.4	-0.9	0.4	2.2	0.9	-1.8	0.0	0.1	0.0	-1.1	-0.7	0.1	
Asian	N	3	2	1	1	1	1	4	7	4	2	0	1	9	9	6	6	8	6	10	7	
	%	1.3	0.9	0.5	0.5	0.5	0.4	1.7	2.8	1.6	0.8	0	0.3	2.6	2.6	1.8	1.6	1.9	1.4	2.2	1.6	0.3
% Change			-0.4	-0.4	0.0	0.0	-0.1	1.3	1.1	-1.2	-0.8	-0.8	0.3	2.3	0.0	-0.8	-0.2	0.3	-0.5	0.8	-0.6	
Total	N	223	220	221	219	216	228	240	248	245	260	266	291	341	348	342	369	421	414	458	435	0.3

TABLE 3.4 Holladay Elementary, Magnet School Designated as Successful

		1996–97	1997–98	1998–99	1999–00	2000–01	2001–02	2002–03	2003–04	2004–05	2005–06	2006–07	2007–08	2008–09	2009–10	2010–11	2011–12	2012–13	2013–14	2014–15	2015–16	Overall change from 1996–2016
White	N	107	102	96	87	85	95	99	96	104	99	89	92	94	81	46	49	36	21	18	17	
	%	46.5	46.2	50	43.3	41.1	45.5	52.9	55.2	46.2	45.6	48.1	43.8	38.7	33.6	24.2	17.9	13.4	8.1	7.1	6.3	
% Change			-0.3	3.8	-6.7	-2.2	4.4	7.4	2.3	-9.0	-0.6	2.5	-4.3	-5.1	-5.1	-9.4	-6.3	-4.5	-5.3	-1.0	-0.8	-40.2
African American	N	27	25	14	16	18	19	22	15	22	24	18	21	23	27	19	26	35	28	36	41	
	%	11.7	11.3	7.3	8	8.7	9.1	11.8	8.6	9.8	11.1	9.7	10	9.5	11.2	10	9.5	13	10.8	14.2	15.1	
% Change			-0.4	-4	0.7	0.7	0.4	2.7	-3.2	1.2	1.3	-1.4	0.3	-0.5	1.7	-1.2	-0.5	3.5	-2.2	3.4	0.9	3.4
Hispanic	N	93	89	80	89	97	91	66	60	94	84	71	90	116	121	117	187	183	194	181	192	
	%	40.4	40.3	41.7	44.3	46.9	43.5	35.3	34.5	41.8	38.7	38.4	42.9	47.7	50.2	61.6	68.2	68	74.6	71.5	70.6	
% Change			-0.1	1.4	2.6	2.6	-3.4	-8.2	-0.8	7.3	-3.1	-0.3	4.5	4.8	2.5	11.4	6.6	-0.2	6.6	-3.1	-0.9	30.2
Native American	N	1	2	2	7	6	4	0	2	2	6	4	5	10	12	7	7	5	7	11	11	
	%	0.4	0.9	1	3.5	2.9	1.9	0	1.1	0.9	2.8	2.2	2.4	4.1	5	3.7	2.6	1.9	2.7	4.3	4	
% Change			0.5	0.1	2.5	-0.6	-1	0	1.1	-0.2	1.9	-0.6	0.2	1.7	0.9	-1.3	-1.1	-0.7	0.8	1.6	-0.3	3.6
Asian	N	2	3	0	2	1	0	0	1	3	4	3	2	1	0	0	0	0	0	0	0	
	%	0.9	1.4	0	1	0.5	0	0	0.6	1.3	1.8	1.6	1	0	0	0	0	0	0	0	0	
% Change			0.5	-1.4	1	-0.5	-0.5	0	0.6	0.7	0.5	-0.2	-0.6	-1	0	0	0	0	0	0	0	-0.9
Total	N	230	221	192	201	207	209	187	174	225	217	185	210	243	241	190	274	269	260	253	272	

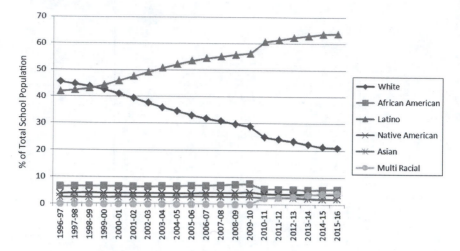

FIGURE 3.1 TUSD multi-year ethnic enrollment based on 100th day count.

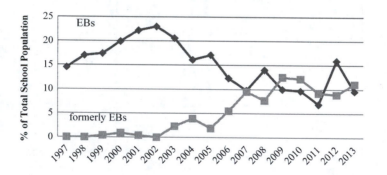

FIGURE 3.2 Proportion of students at Davis Bilingual who spoke a non-English language at home who were labeled as "English Learners" and "Former English Learners."

Note: Fluctuations over time are in part due to changes in the way English learner status has been defined and collected in the state.

English Immersion (SEI). Notably, emergent bilingual (EB) enrollment at Davis (both students who were classified as EBs and reclassified as formerly EB) peaked the school year after the policy changed—a level of enrollment that has been maintained since (see Figure 3.2). Davis Bilingual has historically been at the center of much attention because of its efforts to instill bilingualism and culture as a means to promote achievement for Latino students, in spite of Arizona's efforts to eliminate Mexican American cultural and linguistic heritage in schools with various state policies (see Gándara & Hopkins, 2010; García, Lawton, & Diniz de Figueiredo, 2010; Jiménez-Castellanos, Combs, Martínez, & Gómez, 2013), which is evident in their enrollment (see Table 3.2 and Figure 3.2). Indeed, the relatively high Latino enrollment at Davis Bilingual is in part attributed to the school's emphasis on language and culture, which has a particularly strong appeal to Latino families who select the magnet school so that their children can become biliterate and bicultural (C. Campuzano, personal communication, October 2, 2013). It is also important to note that although Borton and Holladay were considered compliant at the time of the magnet plan, both schools have witnessed the same steady declines in their White student populations (Tables 3.3 and 3.4) as the district overall (see Figure 3.1).

One of the many reasons segregation has been a lasting concern is due to the evidence that it promotes stratification of educational opportunity (Coleman et al., 1966). Despite reflecting a proportion of Latino students that was too high according to the Court's criteria, however, Carrillo and Davis Bilingual have been considered academically rigorous and successful in promoting academic achievement for their students, a majority of whom were identified as Latino. Carrillo is one of only a few TUSD schools to have earned an "A" rating on the state school grading system[6] since 2012. Davis Bilingual, a school that provides blocks of academic literacy instruction in Spanish during the day to promote bilingualism, has consistently earned a "B" since 2012.

Retention of magnet status was updated in January 2015 to reflect both integration and academic growth (see Appendix 3.1). This resulted in the removal of magnet status of six schools: Cholla, Ochoa, Robison, Pueblo, Safford, and Utterback. To be compliant, however, Carrillo and Davis were directed to enroll more White students, which required that they turn away the very students the desegregation order is supposed to protect. Upon inspection of enrollment patterns, this pressure has resulted in slight increases in the number of White students attending Carrillo and Davis (see Tables 3.1 and 3.2), thereby reducing the number of Latino students who have access to these high achieving schools (see Tables 3.1 and 3.2). Although integration, in the spirit of *Brown I*, has merit, the complex situation suggests that integration has come at a cost for Latino youth in TUSD.

Desegregating schools with the use of magnet programs has long been lauded as the answer to segregation (Steele & Levine, 1994), but closer inspection reveals that because success is defined as appealing to White families (Ladson-Billings, 2004), Black and Latino children often do not tend to benefit from the programs. That is, magnet programs deemed successful are those that do not have a concentration of minority students, yet minority students may still reflect disproportionate rates of school failure (Lomotey & Stanley, 1990). The practice of funding desegregation efforts that are centered on the attractiveness of a particular school to White families results in "the ongoing discussion in many communities of color that ask why is it that money and resources follow White middle class children?" (Ladson-Billings, 2004, p. 9).

The practice of having to turn away Latino students when White student enrollment in TUSD is at an all-time low (approximately 21%) and Latino students are excelling at the Latino–dense magnet schools (in spite of the patterns of decreasing White student enrollment) exemplifies the complex issues that surround desegregation orders when they are far removed from their original intent. Whereas the original TUSD desegregation case was consistent with the spirit of *Brown* in its admonition of vestiges of dual systems, the present status of the case points to de facto evidence in supporting its assertion that TUSD is non-compliant. The forces that have prompted the de facto[7] segregation of Latinos in TUSD, often rooted in the propagation of "liberty, rather than equality" (Thompson, 2013, p. 1269), however, are ignored by the Courts to the detriment of Latino youth.

Tensions Surrounding De Jure and De Facto Segregation

Desegregation court orders in American schools stem from the 1954 *Brown v. Board of Education* (*Brown I*) decision that overturned de jure segregation, which had been previously upheld by the "separate but equal" decision in *Plessy v. Ferguson* (1896). Whereas the *Brown I* decision "pronounces the principle of separate as inherently unequal" (Ladson-Billings, 2004, p. 6), *Brown v. Board of Education II* (1955; *Brown II*) placed the burden of formulating a plan to "effectuate a transition to a racially nondiscriminatory school system" on school districts (p. 435–438) and provided lower courts with the authority to evaluate the extent to which school districts had complied (p. 439). *Brown II* set the precedent for District Court oversight of school district compliance with desegregation orders; however, the widespread resistance and apathy toward *Brown II* by school districts was not forcefully decried until the Supreme Court's decision in *Green v. County School Board of New Kent County* (1968), which introduced desegregation criteria that continue to be at the center of desegregation oversight efforts by courts today. In his opinion in *Green*, Justice Brennan explained that the immediate objective of *Brown II* "was with making an initial break in a long-established pattern of excluding Negro children from schools attended by white children" but that "[t]he burden on a school board today is to come forward with a plan that promises realistically to work, and promises realistically to work *now*" (p. 391 U.S. 435).

Most often, courts ordered busing to achieve integration (Frankenberg, Lee, & Orfield, 2003), which in effect integrated students by socioeconomic status because "race and poverty were strongly correlated at that time" (Palardy, 2013, p. 715). Busing, however, received steadfast resistance (Orfield, 1995) and gave way to voluntary[8] desegregation measures with the implementation of magnet schools—schools with a unique focus designed to attract families throughout a district (Metz, 1984). Although there was notable progress in integration from the mid-1960s to the late 1980s, resegregation has been increasing steadily since that time (Orfield et al., 1994).

In her critique of *Brown II*, Ladson-Billings (2004) describes the work of desegregation as "working for the right cause," but asserts that the issue lies in "the remedy, or more specifically, with the implementation of *Brown* as endorsed by the Court" (p. 5). To date, desegregation continues to be defined as the extent to which students of color "attend school with White students" (Orfield et al., 1994, p. 6). Despite exceptions (e.g., Bell, 1976; Ladson-Billings, 2004; Woodward, 2011), this myopic view of desegregation remains largely unchallenged in the extant literature. Moreover, the surge of Latino students in schools due to immigration patterns (García & Frede, 2010) coupled with the rising de facto segregation among Latinos (Fry, 2009) is rarely examined against the continued use of archaic desegregation criteria.

Although recent evidence does not suggest that resegregation is returning us to a pre-*Brown* era (Stroub & Richards, 2013), some scholars have blamed the resegregation of students of color on the dismissal of court oversight (Orfield et al., 1994; Reardon, Grewal, Kalogrides, & Greenberg, 2012). Of the close to 800 desegregation court orders in American school districts, however, close to 400 had yet to be dismissed in 2010.[9] Scholars have also blamed resegregation on the waning of mandatory busing that began in the early 1980s, and argue against the notion of White flight claiming that "there has been no significant redistribution between the sectors of American education" [10](Orfield et al., 1994). There is evidence, however, that early resistance to integration by White families that prompted an increase in enrollment in private schools (Ladson-Billings, 2004) has evolved to present-day White flight in the name of "choice," which often takes the form of mobility into charter schools (Frankenberg, Siegel-Hawley, & Wang, 2011), as well as the use of open enrollment policies across school districts (Stroub & Richards, 2013). There is also ample evidence for the "secession of the successful" (Reich, 1991), or the propensity of White families to leave neighborhoods as the minority population increases—particularly when they have more resources to do so (Crowder, 2000). Indeed, zoning regulations have been found to be central in the "[perpetuation] and [exacerbation of] racial and class inequality" (Rothwell & Massey, 2010). According to Rothwell and Massey, "suburban residents often block the extension of public lines into their municipalities precisely to forestall the entry of poor minority families from the inner city" (p. 1125).

Charter Schools

In her analysis of the "consequences of the *Brown* decision," Ladson-Billings describes a phenomenon she refers to as "White resistance to desegregation" (2004, p. 7). She explains,

> In 1971 about a half million White children attended segregated private schools in the South. Despite the threat these schools posed to the court decision, only a limited number of legal challenges were mounted to combat them, because they did not receive direct public support in the form of tuition grants.
>
> *(2004, p. 7)*

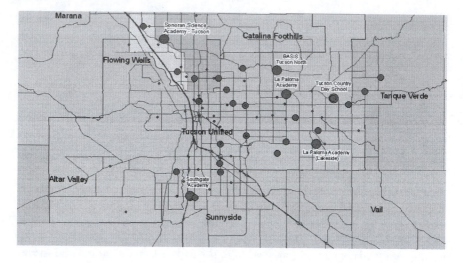

FIGURE 3.3 Distribution of charter schools within Pima County (Scott, 2013).

Resistance to desegregation in more recent times has not only been embodied in private schools (Cowen, Fleming, Witte, & Wolf, 2012), but also in the proliferation of charter schools that purport giving parents choice and, unlike most private schools, do receive direct public support (Roda & Wells, 2013). Arizona passed legislation supporting the charter schools in 1994. To date, the state has the fastest growth of charter schools in the United States. Within TUSD boundaries alone, there are 54 charter schools that comprise over 11,000 students, almost 40% of whom are White (see Figure 3.3). Overall, the four largest charters within the TUSD boundaries reflect between 45–74% White student enrollment, which translates into more than twice to almost four times the White student enrollment in TUSD.

Open Enrollment

Some scholars believe the resegregation promoted by charter schools could be curbed by "creating more viable, racially diverse and undivided (minus the separate and unequal gifted and talented programs) schools" to keep the advantaged families, who tend to be White, in the public education system (Roda & Wells, 2013). There are, however, many advantaged White families who remain in the public education system. As the minority population in a particular area increases, however, they either flee to suburban public schools when they can afford to do so (Crowder, 2000) or, as is the case of students living within TUSD boundaries, use open-enrollment policies to attend public schools in another district within the county.

Within Pima County, there are four majority-White districts—all immediately surrounding TUSD. One of the school districts, Tanque Verde, was established in

2005 and is located on the east side of the county. To date, it remains the most White-dense district in the county with a minority population of 22%. What is particularly noteworthy about the relatively new school district is that it not only, in effect, seceded from TUSD, thereby confiscating a segment of TUSD's White student population, but the district also willfully ignored TUSD policy efforts to comply with desegregation. In 2007, Tanque Verde enrolled a TUSD student, disregarding the TUSD regulation that had prevented students from using open enrollment to attend other districts as an effort to maintain racial balance in TUSD schools (Younger, 2007).

Despite evidence to the contrary, some affirm that the increased segregation of Latino students in particular is not an artifact of "White flight," but is due to "huge changes in birth rates and immigration patterns" (Orfield et al., 1994, p. 7). Immigration trends have certainly changed the ethnic and racial composition of schools; across the United States, schools have been witnessing a sharp increase in the number of Latino students over the past several decades (García & Frede, 2010). As Fry (2009) reports:

> Suburban Hispanic students are increasingly attending schools whose student bodies have a high percentage of Hispanics. In 2006–07, the typical suburban Hispanic student attended a school that was 49% Latino, up from 4% Latino in 1993–94. By contrast, there was little change during this period in the level of racial isolation of black and Asian suburban students.
>
> *(p. ii)*

Although the immigration and birth rates of Latinos have certainly played a role in the changes of school demographics across the United States, it is necessary to also consider the ways "choice" has contributed to school demographics. Without this acknowledgment, desegregation orders will continue to hinder the educational plight of Latinos in TUSD.

Consistent with national trends, TUSD Latino population has grown dramatically. As previously mentioned, the TUSD student population is now 65% Latino (see Figure 3.1). Although the increase in the proportion of Latino families in TUSD has been relatively steady, the exodus of White families has outpaced this increase. Since 1996, there has been a decline of approximately 18,000 White students, whereas the increase of Latino students has only been close to 5,000. Moreover, since 2013, Latino student enrollment has declined by over 1,000 students. As such, not only must the district contend with the White-to-Latino demographic shift in its charge to address vestiges of past discrimination, but also with the overall shrinking student population. Just fifteen years ago, enrollment in the district neared 62,300. The enrollment for the 2015–16 school year in TUSD, however, was less than 48,000 students. The decrease in student enrollment has compelled TUSD to close over twenty schools since 2010 (TUSD 2012, 2013d). Consistent with Fry's (2009) description of Latino enrollment trends, all districts within Pima county are also experiencing growth in their Latino populations—some doubling their proportion of Latino students over the past thirteen years (Scott, 2013). If the growth patterns continue, TUSD will become close to 100% Latino. How will desegregation be defined then?

Arizona Policies That Promote Segregation

In addition to ignoring the de facto forces that have shaped TUSD's demographics, the Court has failed to consider the role of Arizona policies that have undermined integration for Latinos. Many of these policies, although considered de facto given that they address linguistic minority students, are arguably de jure practices (see Donato & Hanson, 2012). As discussed in Chapter 2, Arizona policy expressly requires the segregation of EBs given its self-appointed status as an "English first" state (see Figure 3.4). The SEI model used in Arizona requires that EBs are grouped homogenously to the extent possible based on English proficiency, and that they receive explicit English instruction in four-hour blocks (ADE, 2008). Thus, EBs are segregated from students with different levels of English proficiency as well as from academic content that is covered while they attend the four-hour block of English instruction. What is especially important about the Court's failure to consider state policies that contribute markedly to EBs' educational experiences is that the District Court holds TUSD responsible for EBs' achievement disparities. In reiterating the plaintiff's response, the Court asserted "Most troubling are the low achievement rates by English Language Learners [(ELL)] on the Arizona

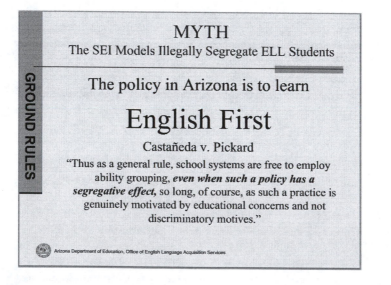

FIGURE 3.4 Arizona Department of Education Office of English Language Acquisition Services training slide.

Instrument to Measure Standards (AIMS) exam" (*Fisher-Mendoza v. TUSD*, 2008). Absent from consideration are the stipulations of Proposition 203 that have both impeded EBs' achievement statewide (Jiménez-Castellano, Combs, Martínez, & Gómez, 2013) and limited the extent to which TUSD can circumvent required practices that are harmful to EBs (see Hakuta, 1998). Notably, also absent from the Court's consideration is the academic success among EBs at both Carrillo and Davis in spite of harmful policies and statewide trends. Indeed, Davis Bilingual has had a history of success with *all* students by promoting "Spanish first" as its magnet focus (Hernandez, 2009)—addressing both issues while vigilantly navigating Arizona policy.

Tensions Surrounding Race, Ethnicity, and Power

The *Brown* decision has been conceptualized by some as an issue of identity based on the Court's reference to Kenneth Clark's (1950) evidence that segregation and racism have generated feelings of inferiority and psychological harm among African American children (Bergner, 2009). Supreme Court Justice Clarence Thomas vehemently disagrees with this position,[11] as exemplified by the following statement found in his concurring opinion for the Supreme Court's *Missouri v. Jenkins* (1995) decision: "It never ceases to amaze me that the courts are so willing to assume that anything that is predominantly black must be inferior" (para. 1). He later continues:

> Without a basis in any real finding of intentional government action, the District Court's imposition of liability upon the State of Missouri improperly rests upon a theory that racial imbalances are unconstitutional ... In effect, the court found that racial imbalances constituted an ongoing constitutional violation that continued to inflict harm on black students. This position appears to rest upon the idea that any school that is black is inferior, and that blacks cannot succeed without the benefit of the company of whites.
>
> *(para. 9)*

Justice Thomas' assertion is particularly salient given the striking parallels between the facts of the *Missouri v. Jenkins*, 1995 case and the *Fisher-Mendoza v. TUSD*, 2011 case. That is, the lower courts have conceptualized successful integration in both cases as contingent on whether White students would deem a particular school appealing. In consideration of the Court's decision in *Missouri v. Jenkins*, 1995, contesting the notion of viewing success for students of color as contingent on the enrollment of White students merits serious consideration for the Latino students of TUSD. The TUSD case is additionally hindered, however, by the archaic method in which ethnicity is monitored by American schools.

As of 2010, the United States Department of Education required schools to collect demographic information on students in a way that would separate ethnicity from race. Accordingly, Hispanics[12] of any race were to be aggregated together for reporting purposes, whereas non-Hispanics would be disaggregated as American Indian or Alaska Native, Asian, Black or African American, Native Hawaiian or Other Pacific Islander, White, or of "two or more races" (ADE, 2011). When a TUSD parent selects "Hispanic" for their child, they are not identified as having two or more races regardless of mixed heritage. Thus, despite the fact that there are students of multiple ethnicities who have Hispanic heritage, the reporting defaults to "Hispanic" in all cases, speciously resulting in schools' non-compliance.

As mentioned in Chapter 2, the U.S. Supreme Court decision in *Hernandez v. Texas* (1954), that was decided the same year as *Brown I*, upheld that Mexican Americans were protected by the 14th Amendment. Having been classified as White, but clearly treated as a subordinate class, the *Hernandez* case acknowledged that ethnic identification had been used "as a basis for exclusion and subordination" (Martinez, 1997, p. 324). Haney-López (2005) asserts that the *Hernandez* case "unambiguously insists, in a way that *Brown* does not, that it is race as subordination, rather than race per se, that demands Constitutional intervention" (p. 62). Although the ways Latinos are identified has changed numerous times across the years, ethnic identification for Latinos continues to be used by the court as a basis for exclusion and subordination. Parents of children with Latino heritage are considered to contribute to the non-compliance of integration regardless of mixed heritage—ironically, one of the most explicit representations of integration that exist.

Redefining Segregation

Despite its label as a Title I school with a large proportion of students who meet the criteria for free or reduced lunch, and 15% of whom are EBs,[13] Carrillo is among the top performing elementary schools in the state. Davis also exemplifies achievement for Latino youth, and additionally provides significant guidance in reframing desegregation. As previously described, despite demographic reports that default to Hispanic, the student population reflects varied ethnic and racial backgrounds; between 15–23% of students are EBs (see Figure 3.2); and students come from varied socioeconomic backgrounds.

It is particularly noteworthy that the school circumvents both the segregation and anti-Spanish practices promoted by "English first" practices that are supported in the current USP with a bilingual approach. Dual language programs, also called two-way bilingual education or two-way bilingual immersion, are designed to promote bilingualism by bringing together a group of children who speak English as their native language and a group of children who share a non-English native language. In dual language programs, language learning is integrated with content instruction with goals to promote bilingualism, academic achievement, and cross-cultural understanding among all students. Indeed, dual language programs are considered the solution to traditional methods of providing equitable learning opportunities to EBs because they are viewed as assets to their peers (Collier & Thomas, 2004), as explained in Chapter 2.

Given the number of schools within TUSD that serve student populations that resemble those at Davis, it is feasible to expand dual language programs, thus addressing the needs of more EBs (who are likely to be Latino in TUSD). Whereas the desegregation order and Hawley's magnet plan conceptualize Latino-dense west side schools as non-compliant, re-conceptualizing one of the desegregation criterions as English proficiency would reframe one of the "unsuccessful" schools that is serving Latino students as exemplars of success which should be strengthened and replicated. By viewing integration in this manner, being Latino and an EB in TUSD is no longer a subordinate position, but one that is an asset to peers.

There are additional criteria that merit consideration when evaluating whether a Latino-majority school is indeed segregated, such as socioeconomic status (Mantil, Perkins, & Aberger, 2012). Orfield and Lee (2005) assert

> One of the common misconceptions over the issue of resegregation of schools is that many people treat it as simply a change in the skin color of the students in a school. If skin color were not systematically linked to other forms of inequality, it would, of course, be of little significance for educational policy. Unfortunately that is not and never has been the nature of our society. Socioeconomic segregation is a stubborn, multidimensional and deeply important cause of educational inequality.
>
> *(2005, p. 4)*

Given that socioeconomic status is perhaps the most egregious of all predictors of academic success and subsequent opportunity, it is necessary to consider its role in desegregation for TUSD (see Figure 3.5). Safier (2013) presents a map of state school grades in Pima County, and asserts in his analysis that they are almost perfectly correlated with socioeconomic status. The fact that Davis Bilingual is an exception to this trend deserves serious consideration. Davis Bilingual's appeal to Latino families includes those who are not considered to be from lower socioeconomic status backgrounds (35% are from a lower socioeconomic status, using free lunch status as a proxy), a fact that indeed should matter if desegregation scholars' claims about the role of socioeconomic status in desegregation (e.g., Orfield & Lee, 2005) have merit. Nevertheless, the status quo in the desegregation literature and the courts' decisions appears to rest on a notion that Latinos are homogenous not only ethnically, but also linguistically and socioeconomically.

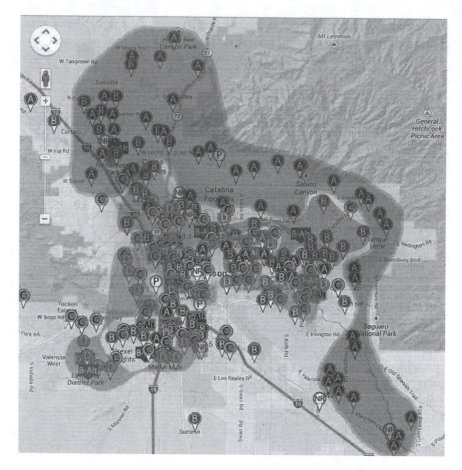

FIGURE 3.5 Distribution of school grades in Pima County (Safier, 2013)

Conclusion

For over four decades, TUSD has been at the center of a desegregation case. As the first district in Arizona to voluntarily desegregate prior to the *Brown* decision, it remains the only district in the state still under court supervision. Although the demographic landscape has changed dramatically since the initial case was decided, the court order remains centered on defining successful integration as the absence of a concentration of Latinos in schools, which is increasingly onerous given the changes in district demographics that are propelled by "choice" in charter schools and open enrollment policies. Demographic shifts continue to reduce the number of White students available to attain racial balance for compliance, compelling schools with high rates of success to *turn away* Latino students. Racial balance is further impeded by the district's use of federal criteria to designate student ethnicity that is reminiscent of the archaic "one drop rule." The practice results in every student with any reported Hispanic heritage to be considered Hispanic, regardless of race or mixed heritage. Moreover, the district must adhere to state policy requiring the segregation of EBs, most of whom are Latino. Given these constraints, TUSD is unlikely to ever be in compliance with the court order so long as desegregation is defined without considering the nuanced context of the district.

Paradoxically, both *Brown II* and *Green* underscored the importance of considering both context and de jure practices when implementing desegregation measures. Indeed, it is the reason *Brown II* and *Green* both placed the burden of identifying desegregation strategies on school boards rather than the courts. In his opinion in the *Green* decision, Justice Brenner stated:

> There is no universal answer to complex problems of desegregation; there is obviously no one plan that will do the job in every case. The matter must be assessed in light of the circumstances present and the options available in each instance. It is incumbent upon the school board to establish that its proposed plan promises meaningful and immediate progress toward disestablishing state-imposed segregation. It is incumbent upon the district court to weigh that claim in light of the facts at hand and in light of any alternatives which may be shown as feasible and more promising in their effectiveness.
>
> *(p. 391 U.S. 439)*

In the spirit of Justice Brenner's opinion, redefining desegregation to capture the nuanced demographics of TUSD (and other majority–minority urban districts), which have in part been shaped by immigration patterns and state policies on choice, can fulfill the goals of *Brown* by providing students educational opportunities that have remained elusive. Indeed, the very notion that a protected class would be hindered from enrolling in schools of their choice runs counter to the spirit of *Brown*.

Although the six schools that lost magnet status were unable to meet both criteria outlined by the Court, Supreme Court precedent in the *Missouri* decision may challenge the District Court. In his Opinion of the Court, Justice Rehnquist stated:

> Just as demographic changes independent of *de jure* segregation will affect the racial composition of student assignments, so too will numerous external factors beyond the control of the Kansas City, Missouri, School District and the State affect minority student achievement. So long as these external factors are not the result of segregation, they do not figure in the remedial calculus.

Notes

1 A version this chapter originally appeared in López, F. (2016). When desegregation limits opportunities to Latino youth: The strange case of the Tucson Unified School District. *Chicana/o Latina/o Law Review, 34*, 1–33.

2 The proportion was based on the Office of Civil Rights criteria.

3 The Supreme Court decision in *Green v. School Board of New Kent County* (1968) shifted compliance with *Brown II* from cursory efforts to explicit racial balance. Among the factors that required consideration are race ratios for students and faculty, as well as equality in facilities, transportation, and extracurricular activities.

4 The 2006 decision in the consolidated cases of *Meredith v. Jefferson County Board of Education* and *Parents v. Seattle School District* states that public school systems could not seek to achieve or maintain integration through measures that take explicit account of a student's race.

5 Other successful magnets include Booth-Fikett K–8; Dodge Middle School; and Palo Verde High School.

6 The A–F school grading system comprises student growth for all students, student growth for the lowest 25% of students, percentage of students passing the state assessment, and the percentage of EBs reclassified as non-EBs (ADE, 2012).

7 Donato and Hanson (2012) challenge "the idea that the segregation of Mexican Americans was de facto" (p. 204). They assert that labeling forced segregation as de facto "allows for easy dismissal of the impact and intentionality of policy decisions made at the local level, and it can hide the deliberate and racial nature of the segregation Mexican Americans experienced" (p. 205).

8 It should be noted that Justice Brenner's opinion of the Court in the Green decision stated that "in desegregating a dual system, a plan utilizing 'freedom of choice' is not an end in itself" (p. 391 U.S.440). Accordingly, voluntary desegregation had been in place prior to the Green decision, but magnet schools were meant to appeal to families as a way to achieve integration.

9 Data from the Common Core of Data cataloged by Reardon, Grewal, Kalogrides, and Greenberg (2012) includes all school districts with at least 2000 students ever under court order for desegregation.

10 For a detailed review of the methodological limitations of this body of work, see Stroub and Richards (2013).

11 Justice Clarence Thomas asserts that "Psychological injury or benefit is irrelevant to the question whether state actors have engaged in intentional discrimination" (1995, para. 13).

12 I use the term Hispanic to be consistent with the reporting criteria used by TUSD. The terms Hispanic, Latino, and Mexican American are used interchangeably in this chapter.

13 Prior to the current practice of labeling EBs as "former English learners," once they are proficient in English, EBs were simply aggregated with students who were never EBs.

References

ADE. (2008). Structured English Immersion EDL Models. Retrieved at http://www.azed.gov/wp-content/uploads/PDF/SEIModels05-14-08.pdf.

ADE. (2011). New federal regulations for race/ethnicity data. Retrieved at http://www.azed.gov/research-evaluation/files/2011/11/fy11federalraceethnicityguidance.pdf.

ADE. (2012). The A–F letter grade system. Retrieved at http://www.azed.gov/research-evaluation/files/2012/08/2012-a-f-letter-grades-guide-for-parents.pdf.

Arizona State Senate Issue Brief. (August 27, 2008). School desegregation in Arizona. Retrieved at http://www.azleg.gov/briefs/Senate/School%20Desegregation%20in%20Arizona.pdf.

Bell, D. A. (1976). Serving two masters: Integration ideals and client interests in school desegregation litigation. *Yale Law Journal, 85*, 470–516.

Bergner, G. (2009). Black children, White preference: Brown v. Board, the doll tests, and the politics of self-esteem. *American Quarterly, 61*, 299–332.

Brousseau, G. C. (1993). Bridging three centuries: The desegregation question 1968–1983. Retrieved at http://www.tusd1.org/contents/distinfo/history/history9310.asp.

Brown, K. D. (1993). The legal rhetorical structure for the conversion of desegregation lawsuits to quality education lawsuits. *The Emory Law Journal, 42*, 791–819.

Brown, S. E. (2012). Desegregation in TUSD: 2012 and beyond. Retrieved at www.tusd1.org/contents/distinfo/deseg/../desegsummer2012.pdf.

Brown v. Board of Education, 347 U.S. 483 (1954).

Cabrera, N. L., Milem, J. F., & Marx, R. W. (2012). *An empirical analysis of the effects of Mexican American Studies participation on student achievement within Tucson Unified School District.* Tucson, AZ: Report to Special Master Dr. Willis D. Hawley on the Tucson Unified School District Desegregation Case. Retrieved at http://works.bepress.com/nolan_l_cabrera/17/.

Clark, K. (1950). *Effect of prejudice and discrimination on personality development.* Midcentury White House conference on children and youth.

Cole-Frieman, K. A. (1996). The ghosts of segregation still haunt Topeka, Kansas: A case study on the role of the federal courts in school desegregation. *The Kansas Journal of Law & Public Policy, 6*, 23–48.

Coleman, J. S., Campbell, E. Q., Hobson, C. J., McPartland, J., Mood, A. M., Weinfeld, F. D., & York, R. L. (1966). *Equality of Educational Opportunity.* U.S. Department of Health, Education, and Welfare.

Collier, V. P., & Thomas, W. P. (2004). The astounding effectiveness of dual language education for all. *NABE Journal of Research and Practice, 2*, 1–20.

Cooper, J. F. (1967). The first hundred years: The history of Tucson School District 1, 1867–1967. Retrieved at http://168.174.252.75/contents/distinfo/history/history100.asp.

Cowen, J. M., Fleming, D. J., Witte, J. F., & Wolf, P. J. (2012). Going public: Who leaves a large, longstanding, and widely available urban voucher program? *American Educational Research Journal, 49*, 231–256.

Crowder, K. (2000). The racial context of white mobility: An individual-level assessment of the white flight hypothesis. *Social Science Research, 29*, 223–257.

Donato, R., & Hanson, J. (2012). Legally white, socially "Mexican": The politics of de jure and de facto school segregation in the American Southwest. *Harvard Educational Review, 82*, 202–225.

Eaton, S. (October 3, 2007). Ruling hinders TUSD's desegregation efforts. *Arizona Daily Star.* Retrieved at http://azstarnet.com/news/opinion/ruling-hinders-tusd-s-desegregation-efforts/article_d36d7ca7-fe03-582b-8b3e-6ce43157d576.html.

Fisher v. Tucson Unified School District, 652 F.3d 1131 (9th Cir. 2011).

Fisher v. Tucson Unified School District Nos. CV 74-90-TUC-DCB, CV 74-204, CV 00090-DCB, (2013).

Fisher v. United States, Nos. CV 74-90-TUC-DCB, CV 74-204-TUC-DCB, 2007 WL 2410351, at *4 (D. Ariz. Aug. 21, 2007).

Fisher-Mendoza v. TUSD, 623 F.2d 1338 (1978).

Frankenberg, E., Lee, C., & Orfield, G. (2003). *A multiracial society with segregated schools: Are we losing the dream?* Cambridge, MA: The Civil Rights Project at Harvard University. Retrieved at http://civilrightsproject.ucla.edu/research/k-12-education/integration-and-diversity/a-multiracial-society-with-segregated-schools-are-we-losing-the-dream/frankenberg-multiracial-society-losing-the-dream.pdf.

Frankenberg, E., Siegel-Hawley, G., & Wang, J. (2011). Choice without equity: Charter school segregation. *Education Policy Analysis Archives, 19*(1).

Fry, R. (2009). *The rapid growth and changing complexion of suburban public schools.* Pew Hispanic Center. Retrieved at http://www.pewhispanic.org/files/reports/105.pdf.

Gándara, P., & Hopkins, M. (Eds.). (2010). *Forbidden language: English learners and restrictive language policies.* New York: Teachers College Press.

Gándara, P., & Orfield, G. (2012). Segregating Arizona's English learners: A return to the "Mexican Room?" *Teachers College Record, 114,* 1–27.

García, E., Lawton, K., & Diniz de Figueiredo, E. H. (2010). *The education of English language learners in Arizona: A legacy of persisting achievement gaps in a restrictive language policy climate.* Los Angeles: UCLA Civil Rights Project.

Garcia, E. E., & Frede, E. C. (2010). *Young English language learners: Current research and emerging directions for practice and policy.* New York: Teachers College Press.

Grant, M. A. (1982). How to desegregate—and like it. *Phi Delta Kappan, 63,* 539.

Green v. County School Board of New Kent County, 391 U.S. 430 (1968).

Hakuta, K. (1998). Supplemental declaration to State of California. Retrieved at http://www.languagepolicy.net/archives/hakuta3.htm.

Haney-López, I. (2005). Race and Colorblindness after *Hernandez* and *Brown. Chicano Latino Law Review, 25,* 61–76.

Hernandez v. Texas, 347 U.S. 475 (1954).

Hernandez, E. M. (2009). The effects of proper implementation of bilingual programs in elementary schools in the United States. In M. S. Plakhotnik, S. M. Nielsen, & D. M. Pane (Eds.), *Proceedings of the Eighth Annual College of Education & GSN Research Conference* (pp. 62–68). Miami: Florida International University.

Huicochea, A. (October 1, 2013). Forums on magnet plans at 3 TUSD schools begin today. *AZ Star Net.* Retrieved at http://azstarnet.com/news/local/education/forums-on-magnet-plans-at-tusd-schools-begin-today/article_68550d2e-b4c8-5705-bb9a-5dc627c322e3.html.

Huicochea, A. (September 9, 2015). Magnet status for 6 TUSD schools in jeopardy. *Arizona Daily Star.* Retrieved at http://tucson.com/news/local/education/magnet-status-for-tusd-schools-in-jeopardy/article_5f3e53e8-b20c-599c-92c7-3e25bd836eaf.html.

Ladson-Billings, G. (2004). Landing on the wrong note: The price we paid for Brown. *Educational Researcher, 33,* 3–13.

Lomotey, K., & Staley, J. (1990). The education of African Americans in the Buffalo public schools. In H. Taylor (Ed.), *African Americans and the rise of Buffalo's post industrial city, 1940 to present* (pp. 157–186). Buffalo: Buffalo Urban League, Inc.

McDermott, K. A., DeBray, E., & Frankenberg, E. (2012). How does Parents Involved in Community Schools matter? Legal and political influence in education politics and policy. *Teachers College Record, 114,* 1–39.

Mantil, A., Perkins, A. G., & Aberger, S. (2012). The challenge of high-poverty schools: How feasible is socioeconomic integration? In R. D. Kahlenberg (Ed.), *The future of school integration: Socioeconomic diversity as an education reform strategy* (pp. 155–222). Washington, DC: The Century Foundation.

Martinez, G. A. (1997). The legal construction of race: Mexican Americans and Whiteness. *Harvard Law Review, 2,* 321–348.

Mendoza v. Tucson Unified School District, 623 F.2d 1338 (1980).

Metz, M. H. (1984). Life course of magnet schools: Organizational and political influences. *Teachers College Record, 85,* 411–430.

Missouri v. Jenkins 93-1823, 515 U.S. 70 (1995).

Ninth Circuit Requires Continued Federal Oversight of School District – *Fisher v. Tucson Unified School District* 652 F.3d 1131 (9th Cir. 2011). (2012). *Harvard Law Review, 125,* 1530–1537.

Orfield, G. (1995). Public opinion and school desegregation. *Teachers College Record, 96,* 654–670.

Orfield, G., & Lee, C. (2005). Why segregation matters: Poverty and educational inequality. *The Civil Rights Project,* Harvard University, Cambridge, MA.

Orfield, G., Schley, S., Glass, D., & Reardon, S. (1994) The growth of segregation in American schools: Changing patterns of separation and poverty since 1968. *Equity & Excellence in Education, 27,* 5–8.

Palardy, G. J. (2013). High school socioeconomic segregation and student attainment. *American Educational Research Journal, 50,* 714–754.

Parents Involved in Community Schools v. Seattle School District No. 1 et al., 551 U.S. 701 (2006).

Plessy v. Ferguson, 163 U.S. 537 (1896).

Ramirez, M., & Castañeda, A. (1974). *Cultural democracy: Biocognitive development and education.* New York, NY: Academic Press.

Reardon, S. F., Grewal, E., Kalogrides, D., & Greenberg, E. (2012). Brown fades: The end of court-ordered school desegregation and the resegregation of American public schools. *Journal of Policy Analysis and Management, 31,* 876–904.

Reich, R. B. (1991). *Secession of the Successful.* New York Times, Jan, 20, 6.

Roda, A., & Wells, A. (2013). School choice policies and racial segregation: Where White parents' good intentions, anxiety, and privilege collide. *American Journal of Education, 119,* 261–293.

Rothwell, J. T., & Massey, D. (2010). Density zoning and class segregation in U.S. metropolitan areas. *Social Science Quarterly, 91,* 1123–1143.

Safier, D. (November 19, 2013). Income Geography and School Grades. Retrieved at http://www.blogforarizona.com/blog/2013/11/income-geography-and-state-school-grades.html.

Scott, D. (March 12, 2013). *Impact of charter schools on the enrollment of Tucson Unified School District Schools.* Department of Accountability and Research, TUSD.

Smith, P. H., Arnot-Hopffer, E., Carmichael, C. M., Murphy El, Valle, A., González, N., & Poveda, A. (2002). Raise a child, not a test score: Perspectives on bilingual education at Davis bilingual magnet school. *Bilingual Research Journal, 26,* 103–121.

Steele, L., & Levine, R. (1994). *Educational innovation in multiracial contexts: The growth of magnet schools in American education.* American Institutes for Research in the Behavioral Sciences, Palo Alto, CA. (ERIC ED370232) Retrieved from http://eric.ed.gov/?id=ED370232.

Stroub, K. J., & Richards, M. P. (2013). From resegregation to reintegration: Trends in the racial/ethnic segregation of metropolitan public schools, 1993–2009. *American Educational Research Journal, 50,* 497–531.

Thompson, K. D. (2013). Is separate always unequal? A philosophical examination of ideas of equality in key cases regarding racial and linguistic minorities in education. *American Educational Research Journal, 50,* 1249–1278.

TUSD. (1978). The desegregation decision and its effect on the Tucson Unified School District. *An Information Service for the Residents of TUSD, 21*(1).

TUSD. (2012). Closed school sites. Retrieved at http://tusd1.org/contents/distinfo/schoolclosures.asp.

TUSD. (2013a). Magnet plan update, special master, and follow-up meeting. Retrieved at http://www.tusd.k12.az.us/contents/distinfo/superletter/Documents/update11-08-13.pdf.

TUSD. (2013b). Magnet Plan Draft. Magnet Office. Retrieved at http://www.tusd1.org/contents/distinfo/deseg/Documents/Magnet_Plan_Draft.pdf.

TUSD. (2013c). Racial/ethnic integration: How do we measure it, report it, and promote it? December 10, 2013 Governing Board Meeting. Retrieved at http://www.tusd1.org/contents/govboard/gbagenda/12-10-13gb.pdf.

TUSD. (2013d). School master plan. Retrieved at http://www.tusd1.org/contents/distinfo/masterplan/qanda_closures.asp.

Woodward, J. R. (2011). How busing burdened Blacks: Critical race theory and busing for desegregation in Nashville-Davidson County. *The Journal of Negro Education, 80*, 22–32.

Younger, J. (October 29, 2007). Tanque Verde schools challenge TUSD. *Arizona Daily Star.* Retrieved at http://azstarnet.com/news/local/education/precollegiate/tanque-verde-schools-challenge-tusd/article_768383cb-949c-5735-9c1b-0fca6965b6cc.html.

APPENDIX 3.1

November 15, 2016
To: The Honorable David Bury
From: Willis Hawley
Re: Withdrawing Magnet Status

In January 2015, the Court established a set of criteria for determining whether magnet schools should retain their magnet status and said that all magnet schools should be both integrated by the 2016–17 school year and should meet specific academic criteria (Doc. 1753).

In the Unitary Status Plan, the plaintiffs and the District agreed that criteria for determining whether a school was integrated would include the provision that no school could have more than 70% of students of a single race/ethnicity. The Court recognized that it would be very difficult to integrate an entire school that was not integrated—i.e., that was "racially concentrated"—so it required that the criteria that magnet schools needed to meet would only apply to the entry grade in that school (i.e., K, 6, and 9) and that that goal should be sustained as the student cohort moved through the school.

The January 2015, Order tasked the Special Master with making recommendations to the Court as to whether individual magnet schools and programs should lose their magnet status if they failed to meet their goals. The Special Master deferred in making recommendations in the fall of 2015 thus providing an opportunity for schools that did not meet the integration criteria established by the Court to do so the following year.

The Special Master examined magnet school enrollment data in 2015–16 and 2016–17 to determine whether the racially concentrated magnet schools had enrolled no more than 70% Latino in their entering classes. Six schools did not meet the criteria for integration in both 2015–16 and 2016–17: Cholla, Ochoa, Robison, Pueblo, Safford, and Utterback. See Table 1 for relevant data.

Three other schools fell short of reaching 70% or less of one race target: Carrillo, Drachman and Roskruge. Carrillo and Drachman have been "A" schools and have experienced some progress in moving toward integration status. Roskruge is a dual language school and dual language is a high priority in the USP.

The Special Master recommends that Cholla, Ochoa, Robison, Pueblo, Safford, and Utterback lose their magnet status this fall of 2016. There is no reasonable way to argue that these six schools met the integration criteria set by the Court.

Magnet funding for the current year may be sustained unless the District proposes otherwise through the established budget reallocation process. Future funding for the six schools will be resolved in the budget process for the 2017–18 school year.

PART II
Theories and Research

4

ALTERING SELF-FULFILLING PROPHECIES

Teacher Beliefs and Teacher Behaviors[1]

Francesca A. López

Ayer, una alumna nueva de tercer año me preguntó, "¿Te puedo hablar en español?" Le dije, "Claro." Me siguió contando que entiende poco inglés y que le da vergüenza hablarlo porque se ríen de ella. Y me dijo, "La maestra nomás me habla en inglés. No me habla en español porque dice que luego no aprendo hablar inglés."

Hoy, me preguntó porque me gustaba hablar en español. Le respondí que yo crecí hablando español y que también porque es el idioma que se habla en el cielo y se fué saltando muy contenta.

Yesterday, a new third grade student asked me, "May I speak to you in Spanish?" I answered, "Of course." She continued to explain that she understands little English and she is embarrassed to speak it because students laugh at her. She told me, "The teacher only speaks to me in English. She won't speak in Spanish because she said I would not learn how to speak English."

Today, she asked me why I liked to speak Spanish. I responded that I grew up speaking Spanish and also because it is the language spoken in heaven. She skipped away happily.

3rd grade teacher

Most educators have heard of self-fulfilling prophecies and can describe what they are. One of the reasons for this is that there is an extensive body of research that has added to our understanding about the ways teachers communicate their expectations to students (e.g., Brophy & Good, 1984), how students perceive differential teacher behaviors (e.g., Weinstein, Marshall, Sharp, & Botkin, 1987), and their effect on students' own perceptions of ability and achievement (Rubie-Davies, 2006). Despite the established presence of this research in teacher preparation programs (e.g., Barnes, 1987) and licensure standards (e.g., Council of Chief State School Officers, 2011), historically marginalized students who face particularly onerous obstacles associated with poverty and prejudice continue to be underrepresented in a vast array of achievement outcomes (e.g., NCES, 2015).

In a separate body of literature, scholars have argued that there are unique competencies that are essential to the effective teaching of historically marginalized students. Among these competencies is *asset-based pedagogy*[2] (ABP) that views students' culture[3] as a strength, countering the more widespread view that inordinate achievement disparities stem from deficiencies in the child and/or child's culture. Cumulatively, ABP scholarship shares a fundamental belief that teachers who possess an understanding of the sociohistorical influences on traditional marginalized students' trajectories (*critical awareness*) are better able to cultivate students' knowledge by building on their culturally influenced prior knowledge (*cultural knowledge*) and incorporating knowledge that validates students' experiences (*cultural content integration*) into their instruction. Accordingly, ABP is believed to help students develop identities that promote achievement outcomes.

Although scholarship reflecting ABP is prominent in the teacher education literature, scholars have urged researchers to address the paucity of studies that explicitly link teachers' ABP beliefs and behaviors to student outcomes (Goldenberg, Rueda, & August, 2008; Jussim & Harber, 2005; Ladson-Billings, 1999; Losey, 1995; Sleeter, 2004, 2012). Along these lines, there is a particular need for quantitative work given that ABP research is "overwhelmingly based on case study approaches and ethnographic or other qualitative methods" (Goldenberg et al., 2008, p.107). That is, although the ABP literature provides detailed depictions of classroom experiences for historically marginalized students that can be overlooked by quantitative studies, quantitative studies are needed to augment existing evidence and more fully inform policy.

Researchers are attending to the need to examine the relationship between aspects of ABP and Latino students' identity and achievement using quantitative methods (Brown & Chu, 2012; Cabrera, Milem, Jaquette, & Marx, 2014; Chun & Dickson, 2011; Rios-Aguilar, 2010); however, evidence remains limited. For example, Chun and Dickson (2011) relied on Latino students' *perceptions* of teachers' practices, excluding measures of teachers' ABP beliefs and behaviors. In contrast, Brown and Chu (2012) did consider both teachers' attitudes about diversity and Latino students' identity and achievement in their study; however, the researchers did not include teachers' ABP behaviors in their study. Although understanding the role of teachers' and Latino students' perceptions of ABP are indisputably important, this prior work has not addressed scholars' appeals for future research to link teachers' ABP beliefs and behaviors to student outcomes. To attend to this need, I applied a *race-reimaged perspective* (Decuir-Gunby & Schutz, 2014) to a traditional framework for examining teacher' beliefs and behaviors and how they influence students' identity and achievement. The race-reimaged perspective that is applied to this framework incorporates critical awareness and

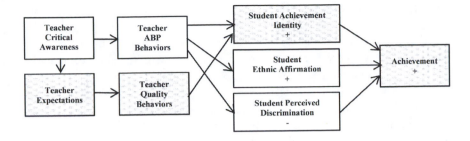

FIGURE 4.1 Conceptual framework of race re-imaged classroom dynamics that incorporate critical awareness, asset-based practices (ABP), and student ethnic identity. Traditional classroom dynamics constructs are shaded to differentiate them from the race re-imaged constructs. Student outcomes variables include "+" and "−" to represent the hypothesized increase or decrease of the constructs.

ABP, as well as students' ethnic identities. A diagram depicting the conceptual framework is represented in Figure 4.1.

In the sections that follow, I provide an overview of the teacher expectations literature and point to inherent flaws and oversights in the assumptions about teacher expectations that fail to consider the historical contexts of minoritized students. To address the flaws and oversights, I also provide an overview of the critical awareness literature—a key prerequisite for ABP. I then describe the findings of my first research question (How are teacher beliefs—expectations and critical awareness—related to Latino students' achievement in reading and mathematics?) and elaborate on why critical awareness is a necessary prerequisite to teacher expectations.

After describing how critical awareness alters teacher expectations, I briefly review the teacher effectiveness research ("teacher quality behaviors" that would be considered "direct" influences in Social Equity Theory (SET), which are not contingent on student ethnicity or race as described in Chapter 1), as well as literature describing ABP. I then describe the findings of my second research question (How are critical awareness and teacher expectancy related to other teacher beliefs and behaviors?).[4]

Teacher Beliefs: Expectations and Critical Awareness

Teacher Expectations

Although "distinguishing knowledge from belief is a daunting undertaking" (Pajares, 1992, p. 309), teacher expectations have been defined as "inferences (based on prior experiences or information) about the level of student performance that is likely to occur in the future" (Good & Nichols, 2001, p. 113). Consequently, they reflect the interplay among affect, evaluation, and knowledge.[5] The potentially deleterious ways in which teacher expectations can influence students' outcomes is often referred to as a "*self-fulfilling prophecy*," defined as "a *false* definition of the situation evoking a new behavior which makes the originally false conception come *true*" (Merton, 1948, p. 195). What began with the observation of potential contamination of interpersonal expectations in a psychology experiment evolved to be known as "Pygmalion Effects in the Classroom" (Rosenthal, 1994, p. 176). In their pivotal study, Rosenthal and Jacobsen (1968) found that students had greater achievement gains when their teachers had been led to believe that the students' scores on an assessment indicated they would show "surprising gains in intellectual competence" (Rosenthal, 1994, p. 176). Although the study was criticized for methodological flaws (Jussim & Harber, 2005) as well as for the lack of information on "the events intervening between the inducement of teacher expectations and the administration of the criterion achievement test" (Brophy & Good, 1970, p. 365), a generation of teacher expectations research ensued.

In their review of decades of research that focused exclusively on teacher expectations effects, Jussim and Harber (2005) concluded that although the "condemnation of teachers for their supposed role in creating injustices" (p. 131) was not warranted by the available evidence, "students who belong to a stigmatized group may be particularly vulnerable to self-fulfilling prophecies" (p. 143). At the time of their review a decade ago, however, only two studies that met their inclusion criteria had examined teacher expectations effects among stigmatized students. Of these, only the study conducted by Jussim, Eccles, and Madon (1996) examined the role of race/ethnicity and social class in teacher expectations effects, where the researchers found that expectations effects for stigmatized groups were "large by any standard" (p. 143). In their examination of whether these effects could be attributed to teachers' biases, however, the researchers concluded that no bias existed among teachers because teacher beliefs were consistent with stigmatized students' performance. The flaw in this inference was presaged by Merton's (1948) discussion on the role of prejudice in self-fulfilling prophecies where he explained how "Americans of good will … experience these beliefs, not as prejudices, not as prejudgments, but as irresistible products of their own observation" (p. 196). Indeed, despite the references to Merton's (1948) self-fulfilling prophecy in teacher expectations work, his discussion of the origin of differential expectations was absent from consideration in earlier research.

> As a result of their failure to comprehend the operation of the self-fulfilling prophecy, many Americans of good will are (sometimes reluctantly) brought to retain enduring ethnic and racial prejudices. They experience these beliefs, not as prejudices, not as prejudgments, but as irresistible products of their own observation. "These facts of the case" permit them no other conclusion … Our unionist fails to see, of course, that he and his kind have produced the very "facts" which he observes.
>
> *(Merton, 1948, p. 196)*

Since Jussim and Harber's (2005) review, scholars have established that teachers' expectations are indeed often biased against students of color (McKown & Weinstein, 2002; Tenenbaum & Ruck, 2007). For the Latino youth who often have teachers with the lowest expectations compared to other marginalized groups (Tenenbaum & Ruck, 2007), this translates into restricted access to rigorous curricula with cognitively demanding work (Moll, 1988, 1990). Consequently, it is necessary to consider ways to abate teachers' biases when examining teachers' expectations. This is the role of critical awareness.

Critical Awareness

Although Merton's (1948) self-fulfilling prophecy had a marked influence in teacher expectations work, the root of differential expectations was not often made explicit in earlier research. Nevertheless, Merton asserted

> The appeal to "education" as a cure-all for the most varied social problems is rooted deep in the mores of America. Yet it is nonetheless illusory for all that. For how would this program of racial education proceed? Who is to do the educating? The teachers in our communities? But, in some measure like many other Americans, the teachers share the very prejudices they are being urged to combat.
>
> *(Meron, 1948, p. 197–198)*

Critical awareness[6] reflects essential knowledge that mitigates bias and prejudice among teachers (Banks, 1993; Darder, 2012; Gay, 2010; Ladson-Billings, 1995b; Valenzuela, 2016). It includes the understanding of the historical context of historically marginalized students; the discrepancy between what is typically validated as knowledge in classrooms and the challenges to those assumptions; and the ways the curriculum in schools serves to replicate the power structure in society (e.g., Apple, 2004; Banks, 1993; Bowles & Gintis, 1976; Darder, 2012; Freire, 1970; Giroux, 1985; Ladson-Billings, 2004). Accordingly, whereas teacher effectiveness work has contributed to our understanding of how teachers' expectations influence student achievement outcomes, critical awareness allows us to consider ways to attenuate the many ways teachers' expectations can otherwise be confounded with students' cultural background (e.g., McKown & Weinstein, 2002; Tenenbaum & Ruck, 2007).

Critical Bicultural Pedagogy.[7] Among the scholars explicit on the role of emancipation is Darder (2012), who elaborates on critical bicultural pedagogy (CBP) based on Mexican American educators Ramirez and Castañeda's (1974) notion of *cultural democracy*:

> [I]ndividuals have the right to be educated in their own language and primary culture, and have the right to cultivate and maintain a bicultural

identity—that is, to retain identification with their culture of origin while learning to survive effectively within the institutional values of the dominant society. Further, this view argues for the necessity of institutional milieus, curricular materials, and educational approaches that are in sync with students' histories, sociopolitical realities, economic contexts, and primary cultural orientation.

(p. xix)

Darder's conceptualization of CBP reflects many of the dimensions evident in the other frameworks, which include: (1) the educational importance of students' language, heritage, cultural values, bicultural[8] identity development, and learning styles reflected in practice and the curriculum; (2) the need for teacher education to provide training in ways to incorporate students' home culture; and (3) the notion that teachers are critical agents of change who work toward changing "the educational style of the school" (Darder, 2012, p. 56). Despite the overlap in Darder's conceptualization of CBP and other asset pedagogies, however, she extends the framework to address the limitations in Ramirez and Castañeda's (1974) model:

> The deficits of the model are most apparent in the fact that it can too easily deteriorate into a positivist instrumentalist modality that perceived culture as predictable, deterministic, neutral, oversimplified, and at moments even relativistic in nature. And although it argues for changing the cultural realities of classrooms, it fails to address critically the necessary shift in power relationships required in schools and society, in order to involve bicultural students in an active process of empowerment, one that can assist them to effectively find their voice, enhance their intellectual formation, and support the development of both individual and collective identity and political solidarity.

(p. 57)

To address this limitation, Darder incorporates *critical democracy* into her framework "to expand on the emancipatory intent" of Ramirez and Castañeda's model (Darder, 2012, p. 57).

Unlike other asset pedagogies, CBP reflects the need to "address critically the necessary shift in power relationships required in schools and society, in order to involve bicultural students in an active process of empowerment" (p. 57). To develop skills necessary for emancipation, students require lived experiences that involve both "preexisting and developing 'funds of knowledge'" (Darder, 2012, p. 64). The ultimate goal is that bicultural students reach cultural negotiation, wherein students "mediate, reconcile, and integrate the reality of lived experiences in an effort to retain the primary cultural identity and orientation while also functioning within the dominant culture for social transformation of the society at large" (p. 52).

Although much of the ABP literature includes both empowerment and emancipatory education as key facets, Darder's conceptualization gives considerable attention to how this can be accomplished. Incorporating the work of Dewey (1916), Foucault (1977), and Giroux (1981, 1983, 1985, 1988a, 1988b), among others, Darder (2012) explains that bicultural students are typically indoctrinated in a hegemonic curriculum that replicates the power structure inherently linked to students' culture:

> At the heart of hegemonic control is political power—a power derived from control of social structures and natural configurations that embody routines and practices inherent in different social relationships resulting from both the content and the manner in which knowledge is structured and produced in society.
>
> *(p. 32)*

Darder also incorporates Freire's (1970) notion of cultural invasion, explained as a process wherein

> The invaders penetrate the cultural context of another group, in disrespect of the latter's potentialities; they impose their own view of the world upon those they invade and inhibit the creativity of the invaded by curbing their expression.
>
> *(p. 150, as cited in Darder, 2012, p. 34)*

Thus, to be able to create critical democracy in classrooms, teachers must understand the "assimilative curriculum of standardized knowledge," Darder emphasizes (p. 80). With this knowledge, teachers can access students' cultural knowledge, integrate their culture into the curriculum in non-essentialist ways, and behave in ways that reflect high expectations of all students.

Developing critical awareness. Scholars involved in the preparation of teachers for historically marginalized students have detailed the importance of developing critical awareness with coursework (e.g., Anderson & Stillman, 2013; Banks, 2001; Darling-Hammond, 2000; Darling-Hammond & Bransford, 2005; Gay, 2005; Gay & Kirkland, 2003; Hollins & Torres-Guzman, 2005; King & Ladson-Billings, 1990; Milner, 2010; Morrison, Robbins, & Rose, 2008; Valenzuela, 2016). Most recently, Valenzuela (2016) has explained that although many universities already have an established presence of coursework that contributes to the development of critical awareness among preservice teachers, it focuses on "language, culture, difference, power, language acquisition, language learning and the like" (p. 19) and is usually accessible only to teachers seeking bilingual or English as a second language certification. The institutionalization of courses that develop critical awareness with sociopolitical content (Milner, 2010;

Valenzuela, 2016) and sociopolitical analysis (Morrell & Duncan-Andrade, 2002; Romero, Arce, & Cammarota, 2009; Stovall, 2006), however, remain elusive. This is acutely problematic since a "lack of political and ideological clarity often translates into teachers uncritically accepting the status quo as 'natural.' It also leads educators down an assimilationist path to learning and teaching … and perpetuates deficit-based views of low-SES, non-White, and linguistic-minority students" (Bartolomé, 2004, p. 100).

Research Findings: How Are Teachers' Expectations and Critical Awareness Related to Student Achievement?

Although scholars have emphasized the importance of critical awareness among teachers (e.g., Anderson & Stillman, 2013; Gay, 2005; Hollins & Torres-Guzman, 2005; Milner, 2010; Morrison et al., 2008; Pohan & Aguilar, 2001), this scholarship has not been considered within more recent work (e.g., McKown 2013; Tenenbaum & Ruck, 2007) that counters earlier assertions regarding the accuracy of teacher expectations (e.g., Jussim et al., 1996). To address this need, I first examined how teachers' expectations and critical awareness are related to student achievement.[9]

In the first analysis, I found that teacher expectations were not a significant predictor of student achievement, but critical awareness *was* related to students' spring reading and mathematics achievement after controlling for fall achievement in each content area. Although the fact that teacher expectations did not predict achievement after controlling for students' prior scores (and critical awareness) may be surprising, these findings are consistent with the literature that I reviewed earlier: there is a robust relationship between students' prior achievement and teacher expectations (e.g., Jussim et al., 1996). This finding—that students' prior achievement explains teachers' expectations—has been used (erroneously) to substantiate the notion that teacher expectations are *accurate*. In other words, some scholars have argued that it is not teacher expectations that influence students' achievement, but that students' achievement informs teachers' expectations. Put another way, by including students' prior achievement in the analysis, teacher expectations are in essence cancelled out because teacher expectations and student achievement are highly correlated—which may seemingly substantiate Jussim and Harber's (2005) conclusion that teacher expectations are not biased, but accurate estimates of students' abilities. Prior research has also demonstrated, however, that teachers can hold biases that are detrimental to students of color (McKown, 2013; Tenenbaum & Ruck, 2007)—which was verified in the first analysis since critical awareness predicted higher achievement above and beyond teacher expectations alone. The role of critical awareness needed to be further explored in my study, so I examined whether critical awareness might play a role in the relationship between teachers' expectations and student achievement.

In the second analysis, I found that critical awareness moderated the relationship between teacher expectations and student achievement (see Figure 4.2).

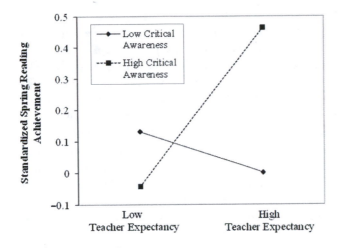

FIGURE 4.2 Moderation of teacher expectations by critical awareness in reading.

Specifically, when teachers had low levels of both expectations and critical awareness, student achievement was consistent with the self-fulfilling prophecy of lower achievement. This finding, which was true for both reading and mathematics, is not surprising. We expect to find that low expectations will translate into behaviors that impede students' learning. When teachers had high expectations and low critical awareness, however, students *also* performed lower in both content areas. Interviews with teachers reveal not only beliefs consistent with the high expectations literature, but also some of the deficit views teachers can hold, even when they believe they have high expectations of all students. The following excerpts, for example, are representative of many teachers' responses when asked what they believe would increase achievement for Latino youth:

3RD GRADE TEACHER: *The difficulties I notice are universal. When students lack persistence or curiosity and or problemsolving skills, it makes achievement difficult.*
4TH GRADE TEACHER: *Parents lack of involvement in child education, not being consistent with interventions, student lack of interest in education, too many problems at home, poverty.*
5TH GRADE TEACHER: *I find that increasing achievement in Latino students is no different than increasing achievement in Anglo students. They need a dedicated teacher who knows how to raise student (all student) achievement.*

Responses by teachers with high expectations but low critical awareness typically blamed parents and/or the students for lower achievement. The first response, for example, exemplifies the belief that student motivation is something that can be willed by the student, without any consideration of the research that has helped us understand the instrumental role of the classroom environment in increasing motivation. The second comment is a representation of responses almost unanimously found across teachers with high expectations but low levels of critical awareness: that parents are not involved and do not value education. This myth has been countered in research (e.g., Moll, 1988, 1990)—but when preservice teachers are not provided with this knowledge during their training, they may come to believe these stereotypes. Overall, teachers with low critical awareness and high expectations place blame *externally*—on parents and students—rather than acknowledge the role they themselves may play in student achievement.

In contrast to the aforementioned findings, it was only when teachers had both high expectations and high levels of critical awareness that students had higher levels of performance. Typical responses of teachers with high levels of critical awareness and expectations when asked what they believe would increase achievement for Latino youth included comments such as:

3RD GRADE TEACHER: *Culture is very important. I make sure to integrate it into social studies, because the children need to see themselves in the culture.*

4TH GRADE TEACHER: *Specific anti-bias education in all schools and at all levels. Cultural awareness education for education professionals. Multicultural education. Variety of assessment measures. Outlaw high stakes standardized testing, especially those tied to punitive consequences for students/teachers. Allow testing in students' primary language when appropriate.*

5TH GRADE TEACHER: *We need a curriculum that understands our students' culture. Students are often not stimulated in school because teachers may not know a student's background or interests and fail to incorporate those into lessons.*

Collectively, these findings suggest that high expectations are indeed important, but without critical awareness, high expectations are susceptible to biases that impede teachers' ability to behave in ways consistent with high expectations. Accordingly, these findings extend the growing literature in support of ABP for historically marginalized students in several ways. First, they add to the evidence against claims that teacher expectations are not biased (e.g., McKown, 2013; Tenenbaum & Ruck, 2007) and counter assertions that the effects from biases that do exist are relatively small (see Jussim & Harber, 2005). Namely, when one considers that disparities between Latino students and their White peers on the 4th grade reading National Assessment of Educational Progress[10] is approximately 1 *SD* (NCES, 2015), it is particularly noteworthy that students with teachers who have high levels of both expectations and critical awareness perform approximately ½ *SD* higher in student reading and mathematics achievement over the course of one academic year. Given the cumulative nature of teacher expectations effects, this effect is substantial and consistent with SET (see McKown, 2013).

The findings also, however, provide quantitative evidence (further substantiated by teacher interviews) that critical awareness plays a key role in maintaining high expectations, supporting the extant literature on critical awareness (e.g., Banks, 1993; Darder, 2012; Gay, 2010; Ladson–Billings, 1995b; Valenzuela, 2016) while addressing limitations raised by scholars (e.g., Goldenberg et al., 2008). Specifically, the research findings underscore that it is insufficient to focus on expectation effects; teachers must possess critical awareness to ensure that their beliefs about students' abilities are not informed solely by students' prior performance. So how do we ensure that teachers receive the necessary knowledge to develop critical awareness? Scholars have found that coursework for teachers designed to increase critical awareness reduces biased beliefs (e.g., Kumar & Hamer, 2013). Unfortunately, preservice teachers often have limited access to coursework that develops critical awareness (Valenzuela, 2016).

Teacher Behaviors

Although the previous section is consistent with other scholars' work demonstrating that critical awareness is associated with Latino students' achievement (Brown & Chu, 2012), there is a still a need to examine *why* this is the case. In other words, how are these particular beliefs related to other beliefs and behaviors? As explained by Pajares (1992) in a synthesis of research examining teacher beliefs,

> Little will have been accomplished if research into educational beliefs fails to provide insights into the relationship between beliefs, on the one hand, and teacher practices, teacher knowledge, and student outcomes on the other. It is easy to urge teacher educators, for instance, to make educational beliefs a primary focus of their teacher preparations programs, but how are they to do this without research findings that identify beliefs that are consistent with effective teaching practices and student cognitive and affective growth, beliefs that are inconsistent with such aims, and beliefs that may play no significant role?
>
> *(p. 327–328)*

Accordingly, I examined how teacher beliefs were related to various ABP teacher beliefs and behaviors. To contextualize the research questions I addressed, I describe prior research that moved beyond expectations by examining teacher behaviors and their relationship to student outcomes in the following sections. This body of research is often known under the overarching theme of teacher effectiveness. I also, however, provide a brief review of asset-based pedagogy that was absent from the teacher expectations literature, but is necessary given the role of critical awareness in student achievement.

Teacher Effectiveness

Whereas teacher expectation research focused on whether teacher beliefs influenced student outcomes, the teacher effectiveness research that was generated between the 1960s and early 2000s focused on how teacher behaviors were related to student outcomes (Brophy, 1986; Brophy & Good, 1984; Good, 2014). Although early research was murky because "no specific teacher behavior had been linked clearly to student achievement" (Brophy, 1986, p. 1069), researchers attended to the limitations raised (Dunkin & Biddle, 1974). What followed was a vast body of work that detailed teacher behaviors such as how they provide and elicit information, the pacing of instruction, along with numerous other behaviors, and how these behaviors were associated with student achievement (Brophy & Good, 1984).

Teacher effectiveness research is particularly noteworthy because of its role in establishing that teacher behaviors are related to student outcomes, addressing pessimism that questioned whether teachers had any effect at all. This body of work also contributed to our understanding of how teachers' beliefs were related to their behaviors and generated research using observation coding systems that operationalized behaviors (Brophy, 1986; Brophy & Good, 1970).

Although there are many observation coding systems used to evaluate teachers, I elaborate on two that were selected in a recent Bill and Melinda Gates' funded study—the largest one ever conducted on teaching in the United States—called the "Measures of Effective Teaching (MET) Project." Of the numerous observation instruments used, the Framework for Teaching (FFT; Danielson, 2013) and the Classroom Assessment Scoring System (CLASS; Pianta & LaParo, & Hamre, 2008), were the only ones that reflected overall classroom quality. One of the things the MET researchers found was that there was substantial overlap in the scores of FFT and the CLASS, as well as the language arts instrument (Kane & Staiger, 2012). Examining the dimensions of both the FFT and CLASS, it is evident that there is similarity in the teacher behaviors evaluated (see Figure 4.3). This is because they both reflect the extant research on teacher effectiveness.

The recent work examining the relationship between teacher behaviors and student achievement has "replicated earlier research and illustrates that many years later, previous findings are highly similar to these new data"

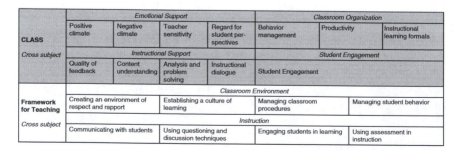

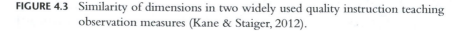

CLASS Cross subject	Emotional Support				Classroom Organization		
	Positive climate	Negative climate	Teacher sensitivity	Regard for student perspectives	Behavior management	Productivity	Instructional learning formats
	Instructional Support				Student Engagement		
	Quality of feedback	Content understanding	Analysis and problem solving	Instructional dialogue	Student Engagement		
Framework for Teaching Cross subject	Classroom Environment			
	Creating an environment of respect and rapport	Establishing a culture of learning	Managing classroom procedures	Managing student behavior
	Instruction			
	Communicating with students	Using questioning and discussion techniques	Engaging students in learning	Using assessment in instruction

FIGURE 4.3 Similarity of dimensions in two widely used quality instruction teaching observation measures (Kane & Staiger, 2012).

(Good, 2014, p. 27). Recalling the fact that quality teaching includes socially transmitted messages that are direct influences (see Introduction), it should not be surprising that observation instruments do not tend to consider signal influences. Given the evidence that general quality teaching behaviors are insufficient to meet the needs of Latino students (López, 2011), it is important to consider the role of ABP in reducing signal influences and as such, that should also be reflected in teacher effectiveness.

Asset-Based Pedagogy

Early attempts to address achievement disparities for poor youth, most of whom were students of color, were rooted in *deficit orientations* that reflect superiority of a group's practices, expectations, and experiences (Banks, 1993; Gutiérrez & Rogoff, 2003; Tharp, 1989). This perspective emerged prominently in education reforms with Lyndon B. Johnson's *War on Poverty* initiative, which provided the first special funding in U.S. history for compensatory programs (Title I) aimed at addressing the "culture of poverty" (Kantor, 1991, p. 65) believed to be inherent among poor youth. The belief reflected in compensatory programs was: "If the environment failed to equip poor children with the cultural resources needed for success at school, many reasoned, the school had to compensate poor children for the disadvantages of being born poor by changing their culture" (Kantor, 1991, p. 66).

Deficit orientations of compensatory programs were challenged as soon as they appeared (e.g., Clark, 1965), but they remain present in both practices believed to address achievement disparities and research initiatives. One contemporary intervention, for example, is focused on addressing students' *noncognitive* factors due to the assumption "that psychological processes and constructs are essentially universal, culture free, and therefore are universally applicable across populations" (Decuir–Gunby & Schutz, 2014, p. 251). Among the noncognitive constructs is *grit*,[11] described as "perseverance and passion for long-term goals ... in challenging circumstances" (Duckworth, Quinn, & Seligman, 2009, p. 541). Grit, however, has received particularly steadfast resistance among equity scholars who assert that it "[misreads] the actual sources of both the achievement and the lack of achievement" (Thomas, 2014, para. 11). Like other noncognitive factors that focus on individuals' behavioral control as the gateway to meeting high expectations and ameliorating achievement disparities (e.g., Kohn, 2008), grit ignores societal demands made on historically marginalized youth, thus perpetuating deficit views of historically marginalized students.

Perspectives that challenged earlier deficit orientations evolved to be known as "*difference orientations*" that reflected the need to consider dissimilarities between the school culture and that of historically marginalized students. Among these approaches were *culturally appropriate* (Au & Jordan, 1981), *culturally congruent* (Au & Mason, 1983), *culturally compatible* (Erickson & Mohatt, 1982), and *culturally responsive education* (Cazden & Leggett, 1981). Difference orientations, however, can often reflect deficiencies as evidenced by a recent study that found "early and wide gaps in cognitive and oral language skills" between Mexican American and White children (Fuller, Bein, Kim, & Rabe-Hesketh, 2015, p. 1). The study was disseminated by numerous media outlets, including National Public Radio (Sanchez, 2015). The image on the transcript of the report[12] depicted two mothers sharing a park bench, each sitting next to their toddler in a stroller. Whereas the Latina mother was reading a fashion magazine,[13] ignoring her child, the White mother was holding a flower and engaging with her child by asking, "Do you know what flower this is?" The image, since removed, highlights how readily differences can be portrayed as deficiencies (for a critique, see Valenzuela, 2015).

In contrast to deficiency perspectives, ABP orientations that have evolved over decades underscore viewing students' differences as *assets*, contesting the ways differences are too often reduced to deficiencies. Among the numerous ABP orientations are *critical bicultural pedagogy* (Darder, 1991, 2012), *equity pedagogy* (Banks, 1993), *culturally relevant pedagogy* (Ladson-Billings, 1995a, 1995b), *culturally responsive teaching* (Gay, 2000, 2010), *cultural connectedness* (Irizarry, 2007), *culturally sustaining pedagogies* (Paris, 2012), and *critical culturally sustaining revitalizing pedagogy* (McCarty & Lee, 2014), among others. These distinct conceptualizations have often focused on different populations of historically marginalized students, highlighting the applicability of ABP across settings. Despite the numerous conceptualizations, however, Gay (2010) asserts, "Although known by many different names … the ideas about why it is important to make classroom instruction more consistent with the cultural orientations of ethnically diverse students, and how this can be done, are virtually identical" (p. 31).

Although distinct conceptualizations of ABP share similarities, scholars have warned about the numerous ways ABP can be minimized to "add-ons, conceptualized as a 'celebration of diversity' rather than as a means of achieving social justice" (Wong et al., 2007, p. 17). Accordingly, although I provide a summary of the overarching themes of ABP scholarship, it is important to consider the sources that have provided a nuanced portrayal of "what culturally responsive pedagogy looks like" (Sleeter, 2012, p. 573) to prevent simplification of ABP as "cultural celebration, trivialization, and essentializing culture" (Sleeter, 2012, p. 568).

As previously mentioned, early teacher effectiveness research was considered unclear because "no specific teacher behavior had been linked clearly to student achievement" (Brophy, 1986, p. 1069). This changed with the abundance of evidence of numerous operationalized behaviors that were examined alongside student achievement (see Brophy & Good, 1984). To date, however, teacher effectiveness work has not considered the ways ABP addresses the unique needs of historically marginalized students. To that end, the operationalization of the discrete dimensions in the ABP literature can be used to examine the ways teachers' ABP beliefs and behaviors are related to student outcomes, thus addressing limitations raised (e.g., Goldenberg et al., 2008; Jussim & Harber, 2005; Ladson-Billings, 1999;

Losey, 1995; Sleeter, 2004, 2012). Collectively, the ABP literature reflects *cultural knowledge, cultural content integration, and language* as necessary pedagogical practices for historically marginalized students. They are briefly described below.

Cultural knowledge. The literature presenting conceptualizations of ABP focused on Latino youth has not drawn solely on the extant work focused on Latino students. For instance, Banks (1993), Ladson-Billings (1995a, 1995b), and Gay (2010) are among the most often cited in the literature focused on ABP for Latino youth (e.g., Antrop-González, Velez, & Garrett, 2004, 2008; Nieto & Irizarry, 2010; Norton & Bentley, 2006; Villegas & Lucas, 2002), although their own work has not focused on this population. Nevertheless, Ladson-Billings (2014) explains the reason she focused on African American students as follows:

> [O]ur work to examine success among the students who had been least successful was likely to reveal important pedagogical principles for achieving success for all students. A literature that tells us what works for middle-class, advantaged students typically fails to reveal the social and cultural advantages that make their success possible. But success among the "least of these" tells us more about what pedagogical choices can support success.
>
> *(p. 76)*

Moreover, even though much of the extant work by scholars who gave us culturally responsive teaching (Gay, 2010) and culturally relevant pedagogy (Ladson-Billings, 1995b) excludes a focus on Latino youth, the foundational premise of culture requires that ABP not be *fixed* but *malleable* to the particular context in which they are applied. The way culture has been represented in practice, however, has proven to be problematic, as reflected by Ladson-Billings (2014) in her statement, "Many practitioners, and those who claim to translate research to practice, seem stuck in very limited and superficial notions of culture" (p. 77). She elaborates, "The idea that adding some books about people of color, having a classroom Kwanzaa celebration, or posting 'diverse' images makes one 'culturally relevant' seem to be what the pedagogy has been reduced to" (Ladson-Billings, 2014, p. 82).

To accurately ground their work in the contexts of students with whom they work, many scholars have addressed the problematic construct of culture that results in scenarios such as those described by Ladson-Billings (2014). Gutiérrez and Rogoff (2003), for example, find that when cultural differences are treated as traits, there is an assumption that "[leads] to a kind of tracking in which instruction is adjusted merely on the basis of group categorization" (p. 20). The treatment of differences as traits, however, may be in part due to the emphasis on differences in ways students learn, and how these merit considerations by teachers. Gay (2002), for example, states that

> Culture encompasses many things, some of which are more important to know than others because they have direct implications for teaching and

learning. Among these are ethnic groups' cultural values, traditions, communication, learning styles, contributions, and relational patterns.

(p. 107)

Although the consideration of cultural values, communication, and relational patterns has support in the extant ABP literature, the notion that an ethic group has a tendency toward a particular learning style is challenged by many. Often cited as one of the earliest conceptualizations of learning differences that merit consideration in classroom practices, Cazden and Leggett (1981) claimed inherent differences in the cognitive styles of emerging bilinguals (EBs) and recommended "multisensory instruction" (p. 86) as one of the teaching strategies that went beyond bilingual education.[14] The notion that an ethnic group shares a particular cognitive style, however, has been contested on the basis that it potentially leads to trait-based beliefs and has no evidence to support its utility (see Gutiérrez & Rogoff, 2003). Banks (1993), for instance, cited a review by Kleinfeld and Nelson (1991) that had not found evidence supporting visual style learning for Indigenous students. Nevertheless, "the paradigm is a contentious one. Both its advocates and its critics are strongly committed to their positions" (Banks, 1993, p. 31).

The ABP literature is consistent in the need to validate students' cultural experiences as knowledge. Avoiding the reduction of cultural experiences as traits, cultural knowledge is also represented in *constructivist views of learning* where "learners use their prior knowledge and beliefs … to make sense of the new input" (Villegas & Lucas, 2002, p. 25). Ladson-Billings (1995b) shares the constructivist view in her conceptions of self and others, where teachers "believed in a Freirean notion of 'teaching as mining' or pulling knowledge out" (p. 479), as well as the "use of student culture as a vehicle for learning" (Ladson-Billings, 1995a, p. 161). It also includes incorporating students' home experiences into classroom instruction (González, Moll, & Amanti, 2005, p. 10) and making "connections between language use in the community and language use in a tradition of literary texts" (Lee, 1995, p. 612). Accessing students' cultural knowledge is also often viewed under the hybridity or third space (Gutiérrez, Baquedano-López, & Tejada, 1999) paradigm, wherein "alternative and competing discourses and positionings transform conflict and difference into rich zones of collaboration and learning" (pp. 286–287). Therefore, the cultural knowledge dimension embodies teachers' ability to access the multiple and dynamic prior knowledge students possess, as well as assess the new knowledge that results, in genuine ways. To this point, Gutierrez and Johnson (2017) warn

it would be a narrow interpretation of learning to understand learning in third spaces as what students can do with assistance, or even what can happen in discrete literacy event with rich social and linguistic interactions. Instead, in the Vygotskian sense, third spaces are collective zones of proximal development.

(p. 252)

Scholars have applied these cultural knowledge frameworks to contribute to our understanding of the importance of student-teacher relationships, with an emphasis on the perspectives of youth (Antrop-González, Velez, & Garrett, 2004, 2008; De Jesus & Antrop-González, 2006; Martin-Beltrán, 2009; Rogriguez, Jones, Pang, & Park, 2004). More recent scholarship has expanded on the seminal conceptualizations, calling for a consideration of the complexities of youth identities that reflect hybridity given "their experiences with peers of many varied identities" (Irizarry, 2007, p. 21) and reflecting the cultural pluralism and "contemporary/evolving community practices" (Paris & Alim, 2014, p. 85).

Cultural content integration. Whereas cultural knowledge reflects the consideration of knowledge students already possess, cultural content integration is about the provision of culture that is not typically validated in the formal curriculum. ABP arose out of the need to address disparities rooted in inequitable treatment based on belonging to a particular group (Banks, 1993). To counter the socially entrenched experiences among historically marginalized students, including that of a hegemonic curriculum, ABP literature requires that teachers incorporate students' culture into the curriculum to affirm "the legitimacy of cultural heritages of different ethnic groups, both as legacies that affect students' dispositions, attitudes, and approaches to learning and as worthy content to be taught in the formal curriculum" (Gay, 2000, p. 29). Accordingly, cultural content integration requires that teachers possess knowledge to determine "what information should be included in the curriculum, how it should be integrated into the existing curriculum, and its location within the curriculum" (Banks, 1993, p. 8).

Scholars have detailed ways to incorporate students' culture in English language arts (e.g., Duncan-Andrade, 2007; Morrell & Duncan-Andrade, 2002), social studies (e.g., Stovall, 2006), mathematics (e.g., Civil & Khan, 2001), and science (e.g., Milner, 2011; for a review, see Aaronson & Laughter, 2016). Although cultural content integration "is probably the most widely implemented but least studied aspect of multicultural education" (Zirkel, 2008, p. 1150), there is evidence on its role in improving student learning and improving interethnic relations (for a review, see Zirkel, 2008). More recent attempts to document the role of cultural content integration have included studies that examine the relationship between ethnic studies curricula and the improved academic outcomes of historically marginalized students (e.g., Cabrera et al., 2014; Dee & Palmer, 2016), as well as the role of multimodal texts in expanding "sophisticated political dialogue" among immigrant and refugee youth (Park, 2016, p. 138).

Language

Within both the cultural knowledge and cultural content integration dimensions is *language* because of its role in students' culture and identity. This view is evident in González's (2001) examination of the identities of Latino children and their mothers in her seminal book, *I Am My Language,* where she asserts, "The ineffable link of language to emotion, to the very core of our being, is one of the ties that bind children to a sense of heritage" (p. xix).

This analysis is shared by Darder (2012) who states, "It is critical that educators recognize the role language plays as one of the most powerful transmitters of culture, and as such, its central role to both intellectual formation and the survival of subordinate cultural populations" (p. 36). As a powerful trasmitter of culture that is central to identity, cultivating a native or heritage languge is not reserved for students who speak a language other than that of the dominant group in society. As pointed out by Perry and Delpit (1998), "language prejudice remains a 'legitimate' prejudice; that is, one can generally say the most appalling things about people's speech without fear of correction or contradiction" (p. 42). Accordingly, language is a key consideration in signal influences that differentially affect historically marginalized students.

Research Findings: How Are Critical Awareness and Teacher Expectations Related to Their ABP Beliefs and Behaviors?

In addition to identifying teachers' beliefs related to expectations and critical awareness, I asked teachers to report beliefs related to ABP (cultural knowledge, cultural content integration, and language), as well as the kind of ABP behaviors in which they engaged.[15] As summarized in Figure 4.4, I found that teachers with critical awareness hold beliefs consistent with ABP and that their beliefs in ABP, in turn, are related to their ABP practices. Teachers who understood Latino students' historical contexts and the importance were much more likely to incorporate (1) visits from members of the Latino community; (2) information from students' assignments to understand their prior knowledge and experiences; and (3) work that requires students to interview family members. They were also much more likely to (1) ensure student participation in activities that integrate a content area with Latino themes; (2) ask students to write about experiences or issues affecting Latinos; (3) incorporate current issues of concern to the Latino community in

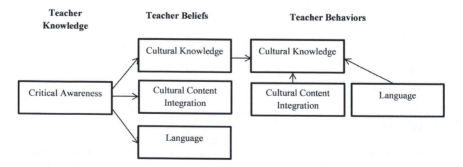

FIGURE 4.4 Summary of results for relationships between teacher beliefs and behaviors.

class; (4) use Spanish in instruction; (5) read literature with Latino themes; and (6) read literature by Latino authors. Drawing once again from the extant literature reviewed earlier in this chapter, it is likely that high levels of critical awareness are consistent with ABP practices because they reflect an understanding of the importance of leveraging students' culture in a setting that too often tends to be devoid of historically marginalized students' lives.

To enhance the analyses I have reviewed here, I again reviewed teacher responses to questions about what they believed would promote their Latino students' achievement, as well as what they believed were the greatest obstacles to Latino students' achievement. Once again, there was a clear pattern that differentiated teachers with high levels of critical awareness (and higher levels of ABP behaviors) from those with lower levels—a pattern that was not as easily discerned by their expectations. For example, the following excerpts represent an overwhelmingly consistent set of responses by teachers with low levels of critical awareness and low levels of ABP that followed a pattern reflecting deficiency views of families and students:

3RD GRADE TEACHER: *When students have parents who work the night shift and they don't spend enough time with their kids, it is a huge obstacle.*

4TH GRADE TEACHER: *I believe educating parents would help increase achievement. When parents value and make education a priority, so do the children. Parents need to understand the importance of school, why their child should be there, and be involved in their child's education.*

5TH GRADE TEACHER: *It seems parents want teachers to do all academic work in school and seldom help with homework. Most kids don't even have chores anymore.*

A few teachers also expressed assimilationist views about achievement, as well as views that perpetuate stratification:

5TH GRADE TEACHER: *I believe teaching the American History will empower Latino students and therefore increase achievement. I believe we should look at students as Americans rather than ethnic groups. I believe grouping students by achievement levels rather than ethnicity.*

In contrast to these views that placed the blame of achievement disparities on parents and students, and were also indicative of little to no attempts to incorporate ABP into instruction, teachers with high levels of critical awareness provided responses that reflected an understanding of institutional and social obstacles, as well as how ABP would enhance educational opportunities:

3RD GRADE TEACHER: *We need to validate language learners by promoting reading and writing in Spanish. I need more bilingual material in my classroom. We need more opportunities to connect with family.*

4TH GRADE TEACHER: *We need a curriculum that understands our students' culture. Students are often not stimulated in school because teachers may not know a student's background or interests and fail to incorporate those into lessons.*

5TH GRADE TEACHER: *I think we need to incorporate Latino leaders, culture, and themes in the classroom, especially dealing with local Tucson history.*

5TH GRADE TEACHER: *I believe Latino students will thrive if we provide rigorous instruction with consistency and promote bilingualism.*

Taken together, these findings shed light on *how* critical awareness and teacher expectations are related to other teacher beliefs and behaviors (see Figure 4.4). Still needed, however, is information on how teacher-reported behaviors are related to student identity and achievement. Namely, whereas teacher critical awareness was found to be related to teachers' beliefs and behaviors about the role of students' culture in instruction (language, cultural knowledge, and cultural content integration), I elaborate on how teachers' behaviors, in turn, were related to changes in Latino students' ethnic and achievement identities over the academic year in the next chapter focused on student identity and achievement.

Notes

1 Portions of this chapter originally appeared in López, F. (2017).
2 To capture the breadth of asset-based educational practices, I use the term "*asset-based pedagogy*" but retain authors' terminology when quoting their work.
3 Here, I use Banks and Banks McGee's (1989) definition of culture: "Most social scientists today view culture as consisting primarily of the symbolic, ideational, and intangible aspects of human societies. The essence of a culture is not its artifacts, tools, or other tangible cultural elements but how the members of the group interpret, use, and perceive them. It is the values, symbols, interpretations, and perspectives that distinguish one people from another in modernized societies; it is not material objects and other tangible aspects of human societies. People within a culture usually interpret the meaning of symbols, artifacts, and behaviors in the same or in similar ways" (p. 8).
4 The ways in which these inform student identity and achievement are presented in Chapter 5.
5 The issue of disentangling beliefs from knowledge was discussed by Pajares (1992) at length, where he also included attitudes, perceptions, dispositions, repertoires of understanding, to name but a few of the terms used interchangeably.
6 Scholars also refer to the requisite knowledge as *equity literacy* (Gorski, 2014) and *critical consciousness* (Valenzuela, 2016).
7 This section originally appeared in López, 2016.
8 Darder (2012) uses the term biculturalism "to project a more accurate picture of the worldview that these students must negotiate" (p. xix). Namely, bicultural students must manage "two cultural/class systems whose values are very often in direct conflict" and "sociopolitical and historical forces" that have perpetuated a subordinate, disempowered status that reflects bicultural students' cultures as deficient. Darder asserts that the conceptualization of biculturalism in CBP is grounded on the political and economic reasons behind inequitable power, and is not synonymous with the "psychological or anthropological paradigms" that are individualistic and relativist.
9 Details on the measures and statistical analyses used in the study are provided in Appendix 4.1.

10 See Figures 1.1–1.4 in Chapter 1.
11 Other issues with the construct of grit in particular involve its portrayal as a fixed trait (Duckworth, Quinn, & Seligman, 2009) and the implicit assumption that accomplishments are an artifact of the amount of grit individuals possess, and as such, that disparities are a result of historically marginalized students not possessing sufficient grit to narrow achievement disparities (see Thomas, 2014).
12 Permission to use the image was requested from the Permissions and Rights department of National Public Radio, but was declined because "the news team does not want to license the graphic" (J. Meade, personal communication, May 4, 2015).
13 The magazine title in the image was *Novedades,* which translates into English as "news" but was the title of a fashion magazine in circulation in Mexico.
14 Cazden and Leggett's (1981) chapter elaborated on Lau Remedies II, which explicitly called for teaching practices that were important for linguistically diverse youth beyond the bilingual education practices that were required at the time.
15 For details on the measures used, see Appendix 4.1.

References

Aaronson, B., & Laughter, J. (2016). The theory and practice of culturally relevant education: A synthesis of research across content areas. *Review of Educational Research, 86,* 163–206.

Anderson, L. M., & Stillman, J. A. (2013). Student teaching's contribution to preservice teacher development: A review of research focused on the preparation of teachers for urban and high-needs contexts. *Review of Educational Research, 83,* 3–69.

Antrop-Gonzalez, R., Velez, W., & Garrett, T. (2004). Challenging the academic (mis)categorization of urban youth: Building a case for Puerto Rican high achievers. *Multiple Voices for Ethnically Diverse Exceptional Learners, 7,* 16–32.

Antrop-González, R., Vélez, W., & Garrett, T. (2008). Examining familial-based academic success factors in urban high school students: The case of Puerto Rican female high achievers. *Marriage & Family Review, 43,* 140–163.

Apple, M. W. (2004). *Ideology and curriculum* (3rd ed.). Boston, MA: Routledge.

Au, K., & Jordan, C. (1981). Teaching reading to Hawaiian children: Finding a culturally appropriate solution. In H. Trueba, G. Guthrie, & K. Au (Eds.), *Culture and the bilingual classroom: Studies in classroom ethnography* (pp. 69–86). Rowley, MA: Newbury House.

Au, K., & Mason, J. M. (1983). Cultural congruence in classroom participation structures: Achieving a balance of rights. *Discourse Processes, 6,* 145–167.

Banks, J. A. (1993). Multicultural education: Historical development, dimensions, and practice. *Review of Research in Education, 19,* 3–49.

Banks, J. A. (2001). Citizenship education and diversity: Implications for teacher education. *Journal of Teacher Education, 52,* 5–16.

Banks, J. A., & Banks McGee, C. A. (1989). *Multicultural education.* Needham Heights, MA: Allyn & Bacon.

Barnes, C. P. (1987). The profile of the beginning teacher. Report of the CSU Committee to Study the Teacher Preparation Curriculum. Retrieved from http://eric.ed.gov/?id=ED282863\

Bartolome, L. I. (2004). Critical pedagogy and teacher education: Radicalizing prospective teachers. *Teacher Education Quarterly, 31,* 97–122.

Black, P., & Wiliam, D. (2009). Developing the theory of formative assessment. *Educational Assessment, Evaluation and Accountability, 21,* 5–31.

Bowles, S., & Gintis, H. (1976). *Schooling in capitalist America: Educational reform and the contradictions of economic life.* New York, NY: Basic Books.

Brophy, J. (1986). Teacher influences on student achievement. *American Psychologist, 41,* 1069–1077.

Brophy, J. E., & Good, T. L. (1970). Teachers' communication of differential expectations for children's classroom performance: Some behavioral data. *Journal of Educational Psychology, 61,* 365.

Brophy, J. E., & Good, T. L. (1984). *Teacher behavior and student achievement.* Occasional Paper No. 73. Retrieved from http://eric.edu.gov/?id=ED251422

Brown, C. S., & Chu, H. (2012). Discrimination, ethnic identity, and academic outcomes of Mexican immigrant children: The importance of school context. *Child Development, 83,* 1477–1485.

Cabrera, N. L., Milem, J. F., Jaquette, O., & Marx, R. W. (2014). Missing the (student achievement) forest for all the (political) trees: Empiricism and the Mexican American studies controversy in Tucson. *American Educational Research Journal, 51,* 1084–1118.

Cammarota, J. (2016). Social justice education project (SJEP): A case example of PAR in a high school classroom. In A. Valenzuela (Ed.), *Growing critically conscious teachers: A social justice curriculum for educators of Latino/a youth* (pp. 90–104). New York, NY: Teachers College Press.

Cazden, C. B., & Leggett, E. L. (1981). Culturally responsive education: Recommendations for achieving Lau remedies. In H. T. Trueba, G. P. Guthrie, & K. H. Au (Eds.), *Culture and the bilingual classroom: Studies in classroom ethnography* (pp. 69–86). Rowley, MA: Newbury House Publishers, Inc.

Chen, Y. H., Thompson, M. S., Kromrey, J. D., & Chang, G. H. (2011). Relations of student perceptions of teacher oral feedback with teacher expectancies and student self-concept. *The Journal of Experimental Education, 79,* 452–477.

Chun, H., & Dickson, G. (2011). A psychoecological model of academic performance among Hispanic adolescents. *Journal of Youth and Adolescence, 40,* 1581–1594.

Civil, M., & Khan, L. H. (2001). Mathematics instruction developed from a garden theme. *Teaching Children Mathematics, 7,* 400–405.

Clark, K. (1965). *Dark ghetto: Dilemmas of social power.* New York, NY: Harper Torchbooks.

Council of Chief State School Officers. (2011). *InTASC model core teaching standards: A resource for state dialogue.* Retrieved from http://www.ccsso.org/documents/2011/intasc_model_core_teaching_standards_2011.pdf

Danielson, C. (2013). The framework for teaching evaluation instrument. Princeton, NJ: The Danielson Group.

Darder, A. (1991). *Culture and power in the classroom: A critical foundation for the education of bicultural students* (1st ed.). Westport, CT: Bergin & Garvey.

Darder, A. (2012). *Culture and power in the classroom: A critical foundation for the education of bicultural students* (2nd ed.). Boulder, CO: Paradigm Press.

Darling-Hammond, L. (2000). How teacher education matters. *Journal of Teacher Education, 51,* 166–173.

Darling-Hammond, L., & Bransford, J. (Eds.). (2005). *Preparing teachers for a changing world: What teachers should learn and be able to do.* San Francisco, CA: Jossey-Bass.

Decuir-Gunby, J., & Schutz, P. (2014). Researching race within educational psychology contexts. *Educational Psychologist, 49,* 244–260.

Dee, T., & Penner, E. (2016). The causal effects of cultural relevance: Evidence from an ethnic studies curriculum. *The National Bureau of Economic Research.* NBER Working Paper No. 21865. Retrieved at http://www.nber.org/papers/w21865

DeGarmo, D. S., & Martinez, C. R. (2006). A culturally informed model of academic well-being for Latino youth: The importance of discriminatory experiences and social support. *Family Relations, 55,* 267–278.

De Jesus, A., & Antrop-González, R. (2006). Instrumental relationships and high expectations: Exploring critical care in two Latino community-based schools. *Intercultural Education, 17,* 281–299.

Dimitrov, D. M. (2010). Testing for factorial invariance in the context of construct validation. *Measurement and Evaluation in Counseling and Development, 43,* 121–149.

Duckworth, A. L., Quinn, P. D., & Seligman, M. E. P. (2009). Positive predictors of teacher effectiveness. *Journal of Positive Psychology, 4,* 540–547.

Duncan-Andrade, J. (2007). Gangstas, wankstas, and ridas: Defining, developing, and supporting effective teachers in urban schools. *International Journal of Qualitative Studies in Education, 20,* 617–638.

Dunkin, M. J., & Biddle, B. J. (1974). *The study of teaching.* New York, NY: Holt, Rinehart & Winston.

Erickson, F., & Mohatt, G. (1982). Cultural organization of participation structures in two classrooms of Indian students. In G. Spindler (Ed.), *Doing the ethnography of schooling: Educational anthropology in action* (pp. 132–174). New York, NY: Holt, Rinehart, and Winston.

Freire, P. (1970). *Pedagogy of the oppressed.* New York, NY: Herder and Herder.

Fuller, B., Bein, E., Kim, Y., & Rabe–Hesketh, S. (2015). Differing cognitive trajectories of Mexican American toddlers: The role of class, nativity, and maternal practices. *Hispanic Journal of Behavioral Sciences, 37,* 139–169.

Gay, G. (2000). *Culturally responsive teaching: Theory, research, and practice* (1st ed). New York, NY: Teachers College Press.

Gay, G. (2005). Politics of multicultural teacher education. *Journal of Teacher Education, 56,* 221–228.

Gay, G. (2010). *Culturally responsive teaching: Theory, research, and practice* (2nd ed). New York, NY: Teachers College Press.

Gay, G., & Kirkland, K. (2003). Developing cultural critical consciousness and self–reflection in preservice teacher education. *Theory into Practice, 42,* 181–187.

Giroux, H. (1985). Teachers as transformative intellectuals. *Social Education, 2,* 376–379.

Goldenberg, C., Rueda, R. S., & August, D. (2008). Sociocultural contexts and literacy development. In D. August & T. Shanahan (Eds.), *Developing reading and writing in second language learners: Lessons from the report of the National Literacy Panel on Language minority children and youth* (pp. 95–130). Washington, DC: Center for Applied Linguistics and Newark, DE: International Reading Association.

González, N. (2001). *I am my language: Discourses of women and children in the borderlands.* Tucson, AZ: University of Arizona Press.

González, N., Moll, L., & Amanti, C. (2005). *Funds of knowledge: Theorizing practices in households, communities, and classrooms.* Mahwah, NJ: Lawrence Erlbaum Associates.

Good, T. (2014). What do we know about how teachers influence student performance on standardized tests: And why do we know so little about other student outcomes? *Teachers College Record, 116,* 1–23.

Good, T., & Nichols, S. (2001). Expectancy effects in the classroom: A special focus on improving the reading performance of minority students in first–grade classrooms. *Educational Psychologist, 36,* 113–126.

Gorski, P. C. (2014). *Reaching and teaching students in poverty: Strategies for erasing the opportunity gap.* New York, NY: Teachers College Press.

Gutiérrez, K. D., Baquedano-López, P., & Tejeda, C. (1999). Rethinking diversity: Hybridity and hybrid language practices in the third space. *Mind, Culture, and Activity, 6,* 286–303.

Gutiérrez, K. D., & Johnson, P. (2017). Understanding identity sampling and cultural repertoires. In D. Paris, & H. S. Alim (Eds.), *Culturally sustaining pedagogies: Teaching and learning for justice in a changing world.* New York, NY: Teachers College Press.

Gutiérrez, K. D., & Rogoff, B. (2003). Cultural ways of learning: Individual traits or repertoires of practice. *Educational Researcher, 32,* 19–25.

Harris, M. J., Rosenthal, R., & Snodgrass, S. E. (1986). The effects of teacher expectations, gender, and behavior on pupil academic performance and self-concept. *The Journal of Educational Research, 79,* 173–179.

Hollins, E., & Torres–Guzman, M. E. (2005). Research on preparing teachers for diverse populations. In M. Cochran–Smith & K. Zeichner (Eds.), *Studying teacher education: The report of the AERA Panel on Research and Teacher Education* (pp. 477–544). Mahwah, NJ: Lawrence Erlbaum Associates.

Hu, L. T., & Bentler, P. M. (1999). Cutoff criteria for fit indexes in covariance structure analysis: Conventional criteria versus new alternatives. *Structural Equation Modeling, 6,* 1–55.

Irizarry, J. G. (2007). Ethnic and urban intersections in the classroom: Latino students, hybrid identities, and culturally responsive pedagogy. *Multicultural Perspectives, 9,* 21–28.

Jussim, L., Eccles, J., & Madon, S. (1996). Social perception, social stereotypes, and teacher expectations: Accuracy and the quest for the powerful self-fulfilling prophecy. *Advances in Experimental Social Psychology, 28,* 281–388.

Jussim, L., & Harber, K. D. (2005). Teacher expectations and self-fulfilling prophecies: Knowns and unknowns, resolved and unresolved controversies. *Personality and Social Psychology Review, 9,* 131–155.

Kantor, H. (1991). Education, social reform, and the state: ESEA and federal education policy in the 1960s. *American Journal of Education, 100,* 47–83.

King, J. E., & Ladson-Billings, G. (1990). The teacher education challenge in elite university settings: Developing critical perspectives for teaching in a democratic and multicultural society. *The European Journal of Intercultural Studies, 1,* 15–30.

Kleinfeld, J., & Nelson, P. (1991). Adapting instruction to Native Americans' learning styles: An iconoclastic view. *Journal of Cross-Cultural Psychology, 22,* 273–282.

Kohn, A. (2008). Why self-discipline is overrated: The (troubling) theory and practice of control from within. *Phi Delta Kappan, 90,* 168–176.

Kumar, R., & Hamer, L. (2013). Preservice teachers' attitudes and beliefs toward student diversity and proposed instructional practices: A sequential design study. *Journal of Teacher Education, 64,* 162–177.

Ladson-Billings, G. (1994). *The dreamkeepers.* San Francisco, CA: Jossey–Bass.

Ladson-Billings, G. (1995a). But that's just good teaching! The case for culturally relevant pedagogy. *Theory into Practice, 34,* 159–165.

Ladson-Billings, G. (1995b). Toward a theory of culturally relevant pedagogy. *American Educational Research Journal, 47,* 465–491.

Ladson-Billings, G. (1999). Preparing teachers for diverse student populations: A critical race theory perspective. *Review of Research in Education, 24,* 211–247.

Ladson-Billings, G. (2004). New directions in multicultural education: Complexities, boundaries, and Critical Race Theory. In J. A. Banks (Ed.), *Handbook of research on multicultural education* (pp. 50–65). San Francisco, CA: Jossey Bass.

Ladson–Billings, G. (2014). Culturally relevant pedagogy 2.0: Aka the remix. *Harvard Educational Review, 84,* 74–84.

Lee, C. D. (1993). Signifying as a scaffold for literary interpretation: The pedagogical implications of an African American discourse genre. Research report series. Urbana, IL: National Council of Teachers of English.

Lee, C. D. (1995). A culturally based cognitive apprenticeship: Teaching African American high school students' skills in literary interpretation. *Reading Research Quarterly, 30,* 608–631.

Lee, C. D. (2007). *Culture, literacy, and learning: Taking bloom in the midst of the whirlwind.* New York, NY: Teachers College Press.

López, F. (2011). The nongeneralizability of classroom dynamics as predictors of achievement for Hispanic Students in upper elementary grades. *Hispanic Journal of Behavioral Sciences, 33,* 350–376.

López, F. (2016). Teacher reports of culturally responsive teaching and Latino students' reading achievement in Arizona. *Teachers College Record, 118*(5).

López, F. (2017). Altering the trajectory of the self–fulfilling prophecy: Asset–based pedagogy and classroom dynamics. *Journal of Teacher Education, 68,* 193–212.

Losey, K. M. (1995). Mexican American students and classroom interaction: An overview and critique. *Review of Educational Research, 65,* 283–318.

McCarty, T. L., & Lee, T. S. (2014). Critical culturally sustaining/revitalizing pedagogy and Indigenous education sovereignty. *Harvard Educational Review, 84,* 101–124.

McKown, C. (2013). Social equity theory and racial-ethnic achievement gaps. *Child Development, 84,* 1120–1136.

McKown, C., & Weinstein, R. S. (2002). Modeling the role of child ethnicity and gender in children's differential responses to teacher expectations. *Journal of Social Psychology, 32,* 159–184.

Martin-Beltrán, M. (2009). Cultivating space for the language boomerang: The interplay of two languages as academic resources. *English Teaching: Practice and Critique, 8,* 25–53.

Merton, R. K. (1948). The self–fulfilling prophecy. *The Antioch Review, 8,* 193–210.

Milner, H. R. (2010). What does teacher education have to do with teaching? Implications for diversity studies. *Journal of Teacher Education, 61,* 118–131.

Milner, H. R. (2011). Culturally relevant pedagogy in a diverse urban classroom. *Urban Review, 43,* 66–89.

Moll, L. C. (1988). Some key issues in teaching Latino students. *Language Arts, 65,* 465–472.

Moll, L. C. (1990). *Social and instructional issues in educating "disadvantaged" students.* (ED314549). Retrieved at http://files.eric.ed.gov/fulltext/ED314549.pdf#page=47

Moll, L. C., & González, N. (2004) Engaging life: A funds of knowledge approach to multicultural education. In J. Banks & C. McGee Banks (Eds.), *Handbook of research on multicultural education* (2nd ed.) (pp. 699–715). San Francisco, CA: Jossey-Bass.

Morrell, E., & Duncan–Andrade, J. M. R. (2002). Promoting academic literacy with urban youth through engaging hip-hop culture. *English Journal, 91,* 88–92.

Morrison, K. A., Robbins, H. H., & Rose, D. G. (2008). Operationalizing culturally relevant pedagogy: A synthesis of classroom-based research. *Equity & Excellence in Education, 41,* 433–452.

Muijs, D., & Reynolds, D. (2002). Teachers' beliefs and behaviors: What really matters? *The Journal of Classroom Interaction, 37,* 3–15.

National Center for Education Statistics (NCES), (2015). The condition of education. Retrieved at http://nces.ed.gov/programs/coe/indicator_cnb.asp

Nieto, S., & Irizarry, J. G. (2012). Instructional practices and approaches. *Journal of the Association of Mexican American Educators, 6,* 17–21.

Norton, N. E. J., & Bentley, C. C. (2006). Making the connection: Extending culturally responsive teaching through home(land) pedagogies. *Feminist Teacher: A Journal of the Practices, Theories, and Scholarship of Feminist Teaching, 17,* 52–70

Pajares, M. F. (1992). Teachers' beliefs and educational research: Cleaning up a messy construct. *Review of Educational Research, 62,* 307–332.

Paris, D. (2012). Culturally sustaining pedagogy: A needed change in stance, terminology, and practice. *Educational Researcher, 41,* 93–97.

Paris, D., & Alim, H. S. (2014). What are we seeking to sustain through culturally sustaining pedagogy? A loving critique forward. *Harvard Educational Review, 84,* 85–100.

Park, J. Y. (2016). Going global and getting graphic: Critical multicultural citizenship education in an afterschool program for immigrant and refugee girls. *International Journal of Multicultural Education, 18,* 126–141.

Perry, T. & Delpit, L. D. (Eds.). (1998). *The real Ebonics debate: Power, language, and the education of African-American children.* Boston, MA: Beacon Press.

Pianta, R. C., La Paro, K. M., & Hamre, B. K. (2008). *Classroom assessment scoring system (CLASS) manual, K–3.* Baltimore, MD: Paul H. Brookes Publishing Company.

Pohan, C. A., & Aguilar, T. E. (2001). Measuring educators' beliefs about diversity in personal and professional contexts. *American Educational Research Journal, 38,* 159–182.

Ponterotto, J. G., Gretchen, D., Utsey, S. O., Stracuzzi, T., & Saya, R. (2003). The multigroup ethnic identity measure (MEIM): Psychometric review and further validity testing. *Educational and Psychological Measurement, 63,* 502–515.

Rios-Aguilar, C. (2010). Measuring funds of knowledge: Contributions to Latina/o students' academic and nonacademic outcomes. *Teachers College Record, 112,* 2209–2257.

Rodriguez, J. L., Jones, E. B, Pang, V. O., & Park, C. D. (2004). Promoting academic achievement and identity development among diverse high school students. *High School Journal, 87,* 44–53.

Romero, A., Arce, S., & Cammarota, J. (2009). A barrio pedagogy: Identity, intellectualism, activism, and academic achievement through the evolution of critically compassionate intellectualism. *Race, Ethnicity, and Education, 12,* 217–233.

Rosenthal, R. (1994). Interpersonal expectancy effects: A 30-year perspective. *Current Directions in Psychological Science, 3,* 176–179.

Rosenthal, R., & Jacobson, L. (1968). Pygmalion in the classroom. *The Urban Review, 3,* 16–20.

Rubie-Davies, C. M. (2006). Teacher expectations and student self-perceptions: Exploring relationships. *Psychology in the Schools, 43,* 537–552.

Sanchez, C. (2015, April 7). Mexican-American toddlers: Understanding the achievement gap. National Public Radio. Retrieved from http://www.npr.org/blogs/ed/2015/04/07/397829916/mexican–american–toddlers–understanding–the–achievement–gap.

Sleeter, C. (2004). Context-conscious portraits and context-blind policy. *Anthropology and Education Quarterly, 35,* 132–136.

Sleeter, C. E. (2012). Confronting the marginalization of culturally responsive pedagogy. *Urban Education, 47,* 562–584.

Stiggins, R. (1988). Make sure your teachers understand student assessment. *Executive Educator, 10,* 24–30.

Stovall, D. (2006). We can relate: Hip-hop culture, critical pedagogy, and the secondary classroom. *Urban Education, 41,* 585–602.

Tenenbaum, H. R., & Ruck, M. D. (2007). Are teachers' expectations different for racial minority than for European American students? A meta-analysis. *Journal of Educational Psychology, 99*, 253–273.

Tharp, R. G. (1989). Psychocultural variables and constants: Effects on teaching and learning in schools. *American Psychologist, 44*, 349–359.

Thomas, P. (2014, January 30). The "grit" narrative, "grit" research, and codes that blind. Retrieved from https://radicalscholarship.wordpress.com/2014/01/30/the-grit-narrative-grit-research-and-codes-that-blind

Valenzuela, A. (2015, April 9). Mexican-American toddlers: (Mis)understanding the achievement gap [Blog post]. Retrieved from http://texasedequity.blogspot.com/2015/04/mexican-american-toddlers-understanding.html

Valenzuela, A. (Ed.). (2016). *Growing critically conscious teachers: A social justice curriculum for Educators of Latino/a Youth.* New York, NY: Teachers College Press.

Villegas, A. M., & Lucas, T. (2002). Preparing culturally responsive teachers: Rethinking the curriculum. *Journal of Teacher Education, 53*, 20–32.

Weinstein, R., Marshall, H., Sharp, L., & Botkin, M. (1987). Pygmalion and the student: Age and classroom differences in children's awareness of teacher expectations. *Child Development, 58*, 1079–1093.

Wong, P. L., Murai, H., Bérta–Ávila, M., William–White, L., Baker, S., Arellano, A., & Echandia, A. (2007). The M/M Center: Meeting the demand for multicultural, multilingual teacher preparation. *Teacher Education Quarterly, 34*, 9–35.

Zirkel, S. (2008). The influence of multicultural education practices on student outcomes and intergroup relations. *Teachers College Record, 110*, 1147–1181.

APPENDIX 4.1

Teacher-Reported Beliefs. Items for the teacher-reported beliefs survey were compiled from Pohan and Aguilar's (2001) *Beliefs about Diversity* scales, and categorized to assess teachers' *beliefs* about the role of each of the four ABP dimensions reflected in the review of the literature (critical awareness, cultural content integration, language, and cultural knowledge), as well as beliefs associated with teacher expectancy and formative assessment. Accordingly, it is included in the present study as a dimension. Teachers were asked to report the extent to which they agree (1 = *strongly agree*, 5 = *strongly disagree*) with twenty-five statements. The validation of the original survey (Pohan & Aguilar, 2001) suggests that the items are cogent representations of the construct of critical awareness as it relates to issues of teachers' beliefs regarding students' race/ethnicity, social class, and language, and are not susceptible to socially desirable bias (see Pohan & Aguilar, 2001). Examples of the items and descriptive statistics are presented in Table A.1.

Teacher-Reported Behaviors. The teacher-reported behaviors survey was designed to assess the degree to which teachers report *incorporating* the domains reported in the beliefs survey. The survey also asks teachers to report their training background, ethnicity, years taught, and certification. The measure is a modified version of the questionnaires developed with content validity input from experts in ABP for the National Indian Education Study (NIES), the only large scale, nationally representative study that has collected information about the degree to which teachers incorporate culture into the educational experiences of Native American students (see López, Heilig, & Schram, 2013). Examples of the Likert-type items and descriptive statistics are presented in Table A.2.

Data Analysis. To address the first research question, a multiple regression analysis was conducted with teacher expectancy and critical awareness as independent

TABLE 4A.1 Teacher–Reported ABP Beliefs, scored 1–5

Dimension	Number of items	Example	α	M	SD
Critical Awareness	11	Historically, education has been monocultural, reflecting only one reality and has been biased toward the dominant (White) group.	0.77	3.89	0.71
Teacher Expectancy	3	Latino students can close achievement gaps if teachers provide them with rigorous instruction.	0.70	4.14	0.88
Cultural Knowledge	3	Teachers should learn about students' home lives and incorporate this knowledge into instruction.	0.77	4.27	0.62
Cultural Content Integration	4	Teachers should incorporate class materials that reflect the contributions made by individuals who share their students' cultural heritage.	0.72	4.30	0.68
Language	3	Students who do not speak English are at an advantage to become bilingual.	0.70	4.39	0.53

variables; student spring reading achievement as the dependent variable; and student fall reading achievement as a control variable. A subsequent block with an interaction term for teacher expectancy and critical awareness entered in the final model.

To address the remaining research questions, LISREL 9.1 software was used to conduct path analysis. Analyses of student measures examine change over the year or use data from the beginning of the year to control for student outcomes. Models were specified from the research questions. Model 1 investigated the direct influences of teachers' critical awareness beliefs (BLCA) and teachers' expectancy (BLTE) on other teacher beliefs and the direct and indirect influences of teacher beliefs on teacher behavior. Model 2 investigated the direct and indirect influences of teacher behavior on student outcomes. Non-significant paths were pruned to arrive at final models.

Model fit was evaluated using absolute and relative measures. Absolute measures of fit indicate the degree to which the model approximates perfect fit. Here, the chi-square statistic (χ^2) and root mean square of approximation (RMSEA) are reported. The chi-square statistic is difficult to use in large-scale studies because there are no standards for fit beyond non-significance and the chi-square is sensitive to sample size, with larger samples more likely to be found significant because of the increased power of the test. However, the relatively small sample in this study allows for meaningful interpretation of chi-square significance. Additionally, RMSEA, the most common absolute fit index, was also examined. MacCallum, Browne, & Sugawara (1996) suggest RMSEA < .05 indicates good fit, while RMSEA < .08 indicates acceptable, but mediocre fit.

TABLE 4A.2 Teacher-Reported ABP Behaviors

Dimension	Number of items	Example	Coefficient alpha	Mean	Standard Deviation	Range
Formative Assessment	4	To what extent do you use performance-based assessments to inform your teaching?	0.81	3.14	0.44	1–4 Not at all to large extent
Critical Awareness	9	To what extent have you acquired knowledge, skills, and information specific to teaching Latino students from college courses with a general focus on diversity?	0.86	2.79	0.71	1–5 Never to every day or almost every day
Cultural Knowledge	2	How often do you assign work that requires students to interview family members?	0.70	3.05	0.11	1–5 Never to every day or almost every day
Cultural Content Integration	9	To what extent do you integrate lessons and materials about current issues affecting Latino people and communities into your curriculum?	0.90	2.98	0.65	1–5 Never to every day or almost every day
Language	3	To what extent do you use Spanish when you teach any core subject (reading, mathematics, science, and social studies)?	0.76	3.36	0.84	1–4 Never to whenever it is feasible

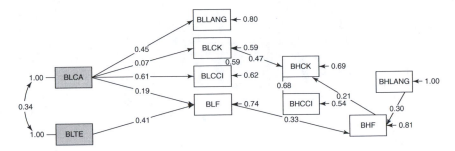

FIGURE 4A.1 Revised model with non-significant paths removed and revised pathways between teacher behavior variables.

Note: BLCA = Critical awareness beliefs; BLTE = teacher expectancy; BLLANG = beliefs about the use of Spanish in instruction; BLCK = cultural knowledge beliefs; BLCCI= cultural content integration beliefs; BLF = formative assessment beliefs; BHCK = cultural knowledge behaviors; BHCCI = cultural content integration beliefs; BHF= formative assessment behaviors; and BHLANG = behaviors reflecting the use of Spanish.

TABLE 4A.3 OLS Regression

	Model 1			Model 2		
	β	SE	p	β	SE	p
Intercept	0.206	0.033	**>0.001**	0.138	0.038	**>0.001**
Fall Reading	0.708	0.035	**>0.001**	0.713	0.034	**>0.001**
Critical Awareness	0.092	0.036	**0.011**	0.072	0.036	**0.047**
Teacher Expectancy	0.014	0.036	0.691	0.094	0.042	**0.027**
Interaction				0.159	0.045	**>0.001**

Relative fit was assessed using the non-normed fit index (NNFI, also known as the Tucker-Lewis index) and comparative fit index (CFI). Both of these relative fit indicators depend on the average size of the correlations among measures in the data and are minimally affected by sample size (Dimitrov, 2010), thus they are useful even with small samples. Models with acceptable fit result in NNFI and CFI values >.90; close fit is indicated by NNFI and CFI >.95 (Hu & Bentler, 1999).

References

Dimitrov, D. M. (2010). Testing for factorial invariance in the context of construct validation. *Measurement and Evaluation in Counseling and Development, 43,* 121–149.

Hu, L. T. & Bentler, P. M. (1999). Cutoff criteria for fit indexes in covariance structure analysis: Conventional criteria versus new alternatives. *Structural Equation Modeling, 6,* 1–55.

López, F., Heilig, J., & Schram, J. (2013). A story within a story: Culturally responsive schooling and American Indian and Alaska Native achievement in the National Indian Education Study. *American Journal of Education, 119,* 513–538.

Maccallum, R. C., Browne, M. W., & Sugawara, H. M. (1996). Power analysis and determination of sample size for covariance structure modeling. *Psychological Methods, 1,* 130–149.

Pohan, C. A. & Aguilar, T. E. (2001). Measuring educators' beliefs about diversity in personal and professional contexts. *American Educational Research Journal, 38,* 159–182.

5

STUDENT IDENTITY[1]

Francesca A. López

> What I love most about my school is that it's really connected around here.
> It really brings out, like, the culture of anybody who's here.
>
> *—5th grade student*

Stereotypes and Identity

Readers may be familiar with the experiment conducted by third-grade teacher Jane Elliot—the "brown eyes, blue eyes experiment" that she conducted after the assassination of Martin Luther King, Jr. For those unfamiliar, Ms. Elliot wanted her students to know what it is like to be on the receiving end of prejudice and devised an experiment. She split up the class into groups: blue eyes and brown eyes. On day one, students with blue eyes were superior; students with brown eyes were inferior and wore a collar to signal their status to the class. The lower status brought with it segregation and name calling,[2] and contributed to a fascinating phenomenon. The image shows Ms. Elliot and the brown-eyed students reviewing phonics cards. On the day the blue-eyed students were superior, they outperformed the brown-eyed students. The next day, when they were the "superior" group, the brown-eyed students surpassed the class record time. What this experiment showed us, as did many experiments carried out more recently (Steele, 2011) that established the phenomenon of *stereotype threat*, is that performance can be impeded simply by belonging to a negatively stereotyped group. It does so by leading those in negatively stereotyped groups to doubt their abilities. In this particular case, academic ability was tied to inferiority based on eye color—but it was an experiment designed to show what inferiority linked to race and ethnicity can do. These social events that "signal to members of negatively stereotyped groups that they are devalued because of their group membership" (McKown, 2013, p. 1125) have powerful implications for historically marginalized youth precisely because they are deleterious to identity. As described by Bandura (2006), we "live in a psychic environment largely of [our] own making" (p. 165).

Identity, broadly speaking, is defined by the answer to the question "Who am I?" (Eccles, 2009; La Guardia, 2009; Wigfield & Karpathian, 1991). As a facet of identity, self-beliefs about academic ability have been central to the examination of achievement outcomes because they reflect "the assumption that individuals' perceptions of themselves and their capabilities are vital forces in their success or failure in achievement settings" (Schunk & Pajares, 2005, p. 85). Indeed, research on teacher expectations has established a robust link between teacher beliefs and students' perceptions of ability (see Good, 1987; Good & Brophy, 2010). In this body of research, teacher beliefs have been found to be reflected in behaviors such as waiting less time for students perceived by teachers to be "low achievers" to answer a question or praising these students less often when they have been successful (Good & Brophy, 2010). Central to teacher expectation research, teacher behaviors have also been found to be internalized by students, shaping their identity in terms of perceptions of ability that influence their subsequent performance.

Academic self-beliefs. Although there are many academic self-beliefs that have been found to be related to student achievement (see Schunk & Pajares, 2005), they include self-efficacy (Bandura, 1986), self-concept (Marsh & Shavelson, 1985), and expectancy value (Eccles et al., 1983). These and other self-beliefs are all believed to develop through students' interpretation of their personal experiences. Certainly, we have substantial evidence not only on the extent to which students can infer teachers' beliefs, but also on the directionality of the relationship (for a review, see Rubie-Davies, 2006). For example, researchers have found that students are quite adept at inferring teachers' expectations (e.g., Weinstein, Marshall, Sharp, & Botkin, 1987) and that teachers' expectations tend to be more influential to students' achievement than the reverse (e.g., Muijis & Reynolds, 2002; Rubie-Davies, 2006), challenging assumptions about the accuracy of teacher expectations. A key finding of this research is that teachers' beliefs reflecting low expectations have stronger implications for students than those of high expectations, making students who are considered low achievers more vulnerable to teacher beliefs (Madon, Jussin, & Eccles, 1997). When this research is considered with evidence that students' self-beliefs predict the extent to which students will take risks for more challenging work, which is known to enhance learning, the consequences of low expectations for minoritized youth can be devastating. Accordingly, the evidence we have underscores the importance of focusing on teacher beliefs (Rubie-Davies, 2006) and teachers' behaviors (Harris, Rosenthal, & Snodgrass, 1986; Chen, Thompson, Kromry, & Chang, 2011) toward Latino youth precisely because they tend to be biased (Tenenbaum & Ruck, 2007) and markedly shape Latino students' academic self-beliefs.

Out of the numerous conceptualizations of academic self-belief, scholastic competence is considered to be one of the strongest predictors of academic achievement (for a review, see López, 2010). Scholastic competence lacks a singular conceptualization (Schunk & Pajares, 2005), but is considered to encompass both self-evaluative ([self-efficacy] Bandura, 1977, 1997) and norm-referenced ([self-concept] Marsh & Shavelson, 1985) views of academic ability. Scholastic competence is also relatively stable even though domain-specific competencies may vary (Marsh & Shavelson, 1985). That is, even if there is slight variation in students' perceptions about their ability in reading, mathematics, science, and so on, all of these micro-focused perceptions about content areas inform an overall belief about academic ability. Although this body of research is embedded in the teacher efficacy literature, which focuses on direct influences that affect all individuals, students' perceptions of ability are also informed by signal influences. As such, other facets of identity must be considered.

Ethnic identity. Ethnic identity is a component of self-concept that reflects the extent to which an individual identifies with their ethnic background (Juang & Syed, 2008; Phinney, 1992). Although asset-based pedagogy (ABP) and teacher expectations research considers children adept at evaluating the behaviors others have toward them within school settings and, as a result, making inferences about their academic abilities, ethnic identity is often grounded in developmental theories that confine it to later stages of development (Phinney, 1992). Attributing her theoretical framework to the work of Erikson (1968) and Marcia (1980), Phinney (1989, 1992) explained that ethnic identity begins with a period in which children give ethnicity little, if any, conscious thought and progresses to an exploration of the ways in which their ethnic group differs from others. In the final stage of ethnic identity development, which is believed to occur in adulthood, individuals are believed to achieve ethnic identity once they successfully resolve challenges that arise from exploration of their ethnicity. Thus, for many scholars, the exploration of ethnic identity is believed to occur in adolescence and fully develop in adulthood. As such, the research examining the role of ethnic identity on students' achievement has been largely restricted to adolescent populations.

Challenging the belief that ethnic identity is limited to later stages of development, Quintana and Scull (2006) explain earlier developmental considerations for minoritized children:

> Their understanding includes the implications of such ethnic attitudes as prejudice in their experience of ethnicity and ethnic self-concepts. During this development period, children are able to understand how others perceive them based on ethnic group status.
>
> *(p. 91)*

In consideration of evidence that children from academically stigmatized groups are not only developmentally capable of perceiving discriminatory behaviors (e.g., Stone & Han, 2005), but also to "show earlier and greater awareness of broadly held stereotypes" (McKown & Weinstein, 2003, p. 511), examining Latino students' ethnic self-concepts and perceptions of discrimination is critical to understanding *how* ABP might address inequity before Latino youth have decided that school settings are not places where they belong. This is consistent with the evidence for socially transmitted signal influences in Social Equity Theory (SET, McKown, 2013) that are contingent on ethnicity.

In addition to developmental considerations, one of the most pervasive issues in the research examining ethnic identity lies in incongruent conceptualizations. That is, when contradictions across studies are more closely examined, it is the lack of consistency in definitions that is often to blame. For example, in one study, a dual ethnic identity (affirmation toward one's own ethnic group as well as the dominant group) was found to be positively related to academic achievement (Oyserman, 2008). Altschul, Oyserman, and Bybee (2008), however, were unable to replicate these findings. Once the ways in which dual ethnic identity was represented in the instrument are evaluated, issues are revealed. First, the psychometric properties of the dual ethnicity domain were consistently low across studies (Altschul, Oyserman, & Bybee, 2008; Oyserman, 2008), suggesting that the items did not represent the same construct. Scrutiny of the items reveals that dual ethnic identity is represented by statements such as "As a member of my group it is important to me to share my culture and traditions with others" and "I am proud to be a member of my group because we as a people have made many contributions to society." These items arguably do *not* represent dual ethnicity, but inclinations toward *influencing* others and ethnic affirmation, respectively. To reflect dual identity more accurately, the construct must be consistent with the *ethnic pluralism model*, where items reflect the preservation of a positive identity with one's ethnic background (in-group ethnic affirmation) while also identifying with the majority culture (other-group ethnic affirmation; Phinney, 1996; Sidanius, Feshbach, Levin, & Pratto, 1997). Indeed, researchers using varied methodologies have found that individuals with an ethnic identity that relates positively to both their ethnic group and the dominant group tend to have higher levels of academic performance (e.g., Hurtado-Ortiz & Gauvain, 2007). Notably, the ethnic pluralism model is related to the concept of biculturalism, wherein minoritized individuals adopt cultural practices consistent with the dominant society, but retain cultural practices of the group with whom they identify. This, in turn, is consistent with the belief that ABP provides a bridge connecting the dominant school culture to students' home culture, thus promoting academic achievement for historically marginalized students.

In consideration of the potential role of signal influences in the development of students' academic and ethnic self-concepts, as well as the research that has found *both* to be positively related to academic outcomes, the relationship between ABP cannot be limited to academic self-concept; both ethnic identity and perceived discrimination must also be considered.

Research Findings: How Are ABP Behaviors Related to Latino Students' Identity and Achievement?

In Chapter 4, I detailed how teachers' beliefs were related to their ABP behaviors. The key question, however, is how these ABP behaviors are related to Latino students' identity and achievement. If we find that ABP teacher behaviors do not promote identities that are consistent with positive outcomes for Latino youth, then what would be the point of ensuring teachers use ABP in their classrooms? In other words, although understanding the relationships between teachers' beliefs and behaviors is important, it is by understanding *why* they are important that we can address limitations raised in prior reviews (e.g., Pajares, 1992).

As shown in Figure 5.1, the research I carried out found that ABP behaviors inform students' cultural and achievement identities, consistent with Ladson-Billings' (1995b) call for "a theoretical model that not only addresses student achievement but also helps students to accept and affirm their cultural identity" (p. 469). Specifically, I found that teachers' cultural knowledge behaviors, which are believed to be important because they validate students' cultural prior knowledge, are strongly associated with an increase in students' self-concept in reading and mathematics. Cultural content integration is also strongly related to an increase in students' affirmation of other groups, which in turn is also strongly associated with and increase students' self-concept in reading and mathematics. This contribution contradicts the argument made by policymakers in the state of Arizona, who asserted that the use of cultural materials can create animus toward other groups (HB 2281, 2010). Indeed, it appears affirming students' culture encourages other-group affirmation (which is also directly informed by students' ethnic affirmation) and has a strong, positive influence on reading and mathematics competence,[3] which have been shown to serve as robust proxies on reading and mathematics achievement itself (Marsh & Shavelson, 1985).

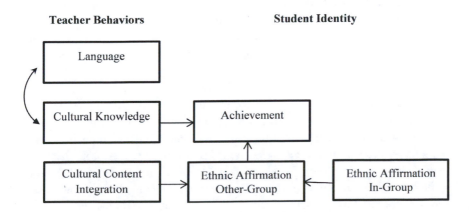

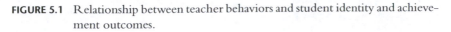

FIGURE 5.1 Relationship between teacher behaviors and student identity and achievement outcomes.

It should be noted that students in the school with the highest levels of ABP had the highest levels of both ethnic affirmation and academic self-competence. Students in the school with the highest levels of ABP, however, also had higher levels of perceived discrimination compared to the other dual language school. Although it may seem counterintuitive, this finding is consistent with prior work finding a positive relationship between students' awareness of discrimination and higher levels of academic self-concept (Altschul, Oyserman, & Bybee, 2006). This is because students who are aware of discrimination are more likely to view these behaviors as faults in those enacting the pejorative behaviors rather than within themselves. The school with the highest levels of ABP engages in discussions about discrimination and ways to promote equity, while supporting students with an explicit focus on honoring students' heritage and others' heritage as well (and accordingly, students at that school also had the highest levels of "other" ethnic identity that contributes to a bicultural identity). As such, the pedagogy reflects a critical awareness described by Ladson-Billings (1995a) that was confirmed by conversations with students. One student stated, "People come to the school and teach us about things that other people don't learn." Another said, "It's really connected around here. And it really brings out like the culture of anybody who's here."

The cultural focus of the school and its link to students' identities was also salient, as summarized by the following statements shared by students:

> Our school is different from other schools. It is bilingual. We have the Cesar Chavez march. We have performances. It is like the best school ever known.
> —*4th grade student*

> I like my school because I know a lot of people here from my elementary school. There's mariachi here and in my elementary school, I played in the mariachi so here I get to practice more and maybe get to be more advanced here. I also like my school cuz it's bilingual and my parents speak Spanish and don't really speak English so they, they know that all the teachers speak Spanish and that's better for them and me too.
>
> —*5th grade student*

When asked what their parents say about their school, or how their school is different from other schools, or what their favorite thing about their school is, students in the high-ABP school often discussed the bilingual emphasis at their school. One student explained, "My school is a better school than other schools because it's bilingual." Several students discussed their parents' desire for them to speak better Spanish and learn about their culture as the primary motivating factor in their school placement. Moreover, many students communicated that both they and their parents valued bilingualism as a tool for academic success and long-term career success. Some examples include:

The teachers are really passionate about their job and some other teachers at other schools, they just do their job and they act like they hate their job.
                                                                           —3rd grade student

Our school has more help than other schools. Um, we have like better teachers that actually, like, help us in our school work when we need it and we can go to, like, a counselor that we have here and stuff if we need help or we can stay after school, come in the morning or grab lunch to get even more extra credit or help.
                                                                           —5th grade student

When the findings presented here are considered with those from Chapter 4, the way ABP promotes students' identity and achievement is uncovered. It is evident that when teachers have an understanding of the numerous social, political, and historical forces that have contributed to Latino youth's current circumstances, as well as knowledge about the ways they can maintain high expectations and make the classroom relevant to their lives, students take notice. Students are also highly aware of the connection language has to their past and present, and how it cultivates parental belonging. Despite the disparaging ways students are at times described (e.g., "unmotivated"), students respect high standards and value the support teachers provide to ensure their success. Students appreciate teachers' efforts to incorporate their lived experiences into learning, but want (and deserve) more than learning—they want to feel that school is a place where they belong. After all, they are often likely to spend more time with teachers than their own family.

Notes

1 Portions of this chapter originally appeared in López, F. (2010) or López, F. (2017).
2 Readers can view the full documentary, "Eye of the Storm," on the PBS Frontline website.
3 Perceived competence and achievement in both reading and mathematics are so highly correlated that they cannot be simultaneously included in analyses. Although reading and mathematics achievement were not included in the analyses, I found reading and mathematics competence to serve as a robust proxy for achievement with the benefit of focusing on students' beliefs in the study.

References

Altschul, I., Oyserman, D., & Bybee, D. (2006). Racial–ethnic identity in mid-adolescence: Content and change as predictors of academic achievement. *Child Development, 77,* 1155–1169.
Altschul, I., Oyserman, D., & Bybee, D. (2008). Racial–ethnic self-schemas and segmented assimilation: Identity and the academic achievement of Hispanic youth. *Social Psychology Quarterly, 71,* 302–320.
Bandura, A. (1977). Self-efficacy: Toward a unifying theory of behavioral change. *Psychological Review, 84,* 181–215.

Bandura, A. (1986). *Social foundations of thought and action: A social-cognitive theory.* Upper Saddle River, NJ: Prentice–Hall.

Bandura, A. (1997). *Self-efficacy: The exercise of control.* New York: Freeman.

Bandura, A. (2006). Toward a psychology of human agency. *Perspectives on Psychological Science, 1,* 164–180.

Chen, Y. H., Thompson, M. S., Kromrey, J. D., & Chang, G. H. (2011). Relations of student perceptions of teacher oral feedback with teacher expectancies and student self-concept. *The Journal of Experimental Education, 79,* 452–477.

Eccles, J. (2009). Who am I and what am I going to do with my life? Personal and collective identities as motivators of action. *Educational Psychologist, 44,* 78–89.

Eccles (Parsons), J., Adler, T. F., Futterman, R., Goff, S. B., Kaczala, C. M., Meece, J. L., & Midgley, C. (1983). Expectancies, values, and academic behaviors. In J. T. Spence (Ed.), *Achievement and achievement motivation* (pp. 75–146). San Francisco, CA: W. H. Freeman.

Erikson, E. (1968). *Identity: Youth and crisis.* New York, NY: Norton.

Good, T. L. (1987). Two decades of research on teacher expectations: Findings and future directions. *Journal of Teacher Education, 38,* 32–47.

Good, T. L., & Brophy, J. (2010). *Looking in classrooms* (10th ed.). Boston, MA: Allyn and Bacon.

Harris, M. J., Rosenthal, R., & Snodgrass, S. E. (1986). The effects of teacher expectations, gender, and behavior on pupil academic performance and self-concept. *The Journal of Educational Research, 79,* 173–179.

Hurtado–Ortiz, M. T., & Gauvain, M. (2007). Postsecondary education among Mexican American youth: Contributions of parents, siblings, acculturation, and generational status. *Hispanic Journal of Behavioral Sciences, 29,* 181–191.

Juang, L., & Syed, M. (2008). Ethnic identity and spirituality. In R. M. Lerner, R. W. Roeser, & E. Phelps (Eds.), *Positive youth development and spirituality: From theory to research.* (pp. 262–284). West Conshohocken, PA: Templeton Foundation Press.

La Guardia, J. (2009). Developing who I am: Self–determination theory approach to the establishment of healthy identities. *Educational Psychologist, 44,* 90–104.

Ladson-Billings, G. (1995a). But that's just good teaching! The case for culturally relevant pedagogy. *Theory into Practice 34,* 159–165.

Ladson-Billings, G. (1995b). Toward a theory of culturally relevant pedagogy. *American Educational Research Journal, 47,* 465–491.

López, F. (2010). Identity and motivation among English language learners in disparate educational contexts. *Education Policy Analysis Archives, 18.* Available at http://epaa.asu.edu/ojs/article/view/717.

López, F. (2017). Altering the trajectory of the self-fulfilling prophecy: Asset-based pedagogy and classroom dynamics. *Journal of Teacher Education, 68,* 193–212.

McKown, C. (2013). Social equity theory and racial-ethnic achievement gaps. *Child Development, 84,* 1120–1136.

McKown, C., & Weinstein, R. S. (2002). Modeling the role of child ethnicity and gender in children's differential responses to teacher expectations. *Journal of Social Psychology, 32,* 159–184.

Madon, S., Jussin, L., & Eccles, J. (1997). In search of the powerful self-fulfilling prophecy. *Journal of Personality and Social Psychology, 72,* 791–809.

Marcia, J. (1980). Identity in adolescence. In J. Adelson (Ed.), *Handbook of adolescent psychology* (pp. 159–187). New York, NY: Wiley.

Marsh, H. W., & Shavelson, R. (1985). Self-concept: Its multifaceted, hierarchical structure. *Educational Psychologist, 20,* 107–123.

Muijs, D., & Reynolds, D. (2002). Teachers' beliefs and behaviors: What really matters? *The Journal of Classroom Interaction, 37*, 3–15.

Oyserman, D. (2008). Racial-ethnic self-schemas: Multidimensional identity-based motivation. *Journal of Research in Personality, 42*, 1186–1198.

Pajares, M. F. (1992). Teachers' beliefs and educational research: Cleaning up a messy construct. *Review of Educational Research, 62*, 307–332.

Phinney, J. S. (1989). Stages of ethnic identity development in minority group adolescents. *The Journal of Early Adolescence, 9*, 34–49.

Phinney, J. S. (1992). The multigroup ethnic identity measure: A new scale for use with adolescents and young adults from diverse groups. *Journal of Adolescent Research, 7*, 156–176.

Phinney, J. S. (1996). When we talk about American ethnic groups, what do we mean? *American Psychologist, 51*, 918.

Quintana, S. M., & Scull, N. C. (2009). Latino ethnic identity. In F. Villarruel, G. Carlo, J. Grau, M. Azmitia, N. Cabrera, & T. Chahin (Eds), *Handbook of US Latino psychology: Developmental and community-based perspectives* (pp. 81–98). Thousand Oaks, CA: Sage.

Rubie-Davies, C. M. (2006). Teacher expectations and student self-perceptions: Exploring relationships. *Psychology in the Schools, 43*, 537–552.

Schunk, D. H, & Pajares, F. (2005). Competence perceptions and academic functioning. In A. J. Elliot & C. S. Dweck (Eds.), *Handbook of competence and motivation* (pp. 85–104). New York, NY: Guilford Press.

Sidanius, J., Feshbach, S., Levin, S., & Pratto, F. (1997). The interface between ethnic and national attachment: Ethnic pluralism or ethnic dominance? *The Public Opinion Quarterly, 61*, 102–133.

Steele, Claude M. (2011). *Whistling Vivaldi: And other clues to how stereotypes affect us (issues of our time)*. New York, NY: W. W. Norton & Company.

Stone, S., & Han, M. (2005). Perceived school environments, perceived discrimination, and school performance among children of Mexican immigrants. *Children and Youth Services Review, 27*, 51–66.

Tenenbaum, H. R., & Ruck, M. D. (2007). Are teachers' expectations different for racial minority than for European American students? A meta-analysis. *Journal of Educational Psychology, 99*, 253–273.

Weinstein, R., Marshall, H., Sharp, L., & Botkin, M. (1987). Pygmalion and the student: Age and classroom differences in children's awareness of teacher expectations. *Child Development, 58*, 1079–1093.

Wigfield, A., & Karpathian, M. (1991). Who am I and what can I do? Children's self-concepts and motivation in achievement situations. *Educational Psychologist, 26*, 233–261.

APPENDIX 5.1

Measures. The following measures were collected for students at the beginning and end of the academic years. All student measures, with the exception of reading benchmarks, were available in Spanish and English. Measures were translated into Spanish; the Spanish translations were back-translated to English and compared to the original measures to assess equivalence. All measures were determined to be equivalent versions of the original English versions. Descriptive statistics disaggregated by grade level are presented in Table A.1.

Reading benchmarks. The Tucson Unified School District uses standardized formative reading assessments that are aligned with the state's academic standards and validated by the Assessment Technology Incorporated (ATI). The assessments are designed to reflect the knowledge students should acquire by the end of the school year. Items are generated based on the difficulty and discrimination parameters that reflect parallel assessments across administrations within each grade level (ATI, 2011, p. 21). The mean marginal reliability was reported as .88. For analyses, normal curve equivalents (NCEs) with a mean of 50 and standard deviation (SD) of 21.06 based on the distribution of scores relative to each grade's norming population were used. The assessment is administered four times throughout the school year between September and May. The first benchmark scores were used to control for prior achievement.[1]

Student achievement identity. To establish students' achievement identity, the reading domain in the *Self-Description Questionnaire I* (Marsh, 1992) was used. The measure was designed to capture different facets of self-concept among children between the ages of 8 and 12 and has been validated extensively (e.g., Marsh, 1990; Marsh & Gouvernet, 1989; Marsh & Holmes, 1990; Marsh, Trautwein, Lüdtke, Köller, & Baumert, 2006). The scale uses Likert-type items that are scored from 1 (*false*) to 5 (*true*). Internal consistency analyses resulted in $\alpha = .89$ for the

TABLE 5A.1 Descriptive Statistics for Latino Students

	Min	*Max*	*Mean*	*Standard Deviation*
Grade 3 (*N* = 160)				
Reading Fall	-3.58	92.93	51.63	21.50
Reading Spring	-14.77	94.72	53.99	24.69
SDQ Reading	1.00	5.00	3.94	0.87
Ethnic In-Group	2.00	4.00	3.45	0.36
Ethnic Other-Group	1.50	4.00	3.27	0.45
Discrimination	0.00	5.00	1.89	0.94
Grade 4 (*N* = 204)				
Reading Fall	9.25	104.23	53.84	15.90
Reading Spring	-4.29	94.72	53.01	16.66
SDQ Reading	1.00	5.00	3.63	0.72
Ethnic In-Group	2.00	4.00	3.40	0.36
Ethnic Other-Group	1.00	4.00	3.27	0.43
Discrimination	0.00	4.20	1.96	0.86
Grade 5 (*N* = 198)				
Reading Fall	-9.43	97.45	50.48	18.77
Reading Spring	-14.77	99.59	57.81	20.90
SDQ Reading	1.75	5.00	3.64	0.69
Ethnic In-Group	2.29	4.00	3.42	0.33
Ethnic Other-Group	1.75	4.00	3.30	0.35
Discrimination	0.00	4.30	1.66	0.79

reading subscale. Items include statements such as "Work in reading is easy for me" and "I am good at reading."

Ethnic affirmation. Phinney's (1992) Multi-Ethnic Identity Measure has been used extensively with various ethnic/racial groups and has robust construct validation evidence (see Ong, Fuller-Rowell, & Phinney, 2010; Ponterotto, Gretchen, Utsey, Stracuzzi, & Saya, 2003). Items are scored from 1 (*strongly disagree*) to 4 (*strongly agree*). To reflect the developmental stage of students, only the in-group ethnic affirmation and other-group ethnic affirmation subscales were used. The in-group ethnic affirmation subscale comprises seven items ($\alpha = 0.82$) that include statements such as "I have a strong sense of belonging to my ethnic group" and "I feel good about my cultural/ethnic background." The other-group affirmation subscale comprises four items ($\alpha = .67$) and includes statements such as "I like meeting and getting to know people from ethnic groups other than my own."

Perceived discrimination. Ten items from the perceived discrimination subscale from the *Societal, Attitudinal, Familial, and Environmental Acculturative Stress Scale for Children* (Chavez, Moran, Reid, & López's, 1997) were used ($\alpha = 82$). Items are scored from 1 (*doesn't bother me*) to 5 (*bothers me a lot*). The scale has been validated and demonstrated to be a robust measure of perceived discrimination among children (Chavez et al., 1997). Items include statements such as "I feel bad when

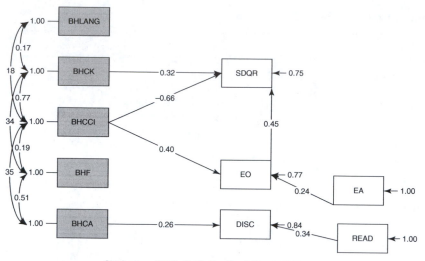

Chi-Square=12.24, df=28, P-value=0.99571, RMSEA=0.000

FIGURE 5A.1 Model 3: Teacher behaviors influence student outcome changes over the course of the academic year.

Note. BHLANG = behaviors reflecting the use of Spanish; BHCK = cultural knowledge behaviors; BHCCI = cultural content integration behaviors; BHF = formative assessment behaviors; BHCA = behaviors regarding acquisition of critical awareness; SDQR = change in students' reading self-competence; EA = change in students' in-group ethnic affirmation; EO = change in students' other-group ethnic affirmation; DISC = change in students' perceptions of discrimination; and READ = change in students' reading achievement.

others make jokes about people who are Latino/Mexican" and "People think badly of me when I practice customs, or I do the 'special things' of my group."

Student-level control variables. Student-level control variables included students' gender (0 = boys, 1 = girls) and English Learner (EL) status (0 = not EL, 1 = EL). It is important to note that EL classification does not reflect students who have been reclassified from EL to non-EL. In Arizona, ELs are assessed in English proficiency twice a year (ADE, 2014). Approximately 80% of ELs in the participating schools are reclassified in a given year according to the participating schools' demographic information.

Note

1   Despite the inherent issues with the use of achievement scores (e.g., Valenzuela, 2005), I use achievement scores as outcomes for two key reasons. One is to be consistent with scholars' assertions that there is a need to link ABP to achievement outcomes to influence policy (Sleeter, 2004). The other is because ignoring the power of achievement scores denies marginalized students access to power (Delpit, 1988).

References

Assessment Technology Incorporated. (2011). Benchmark assessment development in the Galileo K–12 online educational management system. Retrieved from http://www. ati-online.com/ pdfs/researchK12/K12TechManual.pdf.

Chavez, D. V., Moran, V. R., Reid, S. L., & Lopez, M. (1997). Acculturative stress in children: A modification of the SAFE scale. *Hispanic Journal of Behavioral Sciences, 19*, 34–44.

Marsh, H. W. (1990). A multidimensional, hierarchical model of self-concept: Theoretical and empirical justification. *Educational Psychology Review, 2*, 77–172.

Marsh, H. W. (1992). *Self Description Questionnaire (SDQ) II: A theoretical and empirical basis for the measurement of multiple dimensions of adolescent self-concept: An interim test manual and a research monograph.* New South Wales, Australia: University of Western Sydney, Faculty of Education.

Marsh, H. W., & Gouvernet, P. J. (1989). Multidimensional self-concepts and perceptions of control: Construct validation of responses by children. *Journal of Educational Psychology, 81*, 57.

Marsh, H. W., & Holmes, I. W. M. (1990). Multidimensional self-concepts: Construct validation of responses by children. *American Educational Research Journal, 27*, 89–117.

Marsh, H. W., Trautwein, U., Lüdtke, O., Köller, O., & Baumert, J. (2006). Integration of multidimensional self-concept and core personality constructs: Construct validation and relations to well-being and achievement. *Journal of Personality, 74*, 403–456.

Ong, A. D., Fuller-Rowell, T. E., & Phinney, J. S. (2010). Measurement of ethnic identity: Recurrent and emergent issues. *Identity: An International Journal of Theory and Research, 10*, 39–49.

Phinney, J. (1992). The multigroup ethnic identity measure: A new scale for use with adolescents and young adults from diverse groups. *Journal of Adolescent Research, 7*, 156–176.

Ponterotto, J. G., Gretchen, D., Utsey, S. O., Stracuzzi, T., & Saya, R. (2003). The multigroup ethnic identity measure (MEIM): Psychometric review and further validity testing. *Educational and Psychological Measurement, 63*, 502–515.

6

POLICY RECOMMENDATIONS[1]

Francesca A. López

The findings presented here add to the accumulating evidence that supports the serious consideration of asset-based pedagogy (ABP) among policymakers (Sleeter, 2012). Specifically, the findings in the study I describe extend findings from prior research that has relied on students' perceptions of teachers' ABP beliefs (e.g., Chun & Dickson, 2011) or teachers' ABP beliefs (e.g., Brown & Chu, 2012). By examining the ways teachers' ABP beliefs and behaviors are related to student identity and achievement, the study I carried out more fully addresses the appeals made by scholars (Goldenberg et al., 2008; Jussim & Harber, 2005; Ladson-Billings, 1999; Losey, 1995; Sleeter, 2004, 2012). As such, they provide more evidence to support the institutionalization of ABP, leveraging efforts of scholars who have focused on ensuring that teachers possess critical awareness (e.g., Anderson & Stillman, 2013; Gay, 2005; Hollins & Torres-Guzman, 2005; Milner, 2010; Morrison et al., 2008; Pohan & Aguilar, 2001; Valenzuela, 2016).

Although the research I present in this book extends our understanding about how teachers' critical awareness informs their ABP and how this is instrumental for Latino youth's identity and achievement, a glance at the references reveals that we have an abundance of evidence that supports ABP for historically minoritized youth. I use this evidence in my own courses with practicing teachers and school leaders, and am invariably asked, "Why didn't we learn about these things in our teacher training?" The answer is that preservice teachers are not typically provided with knowledge that will help them meet the needs of historically marginalized youth because this knowledge has not been prioritized by those who make curricular decisions. Scholars have long raised issues with the inability to institutionalize practices that have the potential to shape the identities of historically marginalized students (e.g., Gay, 2005; Ladson-Billings, 1999; Sleeter, 2004, 2012).

Although an accumulation of evidence providing an explicit link between ABP and student achievement is useful to inform policy, there is a scarcity of institutional will—particularly in matters that most directly affect historically marginalized students. This is perhaps no clearer than in Arizona, where a discriminatory policy that requires the segregation of EBs (which has no empirical evidence for its implementation) has contributed to egregious dropout rates. The issue, then, is how much longer we will stand by as students with so much potential are made to believe that they are not worthy of upward mobility if they cannot conform to the traditional ways of schooling? In the course of my career, I have met many parents and educators who shy away from challenging educational matters because "they do not want to get political." Standing by in the name of maintaining a curriculum that has served only privileged youth, however, *is* political. Refusing to demand change permits the maintenance of stratification.

With the responsibility we all carry to refuse the status quo, there are implications for both teacher-preparation programs and licensure standards that can transform the opportunities for historically marginalized youth. Echoing Gay's (2005) assertion that "the most viable multicultural teacher education programs combine moral convictions and courage, critical analyses, and political activism with high-quality curriculum and instruction in advocacy and in responding to opposition" (p. 224), the research I detailed in this book suggests a necessary focus on both teachers' critical-awareness development and knowledge about the numerous ways ABP should be incorporated into their classrooms.

Policy Recommendation 1: Nurturing critical awareness. Required coursework is one of the principal ways essential knowledge is provided to preservice teachers (see Darling-Hammond, 2000; Darling-Hammond & Bransford, 2005). Although there are teacher-preparation programs that require all preservice teachers to have some knowledge on the needs of linguistically diverse students, a more robust engagement with this knowledge tends to be limited to those seeking specialist certification (Valenzuela, 2016), thus limiting the extent to which all preservice teachers have opportunities to develop critical awareness. Moreover, compared to coursework focused on the needs of linguistically diverse students, "courses that offer sociopolitical content that addresses policy, politics, social movements, legislative and judicial battles, legal precedents, laws, civil rights history, critical race theory, and the like" (Valenzuela, 2015, p. 19) are even less accessible to preservice teachers despite calls to action (e.g., Milner, 2010).

The need to incorporate coursework that can provide preservice teachers with a deep understanding of sociopolitical factors that influence the lives of their students in differential ways is urgent. Scholars have offered conceptualizations of requisite knowledge that should be required of preservice teachers (e.g., Banks, 2001; Milner, 2010; Valenzuela, 2016) that can inform a revision of teacher preparation content. To enhance a link between this knowledge and practice, however, teacher educators must also engage preservice teachers in sociopolitical analysis with ABP. Some examples can be found in the following:

- Bartolome, L. I. (2004). Critical pedagogy and teacher education: Radicalizing prospective teachers. *Teacher Education Quarterly, 31*, 97–122.
- Morrell, E., & Duncan-Andrade, J. M. R. (2002). Promoting academic literacy with urban youth through engaging hip-hop culture. *English Journal, 91*, 88–92.
- Romero, A., Arce, S., & Cammarota, J. (2009). A barrio pedagogy: Identity, intellectualism, activism, and academic achievement through the evolution of critically compassionate intellectualism. *Race, Ethnicity and Education*, 12, 217–233.
- Stovall, D. (2006). We can relate: Hip-hop culture, critical pedagogy, and the secondary classroom. *Urban Education, 41*, 585–602
- Valenzuela, A. (Ed.). *Growing critically conscious teachers: A social justice curriculum for Educators of Latino/a Youth*. New York, NY: Teachers College Press.

To more fully develop critical awareness, however, students also need to foster an understanding of the historical and contemporary forces that shape the goals of education. The following resources may prove helpful:

- Bowles, S., & Gintis, H. (1976). *Schooling in capitalist America*. New York, NY: Basic Books.
- Darder, A. (1991). *Culture and power in the classroom: A critical foundation for bicultural education*. Boulder, CO: Paradigm Publishers.
- Donato, R., & Hanson, J. (2012). Legally white, socially "Mexican": The politics of de jure and de facto school segregation in the American Southwest. *Harvard Educational Review, 82*, 202–225.
- Gándara, P. C., & Contreras, F. (2009). *The Latino education crisis: The consequences of failed social policies*. Boston, MA: Harvard University Press.
- Haney-Lopez, I. (2014). *Dog whistle politics: How coded racial appeals have reinvented racism and wrecked the middle class*. New York, NY: Oxford University Press.
- Massey, D. S. (2007). *Categorically unequal: The American stratification system*. New York, NY: Russell Sage Foundation.
- Oakes, J. (2005). *Keeping track: How schools structure inequality*. Second Edition. New Haven, CT: Yale University Press.
- San Miguel, G., & Valencia, R. (1998). From the Treaty of Guadalupe Hidalgo to Hopwood: The educational plight and struggle of Mexican Americans in the Southwest. *Harvard Educational Review, 68*, 353–413.
- Tyack, D. B. (1974). *The one best system: A history of American urban education* (Vol. 95). Boston, MA: Harvard University Press.

I offer one additional area of knowledge that all educators must develop to engage with the aforementioned materials: bias reduction. Although we have evidence that multicultural coursework reduces bias (Kumar & Hamer, 2013), an understanding of *how* we develop the biases that so often harm our historically marginalized youth can create the requisite knowledge that can enhance the development of critical awareness. This knowledge includes an understanding of how our brains play a vital role in creating biases. For example, we know our brains use background knowledge to fill in gaps (King, 2017). This is one of the reasons all of the information we filter—consciously and unconsciously—ends up informing our decisions. A critical look at the representation (or lack thereof) in film, television, books, and other media, for example, uncovers the disparaging ways historically marginalized students are often portrayed—which is consistent with many of the stereotypes about historically marginalized youth. Given that these stereotypes and biases are often not benign, teachers must develop an understanding of how they can reverse the effects of being inundated by bias-informing messages on a daily basis. The following are some resources to do just that:

- Banaji, M. R., & Greenwald, A. G. (2016). *Blindspot: Hidden biases of good people.* New York, NY: Random House.
- Coates, T. (2015). *Between the world and me.* New York, NY: Random House.
- Steele, C. 2010. *Whistling Vivaldi: And other clues to how stereotypes affect us.* New York, NY: W. W. Norton & Company, Inc.

Policy Recommendation 2: Cultural knowledge and cultural content integration. As mentioned in Chapter 4, there is a tendency for ABP to be treated as a celebration of cultural differences rather than a way to enact equitable educational practices for historically marginalized youth (Sleeter, 2012; Wong et al., 2007). To avoid its marginalization in the preservice teacher curriculum and enhance preservice teachers' ability to practice ABP in authentic ways, teacher educators must ensure that (a) ABP literature is integrated throughout coursework, (b) preservice teachers are provided with skills to enact ABP across content areas (see Aaronson & Laughter, 2016), and (c) ABP is also applied to field placement (e.g., Pohan et al., 2009). Moreover, teachers must understand what is meant by "culture" to avoid essentializing cultural practices as traits (Gutiérrez & Johnson, 2017). Although the list of references throughout this book represents many of the seminal readings that can help create the necessary background knowledge to engage in authentic ABP, the following resources offer a good place to start:

- Banks, J. A. (1993). Multicultural education: Historical development, dimensions, and practice. *Review of Research in Education, 19,* 3–49.
- Delpit, L. (1988). The silenced dialogue: Power and pedagogy in educating other people's children. *Harvard Educational Review, 58,* 280–299.

- Gay, G. (2010). *Culturally responsive teaching: Theory, research, and practice.* New York, NY: Teachers College Press.
- González, N., Moll, L., & Amanti, C. (2005). *Funds of knowledge: Theorizing practices in households, communities and classrooms.* Mahwah, NJ: Erlbaum.
- Gutiérrez, K., & Rogoff, B. (2003). Cultural ways of learning: Individual traits or repertoires of practice. *Educational Researcher 32,* 19–25.
- Valdés, G. (1996). *Con respeto. Bridging the distances between culturally diverse families and schools. An ethnographic portrait.* New York, NY: Teachers College Press.

Policy Recommendation 3: Language. In addition to language-focused practices, policy, history, legislation, multiculturalism, and parent involvement are all considered essential knowledge for teachers of emergent bilinguals (EBs) (Menken & Antuñez, 2001). These dimensions are consistent with prior work that has established the importance of developing: (1) teachers' foundational understanding of the sociohistorical context of traditionally marginalized youth (Valenzuela, 2016); (2) cultural competencies of teachers so they are able to bring the diversity of students' and families' experiences into the learning and teaching process (Butvilofsky & Sparrow, 2012; Moll, Amanti, Neff, & González, 2005); and (3) an understanding of their own cultural, class, and linguistic identities (Pray & Marx, 2010). As previously mentioned, multicultural coursework that covers these dimensions has been shown to reduce teacher biases (Kumar & Hamer, 2013), which have a marked influence on student achievement (McKown & Weinstein, 2002; Tenenbaum & Ruck, 2001).

Nevertheless, despite evidence that state-level policies that emphasize bilingualism are associated with markedly higher outcomes for EBs (López, McEneaney, & Nieswandt, 2015), as well as evidence that specialist certification is also beneficial to EBs (López, Scanlan, & Gundrum, 2013), few teachers receive the requisite skills to be effective with EBs. In part, the issue stems from the fact that many states do not require specialist certification and thus will not require essential knowledge found to be beneficial for EBs. This issue is particularly salient given that several states have witnessed surges in the number of EBs they serve. Alabama, Arkansas, Kentucky, South Carolina, and Tennessee, for example, are all states with growth in their EB populations ranging from approximately 300 to 700% over the past decade (see Heilig, López, & Torre, 2013). The difficulty of effectively preparing teachers of EBs, however, is not only that many states do not require specialized certification for teachers of EBs (see López et al., 2013) and would thus be unlikely to have requirements stipulating bilingual or English as a Second Language (ESL) methods in schools, but also that states vary markedly in the ways their policies address the educational needs of EBs (see López et al., 2015).

Although state-level language instruction education policies and teacher preparation requirements vary substantially, evidence points to clear advantages for teachers in states that ensure knowledge of best practices for EBs. When teachers are required to have knowledge of asset-based practices related to language, there are advantages to both EBs' achievement and teachers' self-efficacy (López & Santibañez, 2017). Accordingly, although EBs are often ignored in policy debates focused on teacher preparation, state policies should reflect the assets EBs introduce into classrooms and ensure that teachers can capitalize on their potential throughout compulsory schooling. Although some states are moving in the right direction by repealing policies that have failed to fully meet the needs of EBs, such as California and Arizona, others remain deplorably behind.

To more forcefully address the needs of not only EBs, but also other historically marginalized youth, policies that require more robust teacher preparation are necessary. Not only should teachers of EBs have requisite knowledge on language development, but also policy, history, legislation, multiculturalism, and parent involvement. As Valenzuela (1999) cautioned:

> The question of culture is often compromised in bilingual education or dual language programs as if simply teaching in the students' tongue is sufficient for the curriculum to be culturally relevant. While language is a necessary first step toward relevancy, there is more to culture than language.
>
> *(p. 269)*

The following resources may prove helpful to all educators and school leaders in developing an understanding of the importance of language and culture:

- González, N. (2001). *I am my language: Discourses of women and children in the borderlands.* Tucson, AZ: University of Arizona Press.
- Hakuta, K. (1986). *The mirror of language: The debate on bilingualism.* New York, NY: Basic Books Inc.
- Valdés, G. (2001). *Learning and not learning English: Latino Students in American Schools.* New York, NY: Teachers College Press.

Conclusion

Teacher educators have long argued in favor of ABP to meet the needs of historically marginalized students. As detailed in this book, ensuring teachers' development of critical awareness and ABP behaviors holds promise in that together, they can promote the development of ethnic and academic identities of historically marginalized youth. Certainly, there are other facets of teacher preparation that merit serious consideration. Among them are the need to address structural inequities to ensure more teachers of color enter the profession to "take advantage of what they offer our children" (Nieto, 2016, p. x); incorporation of Participatory Action Research in applications of ABP and teacher development (e.g., Cammarota, 2016); and incorporation of knowledge on the ways historically marginalized students interact within an ABP curriculum to co-construct knowledge (Martin-Beltrán, 2009). Although not exhaustive, however, the recommendations presented here provide but a few empirically based examples of the knowledge that teacher educators must consider to more fully transform teacher education. Given the growth in scholarship establishing empirical evidence on how ABP is related to historically marginalized students' outcomes (e.g., Brown & Chu, 2012; Cabrera et al., 2014; Chun & Dickson, 2011; Rios-Aguilar, 2010), it is time for teacher education programs to more forcefully incorporate ABP as an expectation of all teachers.

Note

1   Portions of this chapter originally appeared in López, F. (2017).

References

Anderson, L. M., & Stillman, J. A. (2013). Student teaching's contribution to preservice teacher development: A review of research focused on the preparation of teachers for urban and high–needs contexts. *Review of Educational Research, 83*, 3–69.

Bartolome, L. I. (2004). Critical pedagogy and teacher education: Radicalizing prospective teachers. *Teacher Education Quarterly, 31*, 97–122.

Brown, C. S., & Chu, H. (2012). Discrimination, ethnic identity, and academic outcomes of Mexican immigrant children: The importance of school context. *Child Development, 83*, 1477–1485.

Butvilofsky, S. A., & Sparrow, W. L. (2012). Training teachers to evaluate emerging bilingual students' biliterate writing. *Language and Education, 26*, 383–403.

Cabrera, N. L., Milem, J. F., Jaquette, O., & Marx, R. W. (2014). Missing the (student achievement) forest for all the (political) trees: Empiricism and the Mexican American studies controversy in Tucson. *American Educational Research Journal, 51*, 1084–1118.

Cammarota, J. (2016). Social justice education project (SJEP): A case example of PAR in a high school classroom. In A. Valenzuela (Ed.), *Growing critically conscious teachers: A social justice curriculum for Educators of Latino/a Youth* (pp. 90–104). New York, NY: Teachers College Press.

Chun, H., & Dickson, G. (2011). A psychoecological model of academic performance among Hispanic adolescents. *Journal of Youth and Adolescence, 40*, 1581–1594.

Cruze, A., Cota, M., & López, F. (April, 2017). A decade after Arizona SEI: Teachers' perspectives on implementation of SEI and alternative approaches. Paper presented the annual meetings of the American Educational Research Association, San Antonio, TX.

Darling-Hammond, L. (2000). How teacher education matters. *Journal of Teacher Education, 51*, 166–173.

Darling-Hammond, L., & Bransford, J. (Eds.). (2005). *Preparing teachers for a changing world: What teachers should learn and be able to do.* San Francisco, CA: Jossey-Bass.

Gay, G. (2005). Politics of multicultural teacher education. *Journal of Teacher Education, 56*, 221–228.

Goldenberg, C., Rueda, R. S., & August, D. (2008). Sociocultural contexts and literacy development. In D. August & T. Shanahan (Eds.), *Developing reading and writing in second language learners: Lessons from the Report of the National Literacy Panel on Language Minority Children and Youth* (pp. 95–130). Washington, DC: Center for Applied Linguistics and Newark, DE: International Reading Association.

Gutiérrez, K. D., & Johnson, P. (2017). Understanding identity sampling and cultural repertoires. In D. Paris & H. S. Alim (Eds.), *Culturally sustaining pedagogies: Teaching and learning for justice in a changing world*. New York, NY: Teachers College Press.

Heilig, J., López, F., & Torre, D. (2013). Examining ELL teacher quality, educational policy, and evolving political contexts in Latina/o growth states. In C. M. Wilson & S. D. Horsford (Eds.), *Advancing equity and achievement in diverse U.S. schools* (pp. 41–56). New York, NY: Routledge.

Hollins, E., & Torres-Guzman, M. E. (2005). Research on preparing teachers for diverse populations. In M. Cochran-Smith & K. Zeichner (Eds.), *Studying teacher education: The report of the AERA Panel on Research and Teacher Education* (pp. 477–544). Mahwah, N.J.: Lawrence Erlbaum Associates.

Jussim, L., & Harber, K. D. (2005). Teacher expectations and self-fulfilling prophecies: Knowns and unknowns, resolved and unresolved controversies. *Personality and Social Psychology Review, 9*, 131–155.

King, A. J. (2017). Auditory neuroscience: Filling in the gaps. *Current Biology, 17*, DOI:10.1016/j.cub.2007.07.013

Kumar, R., & Hamer, L. (2013). Preservice teachers' attitudes and beliefs toward student diversity and proposed instructional practices: A sequential design study. *Journal of Teacher Education, 64*, 162–177.

Ladson-Billings, G. J. (1999). Preparing teachers for diverse student populations: A critical race theory perspective. *Review of Research in Education, 24*, 211–247.

López, F. (in press). Altering the trajectory of the self-fulfilling prophecy: Asset-based pedagogy and classroom dynamics. *Journal of Teacher Education.*

López, F., McEneaney, E., & Nieswandt, M. (2015). Language instruction educational programs and academic achievement of Latino English learners: Considerations for states with changing demographics. *American Journal of Education, 121*, 417–450.

López, F., & Santibañez, L. (unpublished manuscript). Teacher preparation to teach English learners and policy implications.

López, F., Scanlan, M., & Gundrum, B. (2013). Preparing teachers of English language learners: Empirical evidence and policy implications. *Education Policy Analysis Archives, 21*, 20.

Losey, K. M. (1995). Mexican American students and classroom interaction: An overview and critique. *Review of Educational Research, 65*, 283–318.

McKown, C., & Weinstein, R. S. (2002). Modeling the role of child ethnicity and gender in children's differential responses to teacher expectations. *Journal of Social Psychology, 32*, 159–184.

Martin-Beltrán, M. (2009). Cultivating space for the language boomerang: The interplay of two languages as academic resources. *English Teaching: Practice and Critique, 8*, 25–53.

Martinez-Wenzl, M., Pérez, K. C., & Gándara, P. (2012). Is Arizona's approach to educating its ELs superior to other forms of instruction. *Teachers College Record, 114*(9), 1–32.

Menken, K., & Antunez, B. (2001). *An overview of the preparation and certification of teachers working with limited English proficient (LEP) students.* Washington, DC: National Clearinghouse for Bilingual Education. Retrieved at http://files.eric.ed.gov/fulltext/ED455231.pdf.

Milner, H. R. (2010). What does teacher education have to do with teaching? Implications for diversity studies. *Journal of Teacher Education, 61*, 118–131.

Moll, L., Amanti, C., Neff, D., & Gonzalez, N. (2005). *Funds of knowledge for teaching: Using a qualitative approach to connect homes and classrooms.* Mahwah, NJ: Lawrence Erlbaum Associates.

Morrell, E., & Duncan-Andrade, J. M. R. (2002). Promoting academic literacy with urban youth through engaging hip-hop culture. *English Journal, 91*, 88–92.

Morrison, K. A., Robbins, H. H., & Rose, D. G. (2008). Operationalizing culturally relevant pedagogy: A synthesis of classroom-based research. *Equity & Excellence in Education, 41*, 433–452.

Nieto, S. (2016). Foreword. In A. Valenzuela (Ed.), *Growing critically conscious teachers: A social justice curriculum for Educators of Latino/a Youth* (pp. ix – xii). New York, NY: Teachers College Press.

Pohan, C. A., & Aguilar, T. E. (2001). Measuring educators' beliefs about diversity in personal and professional contexts. *American Educational Research Journal, 38*, 159–182.

Pohan, C. A., Ward, M., Kouzekanani, K., & Boatright, C. (2009). The impact of field placement sites on preservice teachers' beliefs about teaching diverse students. *School–University Partnerships, 3*, 43–53.

Pray, L., & Marx, S. (2010). ESL teacher education abroad and at home: A cautionary tale. *The Teacher Educator, 45*, 216–229.

Rios-Aguilar, C., Canche, M. S. G., & Moll, L. C. (2012). Implementing structured English immersion in Arizona. *Teachers College Record, 114*(9), 1–18.

Rios-Aguilar, C., González-Canche, M., & Moll, L. C. (2010). A study of Arizona's teachers of English language learners. *Civil Rights Project/Proyecto Derechos Civiles*.

Romero, A., Arce, S., & Cammarota, J. (2009). A barrio pedagogy: Identity, intellectualism, activism, and academic achievement through the evolution of critically compassionate intellectualism. *Race, Ethnicity and Education, 12*, 217–233.

Sleeter, C. (2004). Context-conscious portraits and context-blind policy. *Anthropology and Education Quarterly, 35*, 132–136.

Sleeter, C. E. (2012). Confronting the marginalization of culturally responsive pedagogy. *Urban Education, 47*, 562–584.

Stovall, D. (2006). We can relate: Hip-hop culture, critical pedagogy, and the secondary classroom. *Urban Education, 41*, 585–602.

Tenenbaum, H. R., & Ruck, M. D. (2007). Are teachers' expectations different for racial minority than for European American students? A meta-analysis. *Journal of Educational Psychology, 99*, 253–273.

Valenzuela, A. (2015, April 9). Mexican-American toddlers: (Mis)understanding the achievement gap [Blog post]. Retrieved from http://texasedequity.blogspot.com/2015/04/mexican–american–toddlers–understanding.html.

Valenzuela, A. (Ed.). (2016). *Growing critically conscious teachers: A social justice curriculum for educators of Latino/a youth*. New York, NY: Teachers College Press.

Wong, P. L., Murai, H., Bérta-Ávila, M., William-White, L., Baker, S., Arellano, A., & Echandia, A. (2007). The M/M Center: Meeting the demand for multicultural, multilingual teacher preparation. *Teacher Education Quarterly, 34*, 9–35.

PART III

Teacher Perspective on Asset-Based Pedagogy

7

DECOLONIZING CHICAN@ STUDIES TO REHUMANIZE XICAN@ YOUTH THROUGH INDIGENOUS PEDAGOGIES

Mictlani González

I didn't have the language early in my teaching to articulate the needed transformative space for my minoritized students to thrive. This was so because my teacher preparation program did not teach me anything about culturally responsive pedagogy, but I had the will to create that space as a result of my subtractive schooling experience.

A "Subtractive" Educational Experience

The most persistent memory of my educational experience is riddled in what Angela Valenzuela (1999) regards as "subtractive schooling." An instance of subtractive schooling that I vividly recall was in kindergarten. I was born in Mexico and naturally, my first language was Spanish. My parents moved my two siblings and me to California. Like many families that emigrate in search of economic stability, my parents were in pursuit of the elusive "American Dream." As a result, when I started kindergarten in the United States I did not speak English. Consequently, my teacher would often punish me by ordering me to stand in a corner of the classroom for not speaking English and not being engaged. I recall feelings of shame. My parents recall that I fought them to go to school. Every day I would be screaming and yelling "*No quiero ir!*" "I don't want to go!" Adding to my numerous subtractive experiences in the classroom, I remember going out to the playground and repeatedly being tormented by White students who would call me "wetback." One particular day, a White boy was taunting me, blurting out discriminatory epithets. He grabbed something in his hand and rushed toward me as he proceeded to smash bugs on my back while ordering me to go back to Mexico, calling me a "beaner." This was the beginning of what Valenzuela refers to as a subtractive education that cultivates self-hatred in minoritized students by invalidating our humanity. Thus, schools are a dehumanizing space.

As I went through the public-school system, experiences of discrimination and marginalization accumulated to the extent that I began to marginalize myself by not engaging and resisting, as expressed by Solorzano (2001), in a self-defeating manner. I was disengaging because I had not been equipped by any of my teachers with the necessary skills to engage academically in my classes. Miraculously, I reached high school and graduated with my class. I recall entertaining the idea of higher education but then reconsidering because I believed I was not adequately skilled to succeed in higher education. I remember I was perplexed, wondering whether my lack of skills was indeed my fault despite intuitively knowing that I had not been adequately or equitably educated. Certainly, I had experienced K–12 schooling in a subtractive manner. Like many minoritized students, I remember one of the administrators in my high school condescendingly expressed to me that I would never graduate; the expectation was that I would get pregnant and drop out. She didn't know me, but she was quick to characterize me based on her deficiency-based stereotypes.

It wasn't until after college that I had acquired the language and theories to articulate my subtractive schooling experience and legitimize my resistance—not because I took a class in college that elucidated those theories, but because several years into my career I met and worked alongside some of the most conscious critical educators that would serve as my *maestros* (teachers) who taught me how to, in the spirit of Paulo Freire (1970), "read the world." They exposed me to Xican@[1] history that I was never exposed to in college and certainly not in high school. As a result of studying the history and education of Xican@s, I was able to name my discrimination, marginalization, and resistance, as well as societal and educational racism.

As a newly credentialed teacher, I carried my experiences with me and used them as my strength and purpose for teaching in a manner different from my subtractive experience: a humanizing and loving manner. As a result of both my subtractive experiences, I acquired a sense of critical awareness that López (2017) addresses in her race-reimaged framework as a necessary component for positive student achievement: teacher critical awareness regarding the history of racism and educational racism. I vowed to create a transformative space for my minoritized students where they would be respected, loved, and encouraged to excel academically into competent scholars. Accordingly, I taught them by building on the experiences that they had—a culturally relevant approach (Ladson-Billings, 1995). Moreover, I vowed to provide a space for students to learn to love their humanity by providing a curriculum that would reflect them and their culture positively and validate their lived experiences. I also knew that creating a relationship with students that was rooted in *confianza* (confidence) and *respeto* (respect) was critical and the basis for, what I later learned about, a culturally responsive classroom.

Introduction to Xican@ Studies in Mexican American Raza Studies

About six years into my teaching career, my own two children were going through the public-school system. My oldest daughter, Stephanie, took a Xican@ Studies class with Mr. Arce during her junior year in high school. For the first time in her schooling experience, Stephanie would actually come home excited about doing her homework for her Xican@ Studies class. Some of the homework required that she interview parents, grandparents, and other family members. I of course engaged in her homework with her, which resulted in my own engagement with the content. I couldn't believe the history that I was reading and how it taught me, and my daughter, about the educational injustice toward Xican@s. We learned about political injustice and how Xican@s continued to struggle for educational, political, and social justice. I felt angry that I had not been taught this American history in any of my high school or college classes. I was also angry to read about so many injustices against Mexican Indigenous people as far back as the 1400s.

As my daughter was taking the Xican@ Studies class, I got to know her teacher, Mr. Arce, well. Eventually, he recruited me to work for the Mexican American Studies Department (MAS) in the Tucson Unified School District (TUSD). I was hired as a curriculum specialist and was tasked with writing the curriculum that I was intimately engaged in while working with my daughter on her homework for his class. This was a turning point in my life, because I was propelled on a journey of identity reclamation, specifically Indigenous identity. The MAS department initially consisted of four relentless male educators that were well-versed in Xican@ history and the history of colonization. As the only female MAS teacher at the time, I felt compelled to catch up to their level of knowledge of history, so I read many books on colonization and the history of minoritized people. Due to my emotional investment in meeting the needs of our students and the need to be responsive to our Xican@ students, I vigorously read to develop a consciousness of the history and mis-education so I could, in turn, teach my students their history.

Much of my critical awareness was developed during our MAS professional development, as we engaged in many in-depth studies of the history, including the socio-political history, of Xican@s. Delving into this scholarship helped shape my understanding of the colonization of minoritized people in this country. Moreover, it was during this time that I learned about the effects of colonization—specifically trauma—and how minoritized people suffer from a form of posttraumatic stress disorder given that we carry years of trauma, as we are not post-colonization (as López describes in Chapter 2). As our Maestr@'s team interrogated colonization in our professional development, we learned that *Mexicanos* have been minoritized and made "strangers" in our own land. Moreover, we have been victims of dehumanization practices committed against us for over 500 years, beginning with the Doctrine of Discovery and Christopher Columbus.

Given this history, our team often discussed the need to create an academic program that specifically addressed colonization. Accordingly, our MAS team aimed to create spaces of humanization in our classes that countered the dehumanization that minoritized students experienced in other classes, schooling, and in society in general as colonized, racialized, and minoritized people. Initially, we were able to offer Xican@ studies at only four high schools, four middle schools, and three elementary schools.

In addition to my role in curriculum development, I taught a Xican@ studies class. To prepare myself to teach the courses, I read numerous history books to become an authority in Xican@ Studies. In the process of engaging with the material, I realized that I was steeped in trauma and needed to heal from the countless dehumanizing experiences I had accumulated so that I could be a stable human being and teacher for my students. As I persisted on this personal journey of identity, I gravitated toward an Indigenous identity. I often pondered about life pre-colonization. I was introduced to the profound teaching of Aztec cosmology through several *Mexica* elders. Their teachings exposed an incredible intellectual heritage that I inherited from my ancestors. I knew that this was a heritage that our students also deserved to know and learn about. While we implemented several frameworks to ensure the academic achievement of our students in MAS, I knew that there was something missing that was critical for our students' intellectual and emotional growth in our MAS classes. This Indigenous knowledge was what I believed was missing. Our philosophical underpinnings in MAS were sociopolitical, but severely lacked a connection to our Indigenous history. This, however, became the philosophical divide among those of us in the MAS program. While some of the MAS teachers had been taught a Marxist version of Xican@ studies that became their approach to teaching Xican@ studies, others of us were of the belief that Xican@ Studies had to be decolonized. With that charge in mind, a few of us delved into Xican@ Studies from an Indigenous perspective and proceeded to teach in that vein. Fundamentally, we believed that in order for Xican@ Studies to be transformative, we had to have an understanding of our pre-colonization Indigenous worldview. This knowledge would provide us with a better understanding of colonization, which allows us to more strategically interrogate and counter it. In reflecting on this, I believe that this pedagogical focus provided the necessary transformative element for our predominantly Xican@ student population. This Indigenous-centered pedagogical approach, however, required a different type of assessment to determine and gauge the effectiveness of its implementation. Accordingly, our assessment was centered on our students' development of human measures. The human measures that we focused on were hope, sense of purpose in life, sense of positive ethnic identity, a historical identity, and self-love. Later we learned that by focusing on the development of these human measures, students' academic performance improved to the extent that we abated the opportunity gap (Cabrera, Milem, Jaquette, & Marx, 2014). The human measures encompass the "magic" that is typically ignored when assessing the effectiveness of asset-based pedagogical approaches in education.

Colonization

To establish the context for the imperative of an Indigenous epistemologically rooted pedagogy for Xican@ students, it is imperative to have an understanding of colonization and its horrendous impact on minoritized people. As such, I define colonization as White supremacy, domination, and imperialism through physical, cultural, linguistic, historical, and psychological genocide, and symbolic violence to exert racial supremacy and domination of resources for capital accumulation. This domination of resources includes the minds of minoritized people to ensure colonization in a manner whereby the colonizer no longer has to exert that domination by force, because the colonized have internalized colonization and can marginalize themselves by accepting their place in the stratified system. In this system of colonization, minoritized people are rendered expendable and are designated to occupy the bottom rung of society.

Inherent in colonization is dehumanization. This dehumanization process produces instability. It includes keeping a person from developing their full humanity by taking away that which makes them human (e.g., language, worldview, culture, stability). Freire (1970) speaks of dehumanization in the following manner: "Dehumanization, which marks not only those whose humanity has been stolen, but also (though in a different way) those who have stolen it, is a distortion of the vocation of becoming more fully human" (p. 26). Jack Forbes (2008) speaks of the notion of dehumanization by invoking Freire's conception of "dehumanization" and extends it to the "*wetiko (Whiteness)* psychosis" and "humanization" as the restoration or maintenance of a healthy state of existence. Elements of the *wetiko* psychosis include imperialism, capitalism, and the systems that render certain groups of people as dispensable. Forbes speaks of the need for minoritized groups of people to re-humanize, as does Freire. While they both speak of dehumanization inherent in the colonizing system, neither offers a system for humanizing, despite an insistence on the need to humanize.

One of the forces that maintain colonization is education, given that schooling ensures each member of society plays a role in a particular stratum. As critical educators, however, we must interrogate education as a dehumanizing space for minoritized and racialized students, thus recognizing education as a system of racism. I define educational racism as the dehumanization of minoritized students by the inculcation of racial notions of inferiority and racial subordination, while exalting the properties of Whiteness[2] that maintain educational inequity and ultimately maintain colonization. Although we no longer witness overt educational racism, such as the Carlisle Boarding Schools for the subjugation of Native American students, we continue to witness a system of covert socially acceptable racist educational practices. Examples of racist, but socially acceptable, practices include a Eurocentric curriculum, teachers who impose deficit thinking of minoritized students, implicit bias that results in teacher behavior that is subtractive in nature, and countless others.

Indigenous Epistemologies as Asset-based Pedagogical Methodologies for Teaching Xican@ Youth

A point of clarification is that most of us who worked as MAS teachers in the inception of the MAS program did not set out to "reform education." As a system, education replicates colonization—and there is no reforming a system as sophisticated as colonization. Colonization will, however, continue to be interrogated, as people will continue to recognize the dehumanizing and destructive mechanisms in place that maintain its existence. My personal goal as a critical educator was to elaborate an asset-based pedagogy that interrogated colonization and would provide a transformative space to establish *confianza* with my students where they could find a sense of humanity, humility, and strength, and where they could acquire a sense of hope and responsibility to go back into the community and give back. Other goals were to provide students with the skills to navigate this system of colonization in a manner that allows them to critically analyze society and occupy the necessary spaces (i.e., politically engage as change agents that identify the systems of oppression, understand how they operate to subjugate minoritized people, and eliminated them). In this transformative space created for minoritized students, establishing an academic identity is a byproduct, thereby positively influencing Xican@ student academic achievement. As a side note, we intentionally remained in a public education setting despite the abundance of charter schools (see Chapter 3) because these are the schools that our most vulnerable minoritized students attend.

Indigenous epistemological methodologies are, in their essence, asset-based pedagogies. Given that asset-based pedagogies build on students' strengths, Indigenous epistemologically-rooted pedagogies serve to reintroduce students to their intellectual heritage, one stolen from them through colonization. This is evident in the erasing of Indigenous people's languages and worldview, which is central to identity. As explained by Nieto (2007):

> Precisely, the bridge between the individual and the world is built through the meaning-making process that communication entails. That meaning, which comes embedded in language, serves as the conceptual material with which human beings construct and deconstruct their representations of the world.
>
> *(p. 232)*

Consequently, over 500 years of colonization has resulted in Xican@ students not knowing their Indigenous languages (present-day Indigenous languages continue to be eliminated). As such, students lack a connection to their intellectual heritage. Therefore, whereas other asset-based pedagogies build on students' present lived experiences, Indigenous pedagogies are recursive (Garcia, 2012) in that they rebuild and reintroduce students to their historical collective experience, as well as students' current lived experiences. It is within this space that Xican@ students can reconnect to a worldview that centers their humanity as interdependent with all of creation to impact their stability as human beings.

From Chicano Paradigm to Culturally Humanizing Pedagogy—The Origins of the MAS Indigenous Pedagogy

Initially, one of the asset-based pedagogical frameworks that several of us implemented in our classrooms was the Chicano Paradigm.[3] This framework served to introduce Xican@ youth to a curriculum that was centered on *Indigenous ways of learning* and was implemented by several critical educators in New Mexico and Arizona, and documented by Godina (2003). Those of us who embraced this paradigm by infusing it into our pedagogy did so because it was one of the only paradigms that interrogated colonization and was culturally relevant by centering Mexican Indigenous teachings through the *Nahuatl* language, Aztec *Danza*, and the teachings of the Aztec Calendar. This paradigm provided a purpose for learning that was rooted in acquiring personal inner and outer strength. The narrative that defines the Chicano Paradigm states that *we must acquire knowledge because that knowledge leads to wisdom to develop inner and outer strength to achieve harmony from within and without to acquire stability.* With a history of resistance, minoritized people have had to address colonization as a responsibility that emanates from the love of the people who struggled for us and the love for our people that we must love. Accordingly, a traditional Indigenous belief is that because seven generations of ancestors struggled for us out of love, our students were expected to share their acquired wisdom by going back to serve the community and positively impact seven generations ahead of them. This Indigenous pedagogy served as a critical theoretical basis for the MAS Indigenous-rooted pedagogy that I have named *"Culturally Humanizing Pedagogy."*

Exposing our students to the Chicano paradigm was critical in that it became a "tool" for our students to interrogate colonization. The objective of the Chicano paradigm served to offset the typical cannon of the "American paradigm" that perpetuates individualism and states that education opens up economic opportunities that lead to success, which would then translate to individual power. This paradigm is market based and maintains colonization through its capitalistic objective. We shared with our students that the American paradigm inculcates an individualistic purpose for learning and primes students' minds to accept that our educational system is a meritocracy whereby if you work hard enough, you will have an opportunity at that economic power. But our educational system is not a meritocracy—it is the antithesis. A comparison of the two paradigms reveals that the Chicano paradigm is centered on intrinsic accumulation of knowledge and wisdom; the American paradigm centered on the extrinsic accumulation power.

Nahui Ollin, an Asset-Based Indigenous Pedagogy

I introduced my colleagues to the *Nahui Ollin* (NO), which represents the cyclical movement of nature with respect to the four directions. The phrase comes from the Nahuatl language, *Nahui* meaning four and *Ollin* meaning movement. NO is a fundamental concept in Aztec/Mexica cosmology, a guide for everyday life and decisions. The objective is to constantly strive for balance, especially when there is a struggle. NO uses ancestral cultural concepts representing community, knowledge, education, will power, transformation, and most importantly, self-introspection. NO is composed of traditional Aztec scientific concepts, including the concepts of *Tezcatlipoca* (self-reflection, introspection, analysis, and memory), *Quetzalcoatl* (precious knowledge and stability), *Huitzilopochtli* (our will to act and take positive action), and *Xipe Totec* (transformation)[4]. NO was implemented in some of the MAS classes as a culturally responsive approach to teaching that ultimately supported the development of harmony and balance of our students' mind, body, spirit, and community. The four scientific energies that constitute the *Nahui Ollin* are explained as follows:

- *Tezcatlipoca:* Reflection/Introspection/Analysis/Genetic Memory/Self-love. We do not learn from our experiences alone, but rather we learn from reflecting on our experiences. This reflection process includes a deep analysis of the various elements that have to do with an issue that negatively impacts a person.
- *Xipe Totec:* Transformation. This is a place of cohesion and order to our thoughts whereby clarity is reached as a result of reflection (Tezcatlipoca). Through our reflection we can begin to make sense of the chaos associated with an issue and find order. Finally, by giving order to our thoughts, new perspective is gained that must positively impact our actions.
- *Huitzilopochtli:* Our will. Our actions must reflect our positive transformation. With new perspectives, we must act positively and move forward in a positive manner toward the positive growth of the collective.
- *Quetzalcoatl:* Stability. Gained knowledge acquired through the wisdom that serves to make us stable and balanced human beings. We must constantly draw on that precious knowledge to bring about beauty in our everyday lives.

The cycle of NO provided our students with a system of positive and focused decision-making that offered our students a sense of honor in the decisions that they made. Applying this system of decision-making also provided me a tool to humanize and move forward in a positive manner. NO requires that students' point of reference for all learning centers on their experiences as they are in constant reflection of their present and past experiences. *Tezcatlipoca* demands that we reconcile the past with the present. In fact, a typical classroom mantra was that we strive together to be the best human beings we can be, and as such a poster displayed with the following quote by Arturo Meza reminded us of that: "A true education starts with the knowledge of oneself."

NO is inherently a culturally relevant and responsive pedagogy that centers the lived experiences of the students, both past and present. One example of how I built a curriculum centered on students' past experiences was a unit on the ancient Mexican Indigenous tradition of the day of the dead (*Dia de los Muertos*). An objective of this unit was to identify a family member that had passed on and to recognize that family member's legacy and honor their lives by remembering them through various objects placed on a classroom alter, such as a photo of them and an object that had significance in their lives. Moreover, this was a time to recognize people in history that positively contributed to society such as Emma Tenayuca or Emiliano Zapata.[5]

Implementing NO in the classroom transformed the classroom in many respects: from the culture and climate, to the manner in which students interacted with each other, as well as how they approached their academic work. There was no need to implement typical classroom management strategies, such as the ones that typical teacher-preparation programs offer (e.g., a reward system for good behavior, or other extrinsic rewards). There was also no need for student-engagement strategies because students developed a sense of responsibility and purpose in the classroom driven through a social contract that stated our purpose during our time together. Moreover, our social contract (I developed one every year in collaboration with my students) reflected the teaching of the NO in that we agreed to implement the four elements to result in our positive collective growth (see Figure 7.1). The transformation in my classroom due to NO was evident in the shift in power dynamics in the classroom: this framework fostered more respectful and equitable roles between my students and myself.

Culturally Humanizing Pedagogy

I was fortunate to develop my expertise in applying both a Chicano paradigm and NO frameworks that are epistemologically Indigenous centered and have been documented as effective in influencing Xican@ youth's academic achievement (Godina, 2003). The combination of the Chicano paradigm and NO, however, yielded the creation of what I call "*Culturally Humanizing Pedagogy*" (CHP), a decolonizing pedagogy.

CHP interrogates colonization and provides students a path toward re-humanization through the implementation of the following three components. The first CHP component is engaging students in developing a historical consciousness that exposes the pillars of colonization. In developing a historical consciousness, students are engaged in learning about pre-colonization history,

Our 13 Mexicayotl Agreements

Our goal is to strive to become respectful and loving human beings. We will learn to respect ourselves to in turn respect all other living things. We shall continuously seek the truth as we strive to combat ignorance. We will approach our learning time with an open mind and an open heart so we can learn about where we come from in a reflective manner. We care about nature because without it we could not survive. We must know and understand History to understand our life and our reality to change it.

1   Be honest. Have faith and trust in yourself and others.

2.   Be yourself, follow your heart. Allow yourself to express your true feelings.

3.   Be caring. Care about others as if they were you; *In La Kech* "I am you are me".

4.   Be respectful. Respect and find beauty in everyone and everybody. Apply your Q*uetzalcoatl* consciousness.

5.   Utilize and develop your consciousness; be aware of your surroundings as this is the *Mexicayotl* way.

6.   Be an intellectual warrior. Approach your learning with an open mind and an open heart.

7.   *Panche Be*; always seek the root of the truth.

8.   *Tezcatlipoca*; be reflective. Continue to find clarity in the smokey mirror to understand ourselves better and to learn to love ourselves as this allows us to love others.

9.   We will strive to become loving and respectful human beings as we apply the principles in the *Nahui Ollin.*

10. We will bring about transformation in ourselves, our community and our planet, to the best of our ability, with issues that negatively impact our community

11. Through the guidance of the *Nahui Ollin* we will strive to find balance and harmony in our lives from within and without.

12. Following the *Mexicayotl* allows us to identify what it means to be human. Our humanity is about relationships.

13. Do the right thing. Our heart guides us to take action in a positive and progressive manner for the good of all.

FIGURE 7.1 Mexicayotl Agreements.

specifically the history of their people, with an emphasis on the time period of the Doctrine of Discovery (i.e., the origin of the execution of the colonization template imposed on minoritized people). Additionally, students focus on interrogating the Western canon of history by examining the various perspectives of history post the European invasion. Furthermore, in identifying the pillars of colonization, students are steeped in learning the history of their people at the K–12 levels, making learning relevant and connecting school learning to the lived experiences of our students.

Students must be exposed to the history of minoritized people to understand not only the contributions that minoritized people have provided, but also how they have resisted colonization as they have had to struggle toward equity. In so doing, students acquire the ability to articulate and justify their resistance of colonization. Students also learn to denounce the imposed identity that is assigned to them via colonization—one that typically regards them as criminals.

In denouncing that imposed identity, they work toward establishing an authentic identity centered in self-love or as NO teaches us, *Tezcatlipoca*.

The second CHP component focuses on assisting students in acquiring the tools to combat colonization through re-humanization. One of the critical tools to assist students in re-humanizing is providing opportunities to begin the process of self-love to interrogate internalized oppression. Coupled with self-love is exposing students to "intergenerational wisdom," which serves to reconnect to the wisdom of the students' ancestors. This is vital because, in reconnecting with intergenerational wisdom, students are provided with an opportunity, possibly for the first time, to feel proud of the world-view of their ancestors. This is unlike the typical view of their ancestors as *savage*, as colonization endeavors have explicitly stated. Many of my Xicana/o students were exposed to their intellectual capacity for the first time with CHP. For example, when my students learned for the first time that the Aztec calendar system was, to date, the most accurate calendar system in the world, they realized the intellect that they possessed.

Another tenant in CHP is acquiring conscientization, or specifically allowing students to engage in the process of "reading the world" through the implementation of Freire's "Levels of Consciousness" (Freire, 1970). It is through the implementation of the Levels of Consciousness that students were able to become aware of the constraints on their lives and take action to transform their situation, and thus engage in the process of *conscientization*, whereby students are encouraged to analyze their reality. By developing a critical consciousness, students can critically analyze the numerous historical, cultural, social, political and economic experiences of minoritized groups (Arce, 2016).

Finally, the third component involves supporting students in defining ways to navigate a colonized society. What is meant by *navigating a colonized society* is that critical educators assist students in acquiring the skills to provide them the opportunities they wish to take advantage of. Typically, in a stratified system, minoritized students' dreams are deferred and their life opportunities are limited. Instead, literacy development is focused on developing the requisite skills that allow minoritized youth to engage in discourse, as well as actions, to engage in addressing issues their communities face and improve their communities (Arce, 2016). This includes the need for language development to develop critical thinking, reading, writing, and speaking skills through the study of the experiences of people of color (Arce, 2016).

A major component in the CHP Framework is NO, which provided our students a decision-making cycle that fostered humanization. This cycle was critical in fostering the confidence (*confianza*) that Dr. López describes in her framework. Accordingly, the following teacher dispositions are critical in the implementation of decolonizing methodologies that are essential for establishing an academic culture and climate that nurtures respectful relationships with our students: responding to the impact of colonization, having high standards for our students, denouncing deficit thinking models, and teaching complex thinking. The components of a CHP serve to complete the pedagogical framework that provides students a path toward rehumanization. The CHP components included cultural identity development to cultivate student academic success centered on the development and growth of human measures. The human measures include hope, purpose, and building strong sense of *confianza*. These human measures counter the current educational system that merely seeks to produce proficient test takers who master dominant middle-class culture.

In essence, CHP is centered on humanization; it is a responsive pedagogy that centers *culture*—the lived experiences of youth. In the context of an urban school district, CHP is utilized by teachers to *compassionately* respond to their student's diverse needs and to their lived experiences in a positive and progressive manner. CHP views each child, family, and the communities they come from as assets and builds upon students' cultural wealth (linguistic, aspirational, navigational, familial, social capital, and resistance). CHP considers urban youth as co-creators of knowledge and provides a safe space for growth—cognitively, emotionally, and spiritually (i.e., considers the whole child). CHP also holds all students to high expectations (rigor) and provides the support for the students to achieve academically (access).

An Imperative for Tezcatlipoca: Self-Love Through Reflection and Introspection

Given that a strategy to maintain colonization is self-hate, the most radical decolonizing concept that we can teach our minoritized students is self-love; that is, to help our students learn to love their humanity. Self-hate is essentially internalized colonization/oppression that seeks to foster instability in the lives of minoritized students. This is inevitable for minoritized students as they are constantly bombarded with stereotypical images of their potential (e.g., gangsters, uneducated). Consequences of internalized colonization/oppression include: horizontal violence, the hatred of members of their own ethnic group, and a desire to be like the dominant group in appearance, world-view, and political status.

As stated earlier, the mantra in my classes has always been to engage in the process of self-love guided by the words of professor Arturo Meza who states that a "true education is the knowledge of oneself" (1997). On our path toward self-love, I have always engaged my students in opportunities to research their history often through poetry. Specifically, I have utilized the *I Am From* poem (adapted by Levi Romero). Another strategy for engaging students in researching their history is in interviewing family members and in creating a family tree. By engaging students in this research, it has yielded information that has contributed to the development of their identity, their origin, culture, name, and so on. Students begin to understand that they are a product of the sum of all their experiences and their family members' experiences. Moreover, helping students develop a positive sense of self also requires that they research the contributions of members of their culture to society, along with research of the resistance, resilience and collective strength of members of their cultural group.

The implementation of this Indigenous-rooted pedagogy has produced unprecedented results (e.g., Cabrera et. al., 2014). While we knew that the impact of this pedagogical focus was impressive in terms of how it closed the opportunity gap, our greatest hope was that our program could serve to inform other educational programs for minoritized students through culturally responsive teaching. The following Mexican proverb has been used over again by numerous people describing the MAS struggle for equitable education: "they tried to bury us, but they didn't know we were seeds." Thus, despite the backlash MAS received in Tucson, Arizona, it paved the way for a nationwide Ethnic Studies movement.

Notes

1   I use the "X" instead of the "Ch" because the "X" is pronounced as "sh" and accordingly recognizes our Indigeniety (see Cintli, 1996).
2   Properties of Whiteness include being a member of the dominant culture and benefitting from the privileges.
3   The Chicano paradigm is a teaching tool utilized by Tupac Enrique Acosta in the Xinachtli Project, a project that targeted middle-school students' exposure to Mesoamerican ancestry.
4   This description of the *Nahui Ollin* was collectively written in conversation between myself and Jesus "Chucho" Ruiz in 2008.
5   Emma Tenayuca was a community activist that fought against injustices toward Mexican American women workers. Emiliano Zapata is most remembered for his leadership in the Mexican Revolution, specifically fighting for land rights for the indigenous people of Mexico.

References

Arce, M.S. (2016). Xicana/o indigenous epistemologies: Towards a decolonizing a liberatory education for Xicana/o Youth. In T. L Buenavista, J. R. Marín, A. Ratcliff, & D. Sandoval (Eds.), *Whitewashing American education: The new culture wars in ethnic studies*. Santa Barbara, CA: Praeger Publications.

Cabrera, N. L., Milem, J. F., Jaquette, O., & Marx, R. W. (2014). Missing the (student achievement) forest for all the (political) trees: Empiricism and the Mexican American studies controversy in Tucson. *American Educational Research Journal, 51*(6), 1084–1118.

Forbes, J. D. (2011). *Columbus and other cannibals: The Wetiko disease of exploitation, imperialism, and terrorism*. New York: Seven Stories Press.

Freire, P. (1970). *Pedagogy of the oppressed*. New York: Continuum.

Godina, H. (2003). Mesocentrism and students of Mexican background: A community intervention for culturally relevant instruction. *Journal of Latinos and Education, 2*(3), 141–157.

Ladson-Billings, G. (1995). Toward a theory of culturally relevant pedagogy. *American Educational Research Journal, 32*, 465–491.

López, F. A. (2017). Altering the trajectory of the self-fulfilling prophecy: Asset-based pedagogy and classroom dynamics. *Journal of Teacher Education, 68*(2), 193–212.

Meza, A. (1997). *Tezcatlipoca: Nuestro ser interno*. Universidad Michoacana de San Nicolas de Hidalgo.

Nieto, D. G. (2007). The Emperor's new words: Language and colonization. *Human Architecture, 5*, 231.

Rodríguez, R. (1996). *The X in la Raza*. R. Rodríguez.

Solorzano, D. G., & Bernal, D. D. (2001). Examining transformational resistance through a critical race and LatCrit theory framework: Chicana and Chicano students in an urban context. *Urban education, 36*(3), 308–342.

Valenzuela, A. (2010). *Subtractive schooling: US–Mexican youth and the politics of caring*. Suny Press.

Yosso, T. J. (2006). *Critical race counterstories along the Chicana/Chicano educational pipeline*. New York: Routledge.

8

A COUNTER NARRATIVE

A Pedagogy of Love through Critical Race Theory

José Alberto González

Lalo, a recent arrival from Mexico, was placed in my "green reading group," what my classmates teasingly referred to as the "burros" or academically challenged, reading group. I, having a rudimentary command of Spanish, was assigned to be his translator, thus Lalo's chair was next to mine. Sister Mary Carol, in her despotic tone, shattered the silence demanding to know who was disrupting her class. Lalo had quietly whispered to me asking for instructional clarification. Upon her violent outburst, I quickly looked down at the floor in deference to her authority. Sister Mary Carol demanded I walk to the chalkboard and instructed me to spell the words we had been assigned that week. I froze as I vividly recall looking down at the floor wishing I could disappear. She proceeded to humiliate and verbally accost me, finally ending her diatribe with, "Are you stupid?" As tears streamed down my cheeks, words that were laced in my barrio lexicon came rushing in my defense; however, my upbringing and school decorum filtered my language, and in a wounded voice I looked her in the eye and shouted, "That's not right!" I turned and walked out the door and began to walk home.

The preceding counter narrative is a tenet within Critical Race Theory (CRT), which contests the majoritarian narrative that is officially sanctioned and legitimized as "official knowledge," obfuscating minoritized experiences. The counter-narrative illustrates the micro-aggressions (Sue et al., 2007) I endured during third grade at a local parochial school. Too often, these experiences are not aberrations, but commonplace for *barrio* (neighborhood) youth.

As I reflect on my schooling[1] experiences, I can say I survived. My experiences throughout my elementary and secondary career, which are riddled with similar accounts, are lamentable. Recently, at a family graduation party, my brothers and I were sharing "war-stories" of the schooling experiences we endured at the hands of our teachers and administrators. Interestingly, we laughed. I'm not sure why, as the stories we shared were painful accounts of trauma we live through. Nevertheless, we laughed as we reminisced, with my brother Frank placing our experiences in context. "What we lived through at St. John's are difficult memories. However, those experiences do not capture my loving memories of the friendships I made with my classmates. That's what keeps me going and allows me to move forward." Dixon and Henry (2016) frame these experiences within CRT as "attentive to the sobering realities of racialized suffering and the discursive and material formations that shape and give meaning to a stratified social structure. CRT focuses on exposing and actively dismantling taken-for-granted, regnant racial ideologies and power relations" (p. 224). It is in this spirit that my work and labor of love is centered on. In this chapter, I will explain the asset-based pedagogical approaches I have developed, which are based on CRT and critical pedagogy as not only a theoretical framework, but also a moral code, that I embody and informs my asset-based practice.

Asset-Based Pedagogy

How do I as an urban (barrio) teacher build on the assets or cultural wealth (Yosso, 2002) my students innately possess? How do I begin to (re)imagine, (re)construct the educational experiences of our barrio youth where I see and interact with them as "glasses half full" and not its antithesis? How do we, as members of the teaching profession, rebuke the teacher-centered model and instead use the multitude of asset-based pedagogies that work to transform the educational outcomes of historically underserved populations? Using her race-reimaged classroom dynamics model, López (2017) demonstrates that teachers who use asset-based pedagogies and work to maintain a *critical awareness* can significantly improve student achievement. My own work corroborates this research. In fact, I contend that absent a critical awareness, a pedagogy of love is an impossibility.

As a barrio teacher who works with barrio youth, I work to understand my students lived experiences by maintaining knowledge that informs a socio-political-economic critique (critical awareness) and caring enough to ask critical questions of people in authority: my colleagues, site and district administration, and local and state politicians. I believe that if you are not in trouble with administration, you are not doing your job. Meaning, if I am not challenging the "business as usual" mentality within a school setting, I am complicit in the racialized pain schooling afflicts upon barrio youth. I am clear and resolute in my positionality within our institution; I am a student–parent advocate first and foremost, and will not compromise this responsibility to the community I serve. Consequently, this political stance has been burdensome and brought about unfair scrutiny and oversight throughout the years; however, I have never shied away from this responsibility. The smiles, laughter, love, and determination in my students' faces that permeate my classroom validate this struggle against what I identify as the "big bully" on campus: the *schooling* system.

Having lived and grown up in many of the same barrios my students at Tucson High live in makes my job of studying their barrio history much easier. I often say that to know and love a people, you must know their literature and history. To know and love our Black, Pan-Asian, Indigenous, etc. kin, we must read and study their body of work which captures their struggles and triumphs. This requires research, as these stories and histories are often omitted from the mainstream canon, which is undeniably Eurocentric. I consider this research my homework, which must be carried out before I can engage students in a learning exchange where we co-create knowledge. As a critical component of teaching, it is incumbent upon the teacher to know and understand the environment our students reside in and the history that has shaped them and their community. It is also important to live and raise a family in the same community you serve. I realize this is not always a possibility; however, I feel it is extremely beneficial for both parties involved. What one will discover, though there can be elements of danger, is the beauty of the people, their loving sense of family and community, their work ethic, and their joy for life. These features far outweigh the negative elements that can be part of some communities. For many barrio youth, the "American Dream" is lived in suburbia, far away from the barrio. The dominant narrative for barrio youth, whether implicit or explicit, is to leave once they can. By living among the students one serves, one declares that one is an invested community member.

I recognize that there is difficulty in changing our barrio youth's educational, and thus life, trajectory; however, I know it is possible. Indeed, it is imperative that we engage in this work to change lives. This is work I have been dedicated to over the past twenty-five years.

Sociopolitical/Economic Context

The pathology of poverty and how barrio youth are forced to live/struggle often plays havoc on their life trajectory. The social toxins of domestic and community violence, dilapidated environments (home, community, and schools), household instability, etc. all artifacts of disinvestment; barrio youth are quick to ascertain society has rendered them as disposable. Yet, too often, educators view barrio youth as responsible for their own low academic achievement without any critique of how a system of perpetual inequities impacts their daily lives. I am reminded of Tupac Shakur's acronym THUG LIFE (The Hate U Gave Little Infants F***s Everyone), which speaks to this notion of disposability and the righteous anger it ferments. It epitomizes this uncanny ability of barrio youth to see through society's false façade. Tupac continues, "we have money for war ... but can't feed the poor." It is the hypocrisy within our society that also speaks to our lack of will as a people to end this racialized suffering! Similarly, Olmeca (2012) asserts:

I did not come from a broken home, instead just the opposite … A loving family with problems, a victim of my surroundings … Our biggest obstacle was a lack of education and poverty, forced to do what was needed for a bite of food and security. It's hard to see the warmth of my families' love turn into a cold hug because of money problems unresolved. Two jobs ain't enough and still they grind harder than most … I'm pissed off at the world because we're now not given no choice … Our folks forced out of their home. You must be stupid, no one crosses the desert 'cause they want to … It's a necessity … a sacrifice for the family. You don't call them illegals you call them Economic Refugees. In this part of the song, I would tell you, "imagine how you felt …" but I know you don't need to imagine, cause if you've been poor then you know the feeling real to you, vivid cause you've smelt it, tasted it, felt it … in other words you've lived it!

(Title track)

I have come to know barrio students as *street smart*. Yosso (2002) identifies this as navigational wealth, wherein barrio youth are adept at reading people and society and are quick to "call out" contradictions inherent within a "democratic" society. I recall an example of my own navigational wealth during a second-grade experience with Sister MaryAnn who was everyone's favorite teacher, including mine. She was kind to all her students and treated us with respect and understanding. But my friends and I noticed a pattern Sister MaryAnn had established. Whenever she walked out of the room, she would always ask Angie Polaski, the only Euro-American[2] in our class, to watch her purse. This personal experience, among many others, prompts me to work vigorously toward creating a loving environment for all my students that is *authentic* (Valenzuela, 2010), wherein students are provided with the love and respect they need to flourish as the beautiful flowers that they are meant to be.

Pedagogy of Love

I contend that teaching is an affirmation of love; thus, it is a pedagogy of love, consistent with Ernesto "Che" Guevara's assertion, "at the risk of seeming ridiculous, the revolutionary is guided by a great feeling of love." Teachers who deeply and genuinely care are revolutionaries who are compelled to transform society. This sense of agency driven by the innate emotion of love is the catalyst for improving the human condition and, I argue, what teaching is anchored on. Sadly, as Galeano (2001) astutely reminds us, our world is upside down where our values are inverted, where the notion of love is viewed as a sign of weakness and greed is exalted. I work to (re)center myself as I enter my classroom and diligently strive to establish a utopian classroom where possibility permeates; where risk-taking is encouraged and supported in a constructive, loving manner. I facilitate a classroom which transforms into a (third) space[3] of refuge, a universe where humanization is a possibility and a utopian is reified.

The affirmation of love is the essence of teaching (Freire, 1998), and, as such, is the heart and soul of how I facilitate literacy. It must, however, be an unconditional love. I contend that unconditional love undergirds teaching, which acts as a linchpin to the relationships I make with my students, and thus allows me access to my students' hearts, thereby opening them up the possibility of engaging their minds.

This positionality requires a paradigm shift. As my juniors and seniors enter my class, I comprehend they are *survivors* of their racialized schooling experience. Therefore, I work to develop and refine their literacy skills and critical thinking skills. Additionally, as a former coach, I coach up (*confianza*): I build success through skill development and "*confianza*" through mastery of the skills. I become their biggest cheerleader because I am cognizant many barrio youth have never been praised and acknowledged. At the same time, giving doses of tough love, through an unconditional love filter, is needed on occasion. I teach American History, so my class is heavy on reading, writing, critical dialogue (speaking), and the development of a student's critical consciousness. In describing the liberatory act of a *dialogical method*, Freire (1970) asserts:

> Dialogue cannot exist, however, in the absence of a profound love for the world and for people. The naming of the world, which is an act of creation and re-creation, is not possible if it is not infused with love. Love is at the same time the foundation of dialogue and dialogue itself … Because love is an act of courage, not of fear, love is commitment to others. No matter where the oppressed are found, the act of love is commitment to their cause—the cause of liberation. And this commitment, because it is loving, is dialogical.
>
> *(p. 70)*

Love. In 2012, I team-taught with Mrs. Martinez, a veteran teacher. She approached me to inquire why the students we shared spoke so highly of me and achieved academically in my class, yet not hers. I suggested unconditional love. I stated, "we love each other, in a parental sense, like I love my son." Mrs. Martinez struggled to understand. Our conversation continued with her questions of clarification, and then I asked, "Who are our students who give you the most trouble?" After she provided a list of students, I asked, "Can you love them as your own, and as your own children, can you love them enough to investigate where this behavior is stemming from?" She replied that she was not sure if she was capable, and our conversation came to an end.

Herein lies the problem: teachers, through our formal training, are explicitly instructed to always maintain a "professional" relationship with our students. This is inferred as meaning that at all times, we are to maintain a very clinical, business-like approach to teaching, and at no time should we be the students' friend. "Don't smile until Christmas" syndrome is counterproductive to teaching and working with youth. I argue that, instead, a *parental* love relationship in teaching is the optimal in establishing a critical love (nurturing love; when needed, a tough love), where lifelong bonds are established. By critical love, the teacher can determine which love is necessary for personal growth; a nurturing, supportive, "confianza" building love or from time to time, delivery of a tough love, where critical constructive criticism is necessary for personal growth. Regardless, this entails truly loving all our students—and more specifically, the youth who are in the "most need" of immediate attention, the students who at times make our lives as classroom teachers unbearable. Those are the students who most need to be loved. Truth be told, it requires minimal effort to love and enjoy the academically successful student. The true challenge, however, is learning to ask critical questions as to *why* a student is acting out, and consider how the behavior is a possible sign of distress. Why can't the student write and read at grade level, and how can I bring their skill set up to speed? Do I love the student enough to care to ask? Do I love the student enough to *act*? These reflective questions remind me of the iconic poem by Harlem Renaissance poet, Langston Hughes, as to why I teach:

> What happens to a dream deferred? Does it dry up
> Like a raisin in the sun? Or fester like a sore …
> And then run? Does it stink like rotten meat?
> Or crust and sugar over … Like syrupy sweet?
> Maybe it just sags … Like a heavy load?
> *Or does it explode?*

Too many urban (barrio) youth's dreams are being deferred, thus slowly and methodically eliminated. Society and our institutions of education, government, business, media, religion, and the family all espouse a notion of the United States as a meritocracy. The logic follows: the institution of education is where "dreams" are made. Therefore, if students are diligent and "resilient", they too can gain access to the "American Dream" by attaining high school and university degrees. Yet, it is disturbing how barrio youths' "American dreams" are placed on hold by the socio-political/economic conditions they are forced to live under. More sinister is how barrio youth are set up for a life of heartache and stress, where students and families bear the "scarlet letter" of high school "dropout" when they are actually "pushed out" of their dilapidated, resource-strapped schools or, worse yet, graduate from high school with semiliterate skills and are condemned to a life of mediocrity. Within the field of teacher education and society at large, there exists a failure to comprehend the root cause of this inequality, and it is to the peril of barrio youth and society at large. The persistent lack of structural analysis by those who educate works against the most vulnerable. Darder (2012) reminds us "as teachers continue to buy into the belief that schooling is a neutral and benevolent enterprise, students from oppressed communities are tested, labeled, sorted and tracked, while notions of justice and equality are touted within U.S.

schools, particularly within poor racialized communities" (p. 849). A complete contradiction.

Thus, a pedagogy of love is my moral code and the overarching umbrella that my asset-based pedagogical approach is founded on. Regarding love, I am cognizant and mindful of what Freire (1970) identifies as a *"false generosity*," yet my understanding of love is firmly rooted in the notion "human" justice. As such, if one is disposed to loving the world, a spirit of criticism becomes paramount if we are to continuously grow and flourish. As Franz Fanon states, "Today I believe in the possibility of love; that is why I endeavor to trace its imperfections, its perversions." With an absent critique of our societal imperfections, perversion, or contradiction, "human" justice will never be attained.

Racial Politics and Racialized Literacy

According to a 2016 report by the Department of Education, by 2024, students of color will comprise 56% of the public-school students, yet the teaching and administration force is projected to remain a homogeneous Euro-American population (with teachers overwhelmingly female and administrators overwhelmingly male). Today, many urban school districts, including Tucson Unified School District, have become minority-majority districts. I do not believe civil rights lawyers who argued in the landmark desegregation cases of *Westminster v. Mendez* (1947), and *Brown v. Board* (1954) could have predicted the extent to which Whites[4] would abandon their urban public schools, creating a new phenomenon of "White-flight." What is patently clear, the "browning" of America, particularly within urban public-school settings, is our new social lived reality. The obvious axiological question is, what kind of investment are we willing to make regarding the education we provide to minoritized barrio youth? Do we invest now (Arizona spends roughly $7,000 per pupil) or pay later (Arizona spends roughly $26,000 per inmate)? How is this a moral indictment on our institutional will to live by our "democratic" principles?

If we consider the demographic shift and its future projections, it is undisputable that race matters. Lipsitz (1998) reminds us that although race is considered a cultural construct, the racialized realities of minoritized peoples have "deadly social causes and consequences" (p. 2). That is, we can readily see how racialized politics manifest in the schooling apparatus in terms of suspension and expulsion rates; high school graduation rates; and rates of college matriculation. Examination of these trends allows us to see the lack of quality of life standard our barrio youth face.

Consequently, I argue racialized politics matter. I contend it is obligatory for school officials, specifically teachers and administration, to develop a "racialized literacy," as our schools are filled with minoritized youth whose racialized transgressions in the form of discursive and material formations are being "tested, labeled, sorted, and tracked," thereby codifying our socially engineered, racial hierarchy. Once again, do we have a "profound love for the world and people" to propel us into action?

Critical Race Theory in the Schooling Apparatus

Having been born and raised in Tucson, my phenotype—my dark skin—has stigmatized and thus targeted my life trajectory in our racialized society. Racism and its manifestations in the form of physical, psychological, emotional, spiritual, and discursive violent acts of subordinating my humanity has defined my entire existence. Subsequently, I have always had a racialized literacy. In 2000, while teaching at Cholla High School in Tucson, I was exposed to Derrick Bell's book *Faces at the Bottom of the Well*. This book transformed my life and at the same time revolutionized my teaching. It gave me CRT as a new lens to "read" my word, a language to articulate my racialized experiences that I operationalized as a theoretical foundation for my asset-based approach to teaching.

Before continuing, I feel a working definition of racism is warranted. Here, I define racism as a class or group of people having the institutional power to control the structures of government, media, banking, business, education, and religion by creating policy that provides entitlements to their group, in the abstract and material sense, and subordinating minoritized groups by denying access, in the abstract and material sense. As a direct consequence of European imperialism (settler colonialism) and United States hegemony, racism is White supremacy.

It is within this working definition of racism that I work to develop and sustain a racialized literacy. Yosso's (2006) establishes that "CRT scholars in education have to theorize, examine, and challenge the ways race and racism shape schooling structures, practices, and discourse" (p. 7). It is through this lens and these four precepts (Solórzano, & Delgado Bernal, 2001) of CRT that I center my pedagogy.

The Intercentrality of Race and Racism

This precept is an essential component of CRT; the supposition is that racial acts of subordinating minoritized peoples and acts of normalizing whiteness and its entitlements are an endemic way of life. This demands that I, as a teacher, develop a pedagogy that acknowledges the racialized experiences of my students and equips them in confronting and abating their racialized suffering.

Within this precept is also the concept of the intersection of oppression. Delgado and Stefancic (2001) assert that intersectionality "means the examination of race, sex, class, national origin, and sexual orientation" (p. 51), and how the systems of oppression overlap and are interrelated in their subordination of minoritized youth. Intersectional oppression is important to grapple with, for my students are living with these multiple forms of oppression. For example, this past year, I had students who are female (sexism), transgender (heterosexism), Mexican American (racism), and poor (classism), yet live in a patriarchal world.

The oppression in the form of subordination often can become overwhelming and when we see only a female student who did not submit her homework, we fail to acknowledge the suffering she has endured and is in the process of reconciling.

The Challenge to the Dominant Ideology

This precept confronts the invisibility of White supremacy as a dominant ideology. It challenges the claim that education is a site of neutrality, objectivity, and equal opportunity. Yosso (2006) articulates, "schooling that pretends to be neutral or standardized while implicitly privileging White, U.S.-born, monolingual, English-speaking students" (p. 7) works to the detriment of minoritized youth.

Throughout the year, I develop the ideas of Antoñio Gramsci's (1972) cultural hegemony, which works to expose and challenge the dominant ideology of the ruling class. Cultural hegemony explains how the ruling class, through ideology, dominates the masses by getting the masses to consent and maintain the dominant ideology that consistently works against their self-interest. The masses view the dominant ideology as natural or as commonsense, thus securing the power of the ruling class. The dominant ideology is produced and maintained in the media, church, family, schools, and the political system.

The Commitment to Social Justice

This precept is central to how my class is structured; the expectation is that my students will make this world a better place. Social justice cannot take place without a racialized sociopolitical/economic literacy. This precept addresses the notion of agency and our ability as individuals to make history by shaping our world to be more humane and just. Education is the catalyst for this change.

In this commitment to social justice, I utilize a Freirean (1974) critical consciousness to develop a social/political economic literacy that helps students work toward social justice. There are three fluid categories of *consciousness* that are metacognitive processes, which facilitate a structural or systemic analysis of a given issue or problem. The most common, a *naïve consciousness,* is a byproduct of the dominant ideology and is the default state of cognition. I refer to this state of cognition as lazy thinking, for it requires minimal analysis and a "commonsense" rationale to solving issues or problems. Social justice (change) is impossible as the victim (person or group) is blamed and the real source of the problem is never identified and thus remains unchallenged. A *magical consciousness* focuses the analysis outside the person, but the issue or problem is attributed to "God's will," (i.e., religion) or bad fortune. Like *naïve consciousness,* social justice (i.e., change) is an impossibility in *magical consciousness.* Here, the belief that things are outside of one's control prevents agency. Finally, *critical consciousness* centers analysis on whether an issue or problem is going to be addressed. The locus of control is on the system or structure as the source or root cause. Social justice is a possibility in this consciousness because the root of the problem is identified. Absent a critically conscious state of cognition, love of the world and of people is an impossibility. Today, the *Black Lives Matter* movement has coined a term *"#StayWoke"* that captures this notion.

Critical consciousness has transformed my life by allowing me to be more structural in my own analysis as I engage and interact with the world. Consequently, this process has deeply influenced my pedagogical approach and how I teach critical thinking. Critical consciousness is a skill that, once internalized by students, transforms the culture of our class and makes our interactions, analyses, and discussions much richer and productive. This metacognitive process is amazing to witness as students monitor their own state of cognition by filtering their question and comments ensuring their analysis is structural.

The Centrality of Experiential Knowledge

This precept works to counter the dominant narrative and speaks specifically to the experiential knowledge of minoritized peoples as legitimate, thus the authority or expert in their lived experiences. Yosso (2006) asserts counter narratives "seek to document the persistence of racism from the perspective of those injured and victimized by its legacy" (p.10). It is through counter narratives that barrio youth are empowered to "write back" through *cuentos* (storytelling), family history, biographies, testimonies, and poetry, allowing students to become the authority of their racialized suffering (as opposed to some academician in the academy, far removed from their experiences). Here, their experiences are validated, honored, and legitimized as "official knowledge" in my classes, and students are encouraged to draw on those racialized experiences, as they engage the learning process in my class and in life.

CRT saves lives—and this is not hyperbole. We are living in a time of state-sanctioned lethal violence carried out with impunity. Countless times we see this racial violence manifested in rogue police murders of innocent minoritized people. And because racism affects us all, the modern mentality of juries tends to be "White," resulting in the repeated exoneration of police. Our modern-day situation is reminiscent of southern all-White juries who found Klansmen innocent of murder despite evidence to the contrary, ridiculing the so-called rule of law. For these reasons, among others, teaching students how to live in a racialized world *is* a matter—literally and figuratively—of life and death.

But it is not just the overt acts of racism that take the lives of our minoritized youth. As asserted by Jackson (2011), "People know about the Klan and the overt racism, but the killing of one's soul little by little, day after day, is a lot worse than someone coming in your house and lynching you" (para. 6), That slow death Jackson references is how society sets barrio youth up for failure, blames them for failing, and sits back and bears witness with a "White gaze" to that slow death of their dreams being denied, only to pathologize their will to survive in a world they socially engineered and maintain.

The questions central to my pedagogy are: how do I provide an environment where my racialized students can process their racialized experiences and where I can facilitate the literacy process of teaching American History? How am I responsive to their racialized and intersectional sufferings? How do I meet my barrio youth's social, emotional, physical, psychological needs before I can work with their minds? These questions allow for my pedagogy of love and my life-long relationships to flourish.

Notes

1   Here, I refer to schooling in the spirit of Angela Valenzuela's *Subtractive Schooling* (1999), which reflects the schooling endured by minoritized populations.
2   Euro-American is utilized to denote the heritage of a person who is of European descent.
3   Kris Gutiérrez's Third space notion of zones of student development.
4   "White" is designated here to include Euro-American people who adopt the social construct of a White identity, which has less to do with heritage and more with power. Whether conscious or unconscious, White people forgo their European heritage.

References

Bell, D. (1993). *Faces at the bottom of the well: The permanence of racism*. New York: Basic Books.
Darder, A. (2012). *Culture and power in the classroom: A critical foundation for bicultural education*. New York: Bergin and Garvey.
Delgado, R. (1996). *The Rodrigo chronicles: Conversations about America and race*. New York: New York University Press.
Delgado, R., & Stefancic, J. (2001). *Critical race theory: An introduction*. New York: New York University Press.
Freire, P. (1970). *Pedagogy of the oppressed*. New York: Continuum.
Freire, P. (1974). *Education for critical consciousness*. London: Sheed and Ward.
Freire, P. (1998). *Teachers as cultural workers. letters to those who dare teach. the edge: Critical studies in educational theory*. Boulder, CO: Westview Press.
Galeano, E. (2001). *Upside down: A primer for the looking-glass world*. New York: Macmillan.
Gramsci, A., 1891–1937, Hoare, Q., & Nowell-Smith, G. (1972). *Selections from the prison notebooks of Antonio Gramsci* (1st ed.). New York: International Publishers.
Henry, Jr. & Dixson, A. D. (2016). "Locking the door before we got the keys": Racial realities of the charter school authorization process in post-Katrina New Orleans. *Educational Policy, 30* (1), 218– 240.
Jackson, S. (2011, August 21). Tell it on the mountain top. Retrieved from http://nymag.com/guides/fallpreview/2011/theater/samuel-l-jackson/.
Lipsitz, G. (2006). *The possessive investment in whiteness: How white people profit from identity politics*. Temple University Press.
López, F. A. (2017). Altering the trajectory of the self-fulfilling prophecy: Asset-based pedagogy and classroom dynamics. *Journal of Teacher Education, 68*(2), 193–212.
Olmeca. (2010). Pieces of me: *Pieces of me*. [CD]. Los Angeles, CA: Olmeca.

Solorzano, D. G., & Bernal, D. D. (2001). Examining transformational resistance through a critical race and LatCrit theory framework: Chicana and Chicano students in an urban context. *Urban Education, 36*(3), 308–342.

Valenzuela, A. (2010). *Subtractive schooling: US–Mexican youth and the politics of caring.* Suny Press.

Wynter, S. (1987). On disenchanting discourse "minority" literary criticism and beyond. *Cultural Critique, 7* (Autumn), 207–244.

Yosso, T. J. (2006). *Critical race counterstories along the Chicana/Chicano educational pipeline.* New York: Routledge.

9

CULTURALLY RESPONSIVE PRACTICES IN K–5 CLASSROOMS

Isabel Kelsey

My educational journey has defined my beliefs about traditionally marginalized students' education, specifically emergent bilingual (EB) Latino students living in poverty. More recently, I have experienced teaching in an African American community with a growing number of refugee students from the Middle East and various African countries. My journey, however, begins with my own education, the teaching practices I developed, and the adversities that result from educational policies. Because of my experiences, I've come to understand how US schools have institutionalized segregation by mandating a traditional curriculum, and perpetuated educational policies and practices against marginalized students at the federal, state, and local level.

Over the course of my career, I have witnessed the numerous ways educational policies and desegregation court efforts have influenced the experiences of my EB, Latino students. I have been required to follow specific court mandates that were purported to bring quality and equitable education to the growing community of EB, Latino students living in poverty (*Alvarez-Jasso v. TUSD,* 1994). I have also had to follow a number of requirements resulting from desegregation oversight resulting from *Mendoza v. TUSD* (1980). Although the spirit, as Ladson-Billings described (2004), of the cases had good intentions, the policies that teachers often had to follow did not always meet the needs of EBs. Despite the shortcomings of policies that at least have good intentions, it is Proposition 203 (2001) that has had the greatest negative impact on EB students. With its passing came a traditional curriculum that purposefully excluded the contributions of Latinos, and English became the only means of instruction. It further exacerbated the anti-language sentiment in schools and the general public. At the national level, *No Child Left Behind* (2002) and *Race to the Top* (2009) has intensified high stakes testing and standardized education further.

Hence, my educational experiences include many years of changing policies that often failed to consider the lives of EBs, particularly when they were the target population of a particular policy. Nevertheless, I discovered that teaching was a calling from the time I began teaching in Tucson. My teaching experiences over the course of more than 20 years, from kindergarten through fifth grade, have provided me with the skills to develop culturally responsive practices (CRP). During this time, I have kept a reflective journal in which I annotated teaching practices, beliefs, strategies, research, and other ideas. I also noted my observations on how policies have transformed education and impacted the educational experiences of marginalized students.

My journey is similar to that of many students in schools today. Like many children, I had a caring family and a supportive community. Today, however, restrictive policies have had the effect of desensitizing students from their culture and language, resulting in many marginalized students not having experiences of academic success or feeling part of a community. To counter these policies, I had to develop culturally responsive K–5 practices, which I detail below.

Culturally Responsive Practices

Although the focus of this section is culturally responsive best practices in K–5 classrooms, I begin with a few words on the importance of culturally responsive *leadership* and how a leader's beliefs influence teaching and learning. This is because leadership (which extends to teachers as leaders) is central in understanding and implementing a culturally responsive curriculum (Capper & Frattura, 2009; Gay, 2010). When a leader's personal vision becomes collective, it provides direction to move the school's vision forward. It is thus the collaborative effort of a school leader, teachers, and the community that makes a successful and sustainable school climate culture (Day, 2009).

The four culturally responsive practices I developed have proven to be successful in spite of restrictive policies. They include: shared leadership, inclusive schools, caring, and communities. I provide some examples for each of the practices below. Although some lessons may seem familiar to readers, I used my reflective experiences to generate culturally responsive practices that I then integrated into the existing curriculum. In doing so, I made instruction inclusive and relevant to student experiences.

Shared Leadership

Shared leadership posits that teachers are co-collaborators. In these cases where there is shared leadership, teachers are leaders in the community, school, and classroom. In this section, I discuss Professional Learning Communities (PLCs) that promote leadership responsibility as a collective force to foster a culturally responsive learning community (Portin, Knapp, Dareff, Feldman, Russel, & Samuelson, 2009).

Professional Learning Communities. Today, PLCs are common throughout schools. DuFour, DuFour, and Eaker (2005) define PLCs as

> Educators committed to working collaboratively in ongoing processes of collective inquiry and action research to achieve better results for the students they serve. PLCs operate under the assumption that the key to improved learning for students is continuous, job-embedded learning for educators.

PLCs, however, are primarily focused on data and assessments as explained by Reeves (2005): "The framework of professional learning community is inextricably linked to the effective integration of standards, assessments, and accountability" (p. 47). PLCs that incorporate culturally responsive pedagogy, however, have the additional goal of building community centered on students' culture and language. Therefore, in this section, I discuss several strategies to integrate CRP into a district's curriculum, lesson plans, and daily practices as continuous inquiry for student achievement.

There are three identifiable phases for PLCs; each phase provides specific strategies. Phase I is the planning phase. Phase II further revises goals, involves CPR integration strategies, and incorporates student/parent input during Professional Development (PD). Phase III allows for a team's Retrospective Reflection by revisiting initial CRP goals.

Phase I. The first phase of PLCs requires planning and commitment by the team of teachers and resource personnel. Planning starts in early summer before the school year begins. In the initial phase, the team generates broad themes for the coming school year. To illustrate, some themes of the PLCs I have been involved in are: *sustainability, friendship*, and *civilizations*. Once the team comes to a consensus, we proceed to tentatively plan around the theme for the coming school year. To illustrate using the *sustainability* theme as an example, I explain how this initial idea continues throughout the year resulting in subthemes as the year progresses.

The team decided on the *sustainability* theme because we wanted to develop lessons that demonstrated the interdependence of multiple factors in a system necessary for its sustainability and could be easy integrated with other subjects. The *sustainability* theme permitted us to cultivate students' knowledge by building on students' culturally influenced prior knowledge and validating students' prior experiences. As a result of collaborative and careful planning, the theme was general enough that it led to diverse culturally responsive practices throughout the year.

Once the theme was agreed on by the team, the team proceeded to plan out the integration of culturally responsive practices into state and district standards. My district developed quarterly standards curriculum maps (also known as "pacing calendars"). Although curriculum maps provide guidelines and facilitate the planning process, they can restrict planning flexibility given the requirements to work within quarterly time constraints and targeted benchmark assessments designated by the district. Despite these obstacles, strategic planning permitted successful completion of district mandates and the integration of CRP within a school calendar.

Once the various topics relevant to the themes and subject areas were decided, the next step was planning the first quarter of instruction. The team used first-quarter standards and made sure our schedule for the core subjects, as well as other subjects, were integrated into the school-wide master schedule. This step was crucial at the school site since the school adheres to a dual-language curriculum. The scheduling also called for special attention to weekly music, art, physical education, and gardening classes and ongoing events throughout the year.

Phase II. Phase II involves professional development. To maintain the *sustainability* theme, Phase II involved the discussion of familiar, available, and tangible topics such as: aquaponics, gardening, and the community food bank (among others). This method of teaching concrete to more abstract concepts is supported by Piaget's developmental learning model, "Natural progression of learning starts with more concrete information and gradually becomes more abstract" (Sawyer, 2014, p. 11). Phase II then involved the team's discussion of: 1) student acquisition of depth of knowledge of *sustainability* and 2) the extension of the theme to local and world perspectives.

To illustrate Phase II, I will use two school-wide programs as examples. One is *Exito Bilingue* (Smith & Arnot-Hopffer 1998), which is a dual language literacy immersion program that spans first through fifth grade and integrates core English and Language Arts standards, students' culture, and CRP themes. One of the most effective ways of providing high-quality bilingual language arts instruction is through an inclusive program like *Exito Bilingue*. The school's dual-language bilingual program promotes bilingualism and content knowledge, while also integrating CRP. To wit, both literature circles and guided reading address specific strategies that align to standards, but we infused units that build students' cultural knowledge.

To apply Phase II to *Exito Bilingue*, we taught the required state standards and adhered to the dual-language curriculum, but included a unit on farm workers' rights, which allowed students to study the social injustice experienced by farm workers in Delano, California, that lead to the "Delano grape strike", headed by César Chávez. The goal of the unit was to have students understand the meaning of Chávez's work summarized in his quote:"*Preservation of one's own culture does not require contempt or disrespect for other cultures*" (César Chávez E. Foundation, 2012). The team used the text sets developed during Phase I, focused on Latino Civil Rights such as: *Who Was César Chávez, Harvesting Hope, The Crusades of César Chávez: A Biography, César Chávez: Champion for Civil Rights*. Other civil rights books that narrated similar experiences, like Dolores Huerta's struggle for social justice and authors like Francisco Jiménez were also incorporated in the language arts component. An enrichment and extension of this unit was having Dolores Huerta as part of the school's assembly. The César Chávez unit culminated with a neighborhood march in honor of his civil right leadership.

The other example of how we applied Phase II was with the school's aquaponic program[1] system. Aquaponics easily lends itself to science, but we collaborated with parents and community partners to develop lessons. To infuse sustainability, we also explored the Aztec origins of aquaponics (known as *chinampas*) and how they continue to be used today. (*Chinampas* have roots as a system of agricultural farming and sustainability developed by Aztec people. As a sustainable farming system, *chinampas* are still practiced in Xochimilco, Mexico). Depth of knowledge and theme unit extension was further accomplished through classroom dialogue and literature circles.

Although required district and state assessments feel like a time constraint, they can be used as an effective tool along with classroom assessments and students' self-evaluations when planned appropriately. District and formative assessments can play an important role in assessing student skills and content knowledge (and what we, as teachers, need to do for students to achieve mastery); it is also critical to assess students' cultural awareness. This can be accomplished in numerous ways. For example, in the aquaponic unit, students assisted in developing a rubric grading system for the final presentation that was used in addition to evaluation based on a final\final written paper using the RAFT (Role of Writer, Audience, Format, Topic; Santa, Havens, & Vales, 2004).

Phase III. This phase involved "retrospective reflections," which offers a safe place where teachers can voice their diverse perspectives in a respectful, collaborative setting. At this stage, parent concerns and input are greatly valued and integrated. For example, one of the parents requested that the farm workers' rights lesson be extended to learn about the symbolism of United Farm Workers (UFW) flag. Other parents coordinated the César Chávez march and helped with the UFW T-shirt design. This phase provides cohesiveness to Phase I and II by allowing team members and parents the opportunity to analyze and validate the integration of lessons that connect to students' academic, culture, and language experiences. This requires evaluation, critique, and revisions of initial goals.

To illustrate the significance of Phase III, I will elaborate on its application to the aquaponics program. As a self-sustaining closed system, the aquaponics unit made possible the connection between concrete experiences and a more abstract definition of *sustainability*. By the end of the aquaponics project, students understood that the careful maintenance of its different components was essential to its function. Incidentally, as students were grasping the meaning of *sustainability*, one of the components of the aquaponic system malfunctioned during a holiday break and caused the entire system to fail. Thus, the students understood that each of the components were essential in its performance. During PLC, the team took advantage to turn this incident into a lesson and further developed inquiry questions for our students to extend the meaning of *sustainability*. As a result of effective planning and reflection, the aquaponic unit was successfully completed. Students gave a presentation to teachers, parents, district and community members. Afterwards, we celebrated with tilapia tacos, which were made with one of the components of the aquaponic system (i.e., tilapia).

Also during Phase III, the PLC team reflected on *Exito Bilingue's* UFW lesson and examined whether the lesson had covered stated goals. The team then discussed other emerging themes throughout the year in other curricular areas, aligned them with state standards, and discussed them with students. For example, after revising formative assessments on place value, the team noticed that several students were having difficulty understanding the concept of zero as place value. Therefore, to connect the concept of zero in mathematics with CRP, the team developed a Mayan civilization unit and integrated it with social studies by studying the Mayan culture, language, and the possible causes of its downfall. As a result, not only did students develop an understanding of place value, but also a deeper understanding of the sustainability of a culture. Students learned that a sustainable system could be tangible and simple, like aquaponics, but that sustainability also encompasses the different dimensions of an advanced civilization.

Thus, Phase III reflects our commitment to student learning, which required the team's retrospective reflection by evaluating the needs of students to ensure culturally responsive and inclusive practices were taught and that student/parent input was also considered and integrated. This integration contributed to a culture of trust and respect to develop among students, teachers, families, and the community.

Inclusive Schools

The previous planning phases are essential in building and sustaining an inclusive school environment that uses students' *cultural knowledge* and incorporates *cultural content* relevant to students. In this section, I turn to a focus on CRP teacher practices and how I use them to create academic and culture rigor by addressing the growing diversity of students and making them feel that they belong (Theoharis, 2009).

Generally, inclusive practices have been most prominent in exceptional education where traditional *pull-out* has been replaced by *push-in* practices. CRP inclusive schools, however, address the nation's growing diversity with inclusion. Inclusive practices ensure enrichment opportunities to all students (rather than remedial).

The PLC team made it a priority to create an inclusive climate by developing lessons that extended the cultural knowledge of our students. To do so, we first had to learn about our students' *cultural knowledge*—which we accomplished by visiting students' homes. Home visits were consistent with a "Funds of Knowledge" (Moll, Neff, & Gonzalez, 1992) approach, which provides insight into student's lives and practices that establish long-lasting relationships with families and the community. The purpose of home visits was to engage with students and their family, and learn about students' home culture so we could integrate it into classroom lessons. For example, in one of the home visits I conducted, I learned that the Rivera family sold tamales and each member was involved in the tamale-making process. This was a great opportunity to develop a mini tamale lesson and sell the tamales in our fundraiser bake sale. This knowledge was integrated into a mathematics and economics lesson. Although time is always a constraint, we made it common practice to get to know students and their families. The home visits and our Funds of Knowledge approach solidified the trust between school and home.

In addition to home visits, we developed partnerships with the community to promote deeper relationships with families. One example is our collaboration with the Wellness Center. The Wellness Center provided health and educational resources to the neighborhood and extended its services to English classes and childcare. Another example is our collaboration with *Las Nanas* (the grandmothers), a group of retired grandmothers who brought their expertise to the classroom. A member of Las Nanas was a baker originally from Oaxaca, who was also a *papel picado* paper maker, and a respected elder in her community in Mexico. Her experiences and stories made the *Dia de Los Muertos* (The Day of the Dead is a Mexican holiday that commemorates deceased family members and friends) altar celebration possible. Yet another example is our collaboration with the *Promotoras* (a community base of empowered women), who coordinated and assisted school-wide events. On one occasion, one of the *Promotoras* designed and made performance outfits for all grade level students. She was a seamstress and told stories of how nothing should be wasted. She shared with us how her being the eldest of ten children in a small village in Mexico prompted her to be creative and make clothing out of flour sacks. As a result of her lived experiences, she assisted with the rodeo dance outfits and other festivities that are unique to the Tucson community.

Each of these co-collaborators were an essential home-community-school connection who brought their experiences and knowledge into the school.

Another way of providing inclusive practices in the school is through the partnerships and collaboration of institutions that prove essential to the community. One example is the *Semilla Project* that is a collaboration between the University of Arizona and the school district. Semilla graduate students were native Mexican interns selected from various regions of Mexico who attended the university for a year and co-taught in several local schools. Although the Semilla interns shared cultural and linguistic similarities with many students, their experiences opened a new window into our understanding of culture and education in different parts of Mexico.

In essence, building students' cultural knowledge (as well as teachers) builds a school environment of inclusiveness. When the school and community work collaboratively, students, families, and community members feel valued and develop a sense of belonging.

Caring Communities

Creating an inclusive environment builds a system of caring communities where the relationships among students, faculty, and the community are further strengthened as a single unit coming together for a common goal (Furman, 2004). Caring communities extend beyond the school's boundaries and reach out to the community by extending the shared vision and fostering a sense of belonging. Thus, caring communities celebrate differences within the class and school and integrate students' culture and language.

There are two interdependent elements of caring communities: practices within the school community and practices outside the community. It is important to point out that CRP-practicing schools regard classroom practices as an extension of home. In the following section, I first describe caring communities within the school and provide examples. Then, I continue with caring communities outside school and how they are interconnected with school.

Creating a Caring Environment. Setting a caring environment is a critical initial stage in further developing cultural responsiveness. It is imperative to spend additional time at the beginning of the school year and create a positive, caring message with an environment that is welcoming, well managed, and clean. I developed this practice over the course of my teaching career, when I noted that the best school years were those where parents and students stepped into a caring school environment. Therefore, the school should convey a clear message that the school parents' children will be attending is deeply caring. Setting a caring environment begins with registration, involves planning before the school year begins, focuses on the first day of school, and establishes routines.

Registration. During registration, it is crucial to have registration material read because it sets a tone that the school cares enough to have things well organized. It is an atmosphere that welcomes parents and students by having banners, posters, and signs displayed. In addition, the presence of a sufficient number of personnel, all of whom are friendly and well informed, to direct and clarify issues brings tranquility to a potentially stressful and chaotic event. Having other district personnel or organizations present serves to strengthen community relationships. For example, wellness centers, clothing banks, food banks, busing departments, and other service providers can connect families with needed resources.

Before the school year. Another aspect of caring is ensuring that the school is clean, and that hallways, bathrooms, and bulletin boards are decorated with welcoming signs in the families' languages. "Meet your teacher night" is a very popular, successful evening event where parents and students meet the teachers before the first day of school. At this event, friendly and polite personnel reassure that there is a safe and caring environment, and it is useful to consider inviting community partners (whom I have found to be eager to volunteer to help). Although this might seem like additional work, it sets the tone for the creation of a caring community that bridges school and home.

To begin the year with culturally responsive practices, an additional "before the school year" practice is sending a "welcoming post card" that requests the students to bring a current picture, a family picture, and a small special object to share on the first day of school. The post card could also include a brief questionnaire of students' favorite things and any positive experiences at school they would like to share. This demonstrates that we care enough to make a connection prior to the first day of school. It also helps students think about the lessons that will be implemented the first week of school.

The first day of school. The first day of school sets the tone for the entire school year. On the first day of school, greeting parents and care givers is critical to establishing a positive rapport. Teachers should be prepared to have parents stay the first day and participate in one of the icebreaker activities and help with the day's activities. Including parents allows you to not only welcome them, but also make them a part of the school community. This sends a positive message that you have their child's best interest in mind.

It is good to have the room well decorated with a bulletin board that welcomes students and personalizing it as the week progresses to make them feel special—that they belong and that you care. It is especially useful to get to know students' preferred names and use those from that point forward. The classroom walls should reflect students' culture and work and should be rotated throughout the year to keep it updated.

Expectations and routines. Establishing routines and procedures at the beginning of the school year reassures students of classroom expectations and reduces the possibility of classroom management issues. There are numerous "first day" activities that are great icebreakers and serve to begin the classroom expectations. One in particular is the *name activity.* This is a commonly used lesson that requires students to ask their caregivers questions, which can be made into a culturally responsive lesson by extending the activity to include surnames. The purpose of this caring activity is to build a continuous inclusive, caring environment and foster a positive identity for students. Students are asked to share why they were given their particular name, and are asked to share (after doing some research) the meaning of their last name. I begin this lesson with myself as an example and use the book *My Name Is Maria Isabel.* This book narrates the importance of addressing students by their name. I model the lesson by telling students that I was named after a great aunt who died at a young age. Students then create name tents and on the inside write a brief paragraph about the importance of their name. Eventually, the name tents become a collage of other lessons unique to their name. With primary students, I began the lesson by reading Kevin Henke's *Chrysanthemum* and simplified the lesson by having students illustrate and write a brief passage about themselves. I continue the lesson with their last name and start a classroom family tree. Throughout the year, students add important aspects about themselves on the classroom family tree. The family tree is a reminder to students that they belong in the class and the class is a caring community. Initially, the *name activity* is not an in-depth lesson but a pre-cursor to have students start thinking about future projects. I place the artifact from the *name activity* lesson along on the bulletin board with students' photos. Students can bring a photo of their choosing—but with today's technology, we can easily take students' pictures and have them printed as well.

Another CRP practice that demonstrates a caring community is "caring buckets." This activity may be known by many different names, but it has particular significance to me because the name and idea for "caring buckets" came from one of my students. This student expressed her interest in starting a "caring bucket" because students in the class stood up for her when others were teasing her during recess. She expressed that she was happy to have friends in the class that cared for her feelings. Therefore, the purpose of the "caring bucket" was to acknowledge an individual for a caring act, for instance, an act of kindness, a "thank you," or a "praise." At the end of the day, the kindness notes are read out loud with student consent. The "caring buckets" have been a great caring activity that add to the district's implementation of Positive Behavior Intervention and Support and Restorative Practices. Caring buckets, however, have to be very carefully planned, modeled, and practiced because *all students* need to be recognized for their efforts. Throughout the year, students have to be carefully monitored and reminded of its purpose.

The caring community element is important because it establishes ties between school and homes and values parents as co-collaborators. There are many traditional practices (open house and parent–teacher conferences) that are routine and often done to simply comply with requirements. They all offer, however, an opportunity to build, strengthen, and sustain connections with students and their families.

Conclusion

The previous sections (shared leadership, inclusive classrooms, and caring communities) are essential practices to a school's sustainability. A school's sustainability, however, also depends on the loyalty to its mission, despite waves of policies, mandated standards, and decreasing funding. Culturally responsive schools effectively manage these pressures by implementing high-quality instruction; balancing assessments in today's high-stakes testing environment; and valuing students' culture and language.

Today's increasingly diverse schools require the integration of culturally responsive practices (shared leadership, inclusive schools, caring communities, and sustainable systems) to counterbalance compounding policies and high-stakes testing. Therefore, skillful planning, implementation, and integration of CRP are imperative for schools to address the biases that are still part of the American consciousness.

As an educator, I am aware that administrative support, time, and collaborative planning can be detouring factors. It is not simple to implement CRP. Therefore, I encourage you to start by trying one element (i.e., shared leadership, inclusive schools, caring communities, sustainable systems) at a time and persevering if it's not successful. For example, start by practicing it in your own classroom. If your curriculum is scripted, find different ways of integrating it to assignments or events. Reflect for a moment. If implementing CRP is part of your teaching philosophy and your school or district does not support it, consider transferring to a school that does. Teaching is a calling and a life-long commitment.

Note

1   Aquaponics is a system that combines the raising of aquatic animals with the cultivation of plants in water.

References

Alvarez-Jasso v. Tucson Unified School District, Case No. 4:86–cv–00469–ACM (1994).

Capper, C. A, & Frattura, E. M. (2009). *Meeting the needs of students of all abilities*. Thousand Oaks, CA: Corwin Press.

César E. Chávez Foundation. (2012). Retrieved from: http://chavezfoundation.org.

Darder, A. (2012). *Culture and power in the classroom: Educational foundation for the schooling of bicultural students*. Boulder, CO: Paradigm Publishers.

Day, C. (2009). Building and sustaining successful principalship in England: The importance of trust. *Journal of Educational Administration, 47*(6), 719–730.

Dufour, R., DuFour, R., & Eaker, R. (Eds.) (2005). On common ground: The power of professional learning communities. Bloomington, IN: Solution Tree Press.

Furman, G. C. (2004). The ethic of community. *Journal of Educational Administration. 42*(2), 215–235.

Gay, G. (2010). *Culturally responsive teaching: Theory, research, and practice*. New York. NY: Teachers College Press.

Ladson-Billings, G. (2004). Landing on the wrong note: The price we paid for Brown. *Educational Researcher, 33*, 3–13.

Mendoza v. Tucson Unified School District, 623 F .2d 1338 (1980).

Moll, L. C., Amanti, C., Neff, D., & Gonzalez., N. (1992). Funds of knowledge for teaching: Using a qualitative approach to connect homes and classrooms. *Theory into Practice, 31*(2), 141.

No Child Left Behind Act of 2001, P.L. 107–110, 20 U.S.C. § 6319 (2002).

Portin, B. S., Knapp, M.S., Dareff, S., Feldman, S., Russell, F. A., Samuelson, C., & Ling Yeh, T. (2009). *Leadership for learning improvement in urban schools.* New York: The Wallace Foundation.

Race to the Top: Executive summary. (2009). Washington DC: US Department of Education. Retrieved at https://www2.ed.gov/programs/racetothetop/executive-summary.pdf.

Reeves, D. (2005). Putting it all together: Standards, assessments, and accountability in successful professional learning communities. In R. DuFour, R. Eaker, & R. DuFour (Eds.), *On common ground: The power of professional learning communities* (pp. 45–63). Bloomington, IN: Solution Tree Press.

Santa, C., Havens, L., & Valdes, B. (2004). *Project CRISS: Creating independence through student owned strategies.* Dubuque, IA: Kendall Hunt.

Sawyer, R. K. (2014). *The Cambridge handbook of the learning sciences.* New York, NY: Cambridge University Press.

Short, K. G. (1999). The search for "balance" in a literature-rich classroom. *Theory into Practice, 38,* 130–137.

Smith, P. H., & Arnot-Hopffer, E. (1998). Exito Bilingue: Promoting Spanish literacy in a dual language immersion program. *Bilingual Research Journal, 22*(2–4), 261–277.

Theoharis, G. (2009). *The school leaders our children deserve.* New York, NY: Teachers College Press.

10

ON BECOMING HUMAN IN WHITE SKIN

Julie Elvick

Although I do not feel responsible for the color of my skin, I must begin by acknowledging the myriad ways that fact has provided me with privileges not afforded to others all of my life. As an educator of elementary-aged children in schools that predominantly serve children and families of color, it is imperative that I fight to de-center whiteness in all that I do. It is within this context that I share my testimony that it is in fact possible to become a White educator who is conscious and effective.

Ethnic Affirmation

My "becoming human" story begins with my own ethnic affirmation. During my childhood, I enjoyed being raised in a family wherein the majority of my ancestry is rooted in Scandinavia (specifically Norway and Sweden). My sister and I were born in Tucson, Arizona, but my parents are Arizona transplants, born and raised in Minnesota. The time we spent visiting with extended family each summer always incorporated many aspects of Scandinavian culture, including food, music, stories, and humor. I learned from humble White folks who knew and embraced the culture of their recently emigrated grandparents. Their commitment to sharing their culture caused me to know and to become proud of my roots. The adults in my family worked deliberately to instill familiarity with our ethnic heritage; this allowed me to claim an individual identity with a strong cultural component that continues to develop, and upon which I stand confidently today. I am happy to say that these teachings and traditions mean so much to me (as well as my cousins), that we are now working diligently to provide opportunities for our own children to develop an identity that goes beyond being "White." Learning about my history was a priceless gift from my parents and grandparents. I credit having this knowledge of self for allowing me to develop a sense of confidence, a kind of "rootedness" that I believe has led me to appreciate and find interesting people of backgrounds unlike my own.

That said, there is more to this "becoming human" story than just having a strong sense of my ethnicity. Members of my extended family (cousins, aunts, and uncles), all of whom live in the Northwestern United States (Montana, Wyoming, and Nebraska), express racist attitudes toward people of color and are biased against LGBTQIA[1]. Therefore, though I acknowledge and appreciate the pride my cousins and I share in knowing the cultural practices of our ancestors, I am quite grateful to have been raised in an ethnically and otherwise diverse community like Tucson. This stark difference between me and both my immediate and extended family members who still live in more isolated, segregated communities has caused me to analyze more deeply the reasons I love and embrace people.

Upon reflection, another important influence I believe has helped to shape me and the way I interact with others, including the children and families with whom I work today, is my own educational journey. I attribute the continuation of a developing appreciation of "otherness" to my having attended ethnically and economically diverse schools. I grew up in South-Central Tucson, but moved to the far West side of town at the end of fourth grade. From late elementary school and through high school, I attended schools in the Tucson Unified School District (TUSD) that were diverse both in terms of socioeconomic status and race/ethnicity. Notably, the racial/ethnic makeup of the public schools I attended were much more diverse at the time, when the desegregation order detailed in Chapter 2 was relatively new, than those same schools in this district today. Although I don't think I realized it at the time, in retrospect, spending my formative years with people of different cultural identities and languages was my "normal"; the experience allowed me to learn about, from, and with people who tend to be "the other."

Upon finishing high school in the late 1980s, I decided I would study to become a teacher and attended the University of Arizona. As I began coursework for my major in the College of Education, I decided to make Spanish my minor area of study and worked to become a bilingually certified elementary teacher. At that time, teaching positions in Tucson were not plentiful; I realized that because of the demographics of our community it was likely that I would work with bilingual and Spanish-speaking families. Being bilingual in English and Spanish, then, would be an asset for me in the classroom and would make me better qualified.

In the fall of 1990, I met my first class of second graders in a school that was on the West side of Tucson where I had been educated. Although having the ability to communicate in two languages allowed me to forge more intimate, meaningful relationships with the children and families with whom I was working, I quickly realized that being bilingual did not make me bicultural. It was immediately apparent to me that what I had gleaned about being from a culture other than "White" in my 20 years of living in this Tucson community had been superficial, at best. I think because I had established a "firm footing" of knowing myself and spending my early life living amongst people who enriched my life with experiences that were different from my own, I naturally began to notice that I was lacking a depth of knowing that was limiting the quality of the relationships I was able to build. I knew I needed to learn more, but how? I was a seeker of knowledge from the beginning of my teaching career.

Continuing the Journey

After the first few years as a practicing classroom teacher, I decided to go back to the University of Arizona to pursue a master's degree in Language, Reading, and Culture. During my three years of study, I was exposed to several asset-based pedagogies, but most extensively in Funds of Knowledge (FoK). The central et of FoK is the importance of cultivating an understanding of the richness and competence of families, as well as inquiry-based instruction that centers on the student, including her/his interests and passions, as a focus for instruction.

During my graduate studies, I became a Fellow of the Southern Arizona Writing Project (SAWP), completing the intensive six-week summer institute as part of my graduate coursework. The SAWP institute focuses on strength-based and collaborative structures to enhance the quality of the writing experience. I also took coursework in Literature Study and Miscue Analysis with Dr. Kathy Short and Dr. Yetta and Ken Goodman, respectively. The various courses helped me develop a view of learners through asset-oriented lenses, which has allowed me to improve my ability to support the emergence of young critical beings— individuals who understand the world around them and how they can play active roles—with strong academic identities.

With a Master's degree under my belt, I felt slightly better prepared to be a teacher. Through my coursework, I had gained a deeper understanding of creative ways to facilitate learning and had begun to see families as partners in educating children. The fact remained, however, that I was still a White teacher working with children and families, the majority of whom claimed Mexican and/or Indigenous roots. I knew that if I was to be effective at teaching, I needed to understand more about their lives: their cultures, traditions, and heritage.

Enter Mexican American Studies

By the fall of 2013, my school district had designated the Mexican American Studies (MAS) and African American Studies (AAS) departments charged with creating curricula that presents U.S. history and government from non-Eurocentric perspectives, as well as to provide supports—such as academic tutors—so that children from historically marginalized communities (e.g., Pan-Asian, Native American, African American, and Mexican American) would have more equitable access to education in our public school settings. Amidst my own feelings of inadequacy, I reached out to the MAS department, which consisted of a group of dynamic educators committed to improving the experience of schooling for Mexican American students (students the department referred to as Xicanx). I began attending the annual summer institutes provided by the MAS department, where I learned from young activist-scholars from around the country (as well as other parts of the world) about topics such as the history of the Chicano Movement; the Nahui Ollin, which provides the basis for the Aztec philosophy; the historical influences of colonization in the United States; the school-to-prison pipeline; eco-justice; as well as community activism and organizing.

At the conclusion of each summer institute, MAS staff and educators invited attendees to request department educators to visit their classrooms to conduct guest lessons. Each year, we were also provided with units of lessons created by the various MAS educators that reflected not only the aforementioned topics, but also many others that reflected issues and knowledge that was central to Xicanx students' lives. It was the perfect opportunity for me to receive the mentorship I had been seeking.

Thus, began a collaboration that involved TUSD's renowned MAS program that would ultimately span the better part of my career. Over this time, I have had the opportunity to be in consistent dialogue with and co-teach units on topics such as:

1. "I am from": Participants attended a series of four evening workshops to write poems wherein individuals were prompted to describe a variety of aspects of culture as viewed through their personal lenses.
2. Classroom studies centered on content related to the significance of the day symbols, months, and other aspects of the Aztec calendar.
3. Student-authored amoxtlis (books) that were developed from a series of introspective activities where children identified strengths and wrote about their individual identities centered around reflection and self-love.
4. Student-conducted media critiques: Groups of students analyzed various media sources in terms of the degree to which music, movies, magazines, video games billboards, and television helped to normalize and perpetuate particular beliefs and stereotypes about historically minoritized groups. These activities were engaging for all children, to say the least. It became evident that studying issues of self and social justice appeals to young people. As was the case in my own life, opportunities to develop self-knowledge empowers you to develop knowledge of others. With this knowledge, we can act from a place of confidence to transform that which is harmful.

In my collaboration and learning with MAS, I incorporated five *Nahuatillis* (Guiding Principles) that are essential elements of Indigenous philosophy, which became threads in the fabric that is my teaching pedagogy. They are:

- *Tlahtocan*—Sharing our sacred words.
- *Nemachtilli*—The natural spirit of learning.

- *Nehuan ti nehuan*—I am you are I.
- *Tlanelhualtilztili*—Seeking truth for firmly-rooted stability.
- *Tloque Nahuaque*—Close and together like a hand.

My journey of self-reflection, which includes the examples I have described here so far, reflect one of the five Nahuatilli: *Tlahnelhualtiliztli*, which is seeking truth for firmly rooted stability. Coming to know my Scandinavian roots exemplifies the importance this process played in my own life. In my own classroom, our fifth-grade learning community is *calli*—the word for *home* in the Nahuatl language. *Calli* represents much more than a physical structure; it can be your "house of thoughts," your physical body, and, in the case of our school, it can be a refuge—a safe place where students (and teachers) can reveal their true self. Our morning ritual each day is to meet as a community in a circle, a *tlahtocan*, to share news, thoughts, observations, and so on. It is an intimate gathering of sometimes 30 human beings. Not everyone chooses to share every day, but we protect the first 20 minutes of the morning for this exchange of energy and truth. This is one space in which we are able to humanize one another while cultivating careful listening skills, as well as forging connections and understanding by building empathy and compassion for our fellow *calli*-mates.

The other *Nahuatillis* are infused not only into *tlahtocan*, but also throughout the rest of each day. Included are *nehuan ti nehuan* (I am you are I), which is the epitome of compassion. If I can see myself in you and you can see yourself in me—our strengths, our flaws, our dreams—you and I will learn to be patient with and understand one another. *Tloque nahuaque* supports collaborations that happen during the course of our learning day. In our learning community, this is the idea that we are often smarter together, offering and accepting from one another "loans of knowledge" based on our individual areas of strength and experience. The spirit of learning represented by *nemachtilli* is expressed in our *calli* whenever we read, write, listen, speak, and intuit that which is relevant in our lives outside of school. In other words, the natural spirit of learning infuses students' whole lives into the classroom.

In addition to the five guiding principles, MAS taught me to use the four *Tezcatlipocas* of the *Nahui Ollin* as a framework for praxis and growth. *Tezcatlipoca* (the smoky mirror) represents reflection and introspection; *Xipe Totec* (the shedding of our skin) represents transformation; *Quetzalcoatl* (beautiful knowledge) represents wisdom; and *Huitzilopochtli* (hummingbird-to-the-left) represents our will. Throughout the course of any given day, there are opportunities to reflect, transform, and act, all the while sprinkling in references to characteristics of the 20 day symbols from the calendar. A typical example might be to hear a *calli*-mate express, "That was very *cuetzpalli*, or *tochtli*, or *itzquintli* of you!" Through daily reading of the *Tonalmachoitl* symbol descriptions, the children quickly learn that this reference to *cuetzpalli* means that someone noticed you nurturing someone else, emotionally, socially, and/or academically. Similarly, *tochtli* (rabbit) symbolizes independence with the tendency of caring and providing for others. A reference to *itzquintli* recognizes your loyalty and willingness to stand with a *calli*-mate, to be an accomplice in her/his academic, social, and/or emotional growth.

At this point in my career, I believe I have internalized the varied learning experiences I sought out, which are reflected in my classroom. Not only do I incorporate the cultures of the children and families into my instruction, but I have also adopted some of the practices, values, and beliefs into my own world view. My son is bi-racial. His father, who died three years ago when Benjamin was 11 years old, was Mexican American. The fact that I have come to a strong understanding of my own European-American heritage and have had the aforementioned ongoing opportunities to learn about Mexican/Mexica cultures is useful in that this knowledge of self and "other" allows me to be a more knowledgeable guide as Benjamín Andrés Mejía learns to embrace his complex ethnicity moving toward becoming a bicultural human being.

Yet Another Influence

I consider myself a life-long learner. As such, despite the rich and varied learning opportunities I have engaged in throughout my career, I continue to deepen my understanding of asset-based practices. Accordingly, I would like to briefly describe another asset-oriented approach that I have had the opportunity to study most recently. Over the past seven years at my current elementary school, we have been studying the Reggio-Emilia approach to teaching and learning. Reggio-Emilia is a city in Italy that was all but destroyed during World War II. The adults in the community decided that rather than admit defeat, they would rebuild their city, brick by brick, in the name of children who, for many of us—educators or not—represent all that is hopeful about the future of human kind.

The Reggio-Emilia approach to teaching and learning is centered on the child—each and every child—as the competent and capable protagonist of her/ his learning. Educators inspired by the Reggio-Emilia approach consider themselves equal partners with families in the process of educating all of our children. The founder of the approach, Loris Malaguzzi, wrote extensively about the countless ways children have to learn about the world, as beautifully articulated in his poem, "The Hundred Languages of Children."

In studying this approach with local experts, which included traveling to experience other Reggio-Emilia inspired public elementary schools (e.g., the Opal School inside Portland, Oregon's Children's Museum) as well as learning from consultants traveling to Tucson from Chicago (Karen Haigh), Stockholm (Gunilla Dahlberg), and Reggio-Emilia (Lella Gandini), I have found yet another source of reinforcement for my beliefs and values about what it means to be a human being.

One of the strongest elements of this approach is the opportunity for all children to have access to myriad languages and materials with which to observe and explore the world—to theorize and then test those theories about themselves in relation to the whats and hows and whys of life. Our school, situated in the city of South Tucson, a one-square mile city-within-a-city, serves the families of 225 children, pre-school through 5th grade, the majority of whom claim Mexican, Mexican American, and Indigenous roots. Nearly all of our families are experiencing poverty—98% of our children qualify for free breakfast and lunch under federal guidelines. At Ochoa Community School, we have partnered with the Tucson Children's Project over the past six years, co-directed by Mimi Grey and Teresa Acevedo, to bring exceptional opportunities for young learners to explore identity. The brief descriptions that follow are meant to provide a glimpse into Ochoa's studios—three unique spaces designed by three dynamic educators, each of whom brings incredible skill and expertise to the *atelier* experience.

One studio educator, or *atelierista* as they are known in Reggio-Emilia, is a retired systems engineer. In her work with Ochoa children, Jane Schwartz provides opportunities for computer coding and engineering. Recently, she was awarded a grant with which to purchase Lego Robotics software, which was being installed on our 100 laptop computers for use by all Ochoa children by the Fall of 2017.

We also boast an Experimental Rhythm and Beats studio, directed by a talented percussionist and an innovator, Alfredo "Quiahuitl" Emiliano Villegas (Mr. Q, for short). This studio, filled with all recycled materials, offers learners, ages four through eleven, a plethora of opportunities to experience sound. In his recent "The Hundred Languages of Sound" exhibit at a local gallery, Mr. Q displayed photographs and regalia depicting young explorers theory making and testing within his studio space.

Our third studio, the Materials studio, is facilitated by Ruth Marblestone. The studio offers visual and tactile experiences to Ochoa children as possible two- and three-dimensional ways of knowing themselves and their relationship to others and the natural world. Although at first glance, visitors may feel as though they have entered an art studio, the Materials studio in the Reggio-Emilia tradition has a very different intent. In this studio, young learners are offered clay, wire, light, sand, and countless other materials meant to provoke interest in and study of their own identities, as well as to undertake studies of subjects of their own interests.

In short, at Ochoa Community School, in the resilient spirit of the resolute parents of the demolished city of Reggio-Emilia, we are committed to being accomplices in the struggle with the families and children of this neighborhood. With continuing support from Tucson Children's Project, we strive to provide the richest, most varied opportunities for our children to read and write in the broadest, most relevant sense: focusing on themselves and their world.

Given that I have shared my educational journey and how it has influenced my classroom practice, I would like to close with a reflection about the impact of Gunilla Dahlberg's book *Ethics and Politics in Early Childhood Education*. In particular, Chapter 3 ("What Ethics?") has had an instrumental role in shaping my ability to identify the essential parts of my "becoming human" story. So much of her synthesis of post-modern scholars' thought around "an ethics of care" resonates for me. I attribute much of the aforementioned ways in which my identity and world view have been and continue to be shaped to the ideas presented in that chapter. Specifically, in the "Connections" section of the chapter, Dahlberg identifies three themes that emerge from her study of this body of thought. The first theme is *responsibility as care or responsiveness to "other,"* an idea which places each one of us at the center in relation to all other people, as well as all other life, including the natural environment. The second theme, with which I deeply identify, is *responsibility as respect for "other,"* described as a non-smothering care for others, an act of listening with the intention of maintaining space for difference to unfold in all its particularity. The third theme that Dahlberg recognizes in her synthesis of post-modern schools of thought is the concept of a "rejection of calculative and rational thinking in relations with the other," meaning that it is not a "balancing up" nor an "I versus the other" relationship that we seek to fulfill our lives. If one ascribes to rejection of this belief, the individual acts from a place of agency: we have an urge to care, which has no expectation of reciprocation. To me, this means love.

Note

1   An abbreviation for Lesbian, Gay, Bisexual, Transgender, Queer, Intersex, and Asexual communities.

11
CHICANISMO AND CARNALISMO

An Asset-Based Curriculum and Pedagogy

Alexandro Salomón Escamilla

> Brotherhood unites us, and love for our brothers makes us a people whose time has come and whose struggles against the foreigner "gabacho" who exploits our riches and destroys our culture. With our heart in our hands and our hands in the soil, we declare the independence of our mestizo nation. We are a bronze people with a bronze culture. Before the world, before all of North American, before all of our brothers in the bronze continent, we are a nation, we are a union of free pueblos, we are Aztlan.
>
> *Alurista El Plan Espiritual de Aztlan 1969*
> *Chicano Youth Liberation Conference*

> You have to understand that in order to make progress, in order to gain justice from any society, you have to take a stand. So when we talk about organizing people ... organizing Chicanos ... La Raza ... we have to know about the history of our people ... what our contributions were to this area and this continent. We aren't just Chicanos, a minority in the United States of America; we are Chicanos and Latinos who are a majority of Aztlán, of Mexico, Central America and South America.
>
> *Rodolfo "Corky" Gonzales Bicentennial*
> *Speech Colorado Springs, CO*

The Chicano Movement of the 1960s and 1970s left a great legacy for the Mexican American community because it re-established a tradition of struggle for social justice and consciousness, but its lessons are often forgotten or ignored by educators who work with Xicano/Raza youth. *Chicanismo* and *carnalismo* were the concepts that brought masses of Xicano/Raza together in the fight against oppression. In this chapter, I argue that if we are serious about ending the achievement disparities for Xicano/Raza students, then we must implement a curriculum that is based on *Chicanismo* and a pedagogy that emphasizes *carnalismo*.

During the Chicano Movement, *Chicanismo* and *carnalismo* provided Corky Gonzales and other leaders with the foundation for a philosophy that called for the liberation of *Aztlan*. To many Xican@s this simply meant that our community would move forward and overcome various forces of oppression by coming together collectively. These two concepts became the major pillars of the Chicano Movement, inspiring a renaissance of activism, art, and literature in the Chicano community that continues to thrive across the United States and the world. Even today in *barrios* (neighborhoods) across this nation, these concepts are alive and well and help to drive cultural affirmation, resistance, activism, and transformation in our communities. *Chicanismo* is the idea that as Mexican/Xicano/Raza people we must be proud of the *raices* (roots) that make us who we are and that it is our responsibility to not only be knowledgeable of our history and culture, but also to actively engage in the struggle/movement for the self-determination and liberation of our people. Additionally, it is the idea that through the process of engaging in this struggle we will grow into strong and confident human beings. *Carnalismo* is the power behind *Chicanismo*, for only through unity (brother/sisterhood) can Raza expect to have any power like the MEChA (Movimiento Estudiantil Chicano de Aztlan) *dicho* (saying) "*la union hace la fuerza*" (through unity there is strength). It is the belief that we must build unity among our Raza and work to create peace and understanding in our community. It is also the idea that as Xican@s, we can only have strength when we are unified and determined to stand up for one another in the fight for social justice and critical consciousness. Throughout my career as an educator, I have worked to merge these two concepts into an asset-based pedagogy and curriculum that successfully transforms students into intellectual warriors with strong cultural and academic identities.

As a Chicano youth in the 1990s, I have first-hand knowledge of the potential academic transformation that exposure to Chicano history and literature can have on a young man who is struggling to find purpose in his education. During my freshman year at Centaurus High School in Lafayette, Colorado, I was barely passing my classes, earning a 1.6 GPA and lacking any motivation to improve. It didn't matter that both of my parents had earned doctorates; I didn't see myself in the curriculum, so I didn't really care to put forth much of an effort. Like *I Am Joaquin*,[1] I was "lost in a world of confusion, caught up in the whirl of a gringo society," the result being that like many of my Chicano and Chicana peers I was trapped in a state of mediocrity like the poem says so eloquently, "I shed a tear of anguish as I see my children disappear behind the shroud of mediocrity never to look back to remember me" (Esquibel, 2001). It wasn't until the spirit of *Chicanismo* and *carnalismo* hit me like a lightning bolt when I attended the 1992 La Raza Male Youth Leadership Conference at Denver's Auraria Campus. During the general assembly, I remember the electric feeling I had as I joined the crowd of about 1,000 Xicano youth as we chanted *gritos* of "Chicano Power!" and

"*Que Viva la Raza!*" (long live the people). I especially remember the Chicano Movement workshop I attended, which was taught by Corky Gonzales' son-in-law, Arturo "Bones" Rodriguez, who encouraged me to read books like *Occupied America* by Rodolfo Acuña and would later connect me to various activities that would expand my knowledge and understanding of *Chicanismo* and *carnalismo*. It was a very empowering experience that truly had a transformative impact on my life because I left the conference with a new determination to not only read about Chicano history and culture and become a leader in my school and community, but I was also committed to excelling in my classes and pursuing higher education.

Thanks to my newfound purpose, I improved my reading and writing skills because my interests now extended beyond the classroom walls—eventually earning me admission into the University of Arizona (UA), where I received my Bachelor's degree in Education. It is because of this experience during my youth that throughout my time in the college of education at the UA and my career as a teacher in Tucson Unified School District (TUSD), I felt obligated to implement a teaching pedagogy and curriculum that had a heavy focus and emphasis on *Chicanismo* and *carnalismo*. Thus, I saw my role as a teacher as serving the overall goals of the Chicano movement, which instilled within me a love and passion for learning and education. Naturally, it seemed that the best way to motivate my students, who were/are for the most part Xican@ and Raza youth, was through the use of materials that highlighted their historical and cultural legacy. I engaged them in academic activities and interactions that reflected and utilized their Xicano/Raza cultural capital as an asset that could help strengthen their academic development. This emphasis on *Chicanismo* and *carnalismo* helped me to develop a *barrio* pedagogy that was responsive to Xicano/Raza culture and a curriculum that was relevant to the historical experiences of Xicano/Raza people in the United States. Consequently, it was because of this focus that my students from *Barrio Chicano* who attended my Chicano Studies classes at Wakefield Middle School in South Tucson, Arizona (or in the spirit of *Chicanismo: La Tusa, Ariza y que!*), typically made great strides in their reading, writing, and math scores.

Chicanismo and Carnalismo: The Foundation of My Success as a Teacher

Reflecting on my career before I was recruited to the Mexican American/Raza Studies Department (MARSD) in TUSD, I remember teaching a 7th Grade guided reading class, which was a four-hour block in which the students rotated from station to station. At one table, I would work one-on-one with a small group of students as we read from various texts that ranged from Xicano history and literature, issues of social justice, and even comic books like Calvin and Hobbes. At other tables, students worked independently on everything from social studies and current events to independent reading and writing activities. It was a new program that was enthusiastically spearheaded by our principal, Maria Patterson, who firmly believed that if the students of Wakefield could improve their reading skills, they would have a chance to graduate from Pueblo High School. Wakefield was about 99% Xicano/a, Mexicano/a, Tohono O'odham and Yaqui and had the highest number of students on free or reduced lunch in the district. By the second semester, my students were showing incredible growth in reading: 92% improved by at least one grade level and 62% improved by at least two grade levels. The curriculum specialist visited me during my planning period one day to find out what exactly I had done to inspire these results (inquiring to find out if it was possibly due to district training). For the first time in my career, I had concrete evidence that demonstrated the positive outcomes of pedagogy, curriculum, and instruction based on *Chicanismo* and *carnalismo*. Deep down I always knew, even when I was an undergraduate, that exposure to Xicano culture and history would have a positive impact on Xican@ youth because of the impact it had in my own educational life. I explained to her that my students' improvement in reading was probably a result of two factors: 1) the implementation of materials that reflected Xicano/a history and culture and emphasized social justice, and 2) we created a classroom environment that was more like a *familia* (family) based on mutual love and respect for one another.

As a project specialist for TUSD's MARSD, I joined a team of colleagues that firmly believed in an asset-based approach. It was a small but diverse group of teachers. Although we each had different perspectives on how to implement Mexican American/Raza Studies and the topics on which to focus, we all agreed that the foundation must be on creating academic safe spaces for Xicano/Raza students based on curriculum that is culturally relevant to the history and literature of the Xicano/a community. TUSD's MARSD students were able to shatter the achievement gap (aka the opportunity gap) because they were taught to embrace their culture and history and utilize it as an asset in their life. Our students were able to graduate from high school and matriculate into college at higher rates because of our asset-based pedagogy and curriculum that are consistent with the ideas of *Chicanismo* and *carnalismo*, concepts that have historical roots in *barrios* across *Aztlan* (ancient homeland of the Aztecs, considered by Xican@s to be anywhere in the U.S. where Xican@s reside). These concepts were born out of the *pachucada* (zoot suiter lifestyle) of the 1940s in which Xican@ youth developed a rebel culture through the development of language (*Caló*) and a way of dress (the *pachuco/cholo* style) that represented the experiences of both sides of the U.S.-Mexico border. They blossomed during the Chicano Movement of the 1960s and 1970s with the development of a scholarly framework and ideology based on the collective *gritos* (demands) of Chicano and Chicana activists from all over the country. They are, however, undying values that continue to have relevancy in our communities, often re-emerging in various forms from time to time.

Establishing Carnalismo in the Classroom

Any committed teacher knows that before they can present their content to students, whether calculus or history, they must first establish community with and amongst his or her students. Before we can spark learning and growth in our students, we have to show them that we have love for them and that we value the families and communities that they come from. Our students must understand that we "have their back" and will support them as they strive to accomplish their goals so that they can pursue their hopes and dreams. As a Xicano, I have always understood this idea to be *carnalismo*—a term that derives from carnal/a, literally meaning "my blood" but used by many Mexican people to refer to a brother/sister, or close friend (homeboy/girl). This can manifest itself in many ways including being friendly to someone, helping a neighbor or friend with something or simply offering support to someone in need. Many Xicano@s claim that the word homeboy/girl has ancestral significance originating from the Nahuatl peoples of ancient Anahuac and was also used by revolutionary leader Emiliano Zapata, who referred to his closest friends as *chantlaca* (men from my home) and *chancihuatl* (women from my home). Many teachers may hesitate to use the word *homie* or even *friend* when describing their students, but as a teacher, I see myself as the "big homie" in the classroom there to help the "little homies" find meaning and purpose in their education and life. As a Xicano teacher, I have relied on the concept of *carnalismo* to develop a teaching pedagogy that is based on traditions of friendship and sister/brotherhood that originate in *barrios* across the United States, particularly in West and South Tucson. Due to the cultural connection to *carnalismo*, especially in *barrio* schools of Tucson, it is worthwhile to create a standard of behavior that is familiar to students and is based on a system of mutual respect and love between and among teachers and students.

The first step in establishing a teaching pedagogy based on *carnalismo* is to throw the traditional classroom rulebook in the *basura* (trash). Instead of focusing on rules and regulations, I promoted guidelines that encouraged students to strive for unity and understanding. Borrowing from my colleague and *carnal* Dr. Curtis Acosta, I have my students recite the words of a poem by Luis Valdez called *In Lak 'ech*. The poem is based on an ancient Maya philosophy known as *In Lak 'ech*, literally meaning "you are the other me." Similar to the golden rule, it is a philosophy that seeks to create peace and understanding between people.

> Tú eres mi otro yo/ You are my other me.
> Si te hago daño a ti/ If I do harm to you,
> Me hago daño a mí mismo/ I do harm to myself;
> Si te amo y respeto/ If I love and respect you,
> Me amo y respeto yo/ I love and respect myself.
>
> *(Valdez, 1971)*

Next students recite an interpretation of the Nahuatl concepts known as the *Nahui Ollin* created by Dr. Curtis Acosta and his Chicano Lit students at Tucson High in 2009.

Tezkatlipoka: self-reflection. Smoking mirror. We must vigorously search within ourselves, by silencing the distractions and obstacles in our lives, in order to be warriors for our gente and justice. Quetzalkoatl: precious and beautiful knowledge. Gaining perspective on events and experiences that our ancestors endured, allows us to become more fully realized human beings. We must listen to each other and our elders with humility and love in order to hear the Indigenous wisdom in our hearts. Huitzilopochtli: the will to act. As we grow in consciousness, we must be willing to act with a revolutionary spirit that is positive, progressive and creative. Xipe Totek: transformation. Our source of strength that allows us to transform and renew. We must have the strength to shed the old, which may hinder us, while embracing and accepting our new consciousness in order to transform the world.

(Escamilla, 2011)

The *Nahui Ollin* is based on the central space of the Aztec calendar representing the "four movements" and each have philosophical, physical, spatial, and scientific meanings. Within the *Nahui Ollin* are the four key components of *Tezcatlipoca, Quetzalcoatl, Huitzilopochtli, and Xipe Totec.*

Tezcatlipoca. This process begins with the concept of *Tezcatlipoca*, which literally means "the smoking mirror" but metaphorically represents memory and self-reflection of the past. Xicano Nation elder, community/Indigenous/human rights activist, and practitioner of the *Nahuatl* tradition explains the concept of *Tezcatlipoca* as

[a] reflection, a moment of reconciliation of the past with the possibilities of the future–not a vision of life but an awareness of the shadow that is the smoke of light's passing. It is the smoking mirror into which the individual, the family, the clan, the barrio, the tribe and the nation must gaze to acquire a history that calls for liberation.

(as cited in Arce, 2016, p. 32)

It is a critical reflection that leads to individual and collective liberation because it encourages Xican@ youth to embrace and accept their communal, familial, and community histories and acts as a foundation for which to build their own futures (Arce, 2016).

Quetzalcoatl. The next step in this process is *Quetzalcoatl*, a concept meaning precious/beautiful knowledge emphasizing the importance of scholarship and education in life. According to Acosta:

From the memory of our identity, the knowledge of our collective history we draw the perspective that draws us to the contemporary reality. From this orientation we achieve stability, a direction found in time tested precepts that allows our awareness and knowledge of the surrounding environment to develop. This awareness and knowledge merge to form the "conciencia" of a mature human being...

(as cited in Arce, 2016, p. 33)

This is important because it sends the message that learning and education are not only about the grade one earns but about the knowledge and awareness that one gains. Students are taught that they must have an understanding of their collective historical memory with a connection to the contemporary realities.

Huitzilopochtli. The next part of this philosophy poses that the processes of self-reflection (*Tezcatlipoca*) and creating knowledge and awareness (*Quetzalcoatl*) are inadequate unless they are utilized through direct action on the part of the individual, family, and community. Tupac Acosta states that *Huitzilopochtli* is

La voluntad. Will. The Warrior spirit born with the first breath taken by each newborn infant in the realization that this human life we are blessed with is a struggle requiring physical effort for survival. The exertion of this life sustaining effort evolves into a discipline, a means of maximizing the energy resources available at the human command which in order to have their full effect must be synchronized with the natural cycles ...

(as cited in Arce, 2016, p. 34)

In *Nahuatl, Huitzilopochtli* literally means "the humming bird to the left." It is a reference to the heart being on the left side of the body as well as the humming bird's energetic nature and the strength of its will (Arce, 2016). This concept teaches students that to become disciplined human beings they must exert effort and will power so that they can create change in their lives, family, and communities.

Xipe Totek. The ultimate goal of the *Nahui Ollin* is the movement of transformation which is represented by the concept of *Xipe Totek*. This concept is a great resource as a tool for *carnalismo* pedagogy because it promotes the liberation of our students by presenting a model that is adaptable, fluid and transformative. Tupac Acosta explains, "*Xipe Totek*-transformation. Identified as our source of strength that allows us to transform and renew. We can achieve this transformation only when we have learned to have trust in ourselves" (as cited in Arce, 2016, p. 35). *Xipe Totek* synchronizes the three concepts of *Tezcatlipoca, Quetzalcoatl,* and *Huitzilopochtli* to create a scholarly *chantlaca or chancihuatl* (homeboy/homegirl) that is confident to take the risks necessary to create positive transformation in his/her life, family and world.

Having students reflect on these concepts each day emphasizes the importance of students taking ownership of the idea of scholarship in their academic lives. In fact, in 2010 at La Cosecha Dual Language Conference in Santa Fé, New Mexico, my MARSD students from Wakefield Middle School and I presented the concepts of the *Nahui Ollin* and its important role in our Chicano Studies classes. Reflecting on the *Nahui Ollin* concepts sends the message that in a Chicano Studies class, discipline means hard work and dedication to a task—not punishment. Through this philosophy students are taught to become disciplined human beings by engaging in a process that leads to transformation and liberation. This process teaches that if a human being is able to reflect on their past, acquire a sense of collective history and awareness of contemporary issues with others in his or her community, and finally, exert will power and effort into becoming a disciplined human being, then they will create positive change in their lives, community, and world.

Since then, I have continued to use it as a way to get my students to understand the responsibility behind the spirit of *carnalismo*. They are liberating and decolonizing pedagogies that are based on a Xican@/Indigenous epistemology that stresses the importance of students taking ownership of their lives. Through this philosophy students are taught to become disciplined human beings by engaging in a process that leads to transformation.

Having students say the words of the *In Lak 'ech* and the Four *Tezcatlipocas* aloud each day before the start of class re-establishes the spirit of *carnalismo*. It creates an academic safe space in which students are taught that they are part of a collective group of students and educators that will support them as they navigate their way through their education. Including a Chicano clap (also known as a unity clap)[2] is like the "cherry on top" to this daily routine, physically symbolizing a unifying effort to energize the students and teachers in the class so that everyone is awake and ready to engage at a high level in the day's activities. Although the *In Lak 'ech* and *Tezcatlipocas* is a good foundation, *carnalismo* pedagogy has to go beyond classroom routines and procedures. In order to incorporate a *carnalismo* pedagogy, a teacher (or in Caló, a *profe*) must serve as the "big homie" in the classroom. This role comes with great responsibility because it means that the teacher must show his or her willingness to model the type of risks that they will expect their students to make during their course of study. There are many ways to do this, but one way is for the teacher to model some sort of creative thought and expression that the students will also engage in. For example, my students start by writing and sharing a poem that expresses their backgrounds and personalities as well as their hopes and dreams for their future. Teachers need to show their students that they themselves have hopes and dreams as well as people that they represent and love. Every year, our first assignment is to write an "I Am" poem that each student presents to the class. As the "big homie," I am always the first to present three poems that express my identity at different stages in my life, with the hope of inspiring my students to write their own poem and express themselves in their own way. The following is an excerpt from one of these poems, "Yo Soy Xicano":

> Un hijo de los Mexicanos
> My people are proud and noble,
> they have survived 500 years of injustice, violence and heartache
> Yo soy Xicano
> Although many say that I do not exist, I do!!!
> I exist in the hearts, spirits and minds of LA RAZA
> In all the barrios, ranchos, and campos
> Of those who have been ashamed of who they are
> but now rise with pride to realize the great legacy
> WE have inherited.
> Yo Soy Xicano.

This poem expresses a militancy I felt especially strongly about as a young teacher who was fresh out of college and the experiences I had as a Xicano student activist at the University of Arizona's chapter of MEChA. However, as I continued to grow as a teacher, I decided that I should incorporate a poem that expressed the sentiments I had as a 14-year-old Xicano youth. After searching through boxes that contained some of my writings as a youth, I found a composition notebook from my freshmen year in high school that had poems representing this stage in my life. The one that stood out was a rap inspired by Chicano rap artists like Lighter Shade of Brown and Kid Frost, as well as Black rappers like NWA (Eazy-E, Ice Cube and Dr. Dre) and Tupac Shakur that I would later type up and revise for my class, which I called "Salo's Rap":

> Salo's here with some funky rhymes
> and as you know I'm having a good time
> I'm a Chicano and I have lots of power
> and girls I get smell like flowers
> rosas, I like cholas and the rolas I kick are bigger than life
> I'm puro Azteca and when cinco de mayo comes around
> I feel fresca and eat menudo at my mesa
> so if you ever step you better respect
> cuz I'm down and brown and rep all over town.

Although I removed some explicit language from the version I present to my students, anyone that listened to hip hop in the early 1990s (especially Chicano rap) can relate to the banal flow in this poem. Performing this *rola* (song) for my students, however, always goes a long way in establishing *carnalismo* because they get a picture of me—their teacher—when I was about their age. It also gives me a chance to tell them how, when I originally wrote the poem, I envisioned myself as part of an epic rap group like NWA or Lighter Shade of Brown, a vision that resonates with their own desires. They never fail to remind me, however, that it is a good thing I found a profession in education because I would not make it in the rap game.

Finally, I share a poem that expresses my current identity as a father, told through the perspective of my first daughter, Victoria Renae Escamilla, when she was a newborn. The poem reflects the feelings I had as a new father, my hopes and dreams that she would grow to be an empowered Chicana of the twenty-first century as well as my desire to protect and provide for her. The tone of the poem also reflects an attitude common in rap and hip-hop music that is not intended to be insulting but rather express a stylistic element.

> My name is Victoria and I am very pretty
> I come from a place called the Tucson City
> People say I'm cool, people say I'm bad
> well that is because I have a great mom and dad
> I like to chill I love to kick back
> but if you mess with me I'm going to attack
> and smack any fool that gets in my way
> if you are smart you never will betray
> this cute little girl that likes the Oakland Raiders
> All the other teams are nothing but haters
> take my advice and always be nice
> to me and my family or you will pay the price
> cuz you know that I'm a down Chicanita with a real firme flow
> now that you know what I'm all about
> I hope that I never have to knock you out.

The poems, as well as other community building activities where teachers and students engage in various forms of self-expression create a sense of *familia* by allowing everyone involved to get to know one another at a deeper level. Activities, like the one I described, are necessary if a teacher wishes to create an atmosphere of *carnalismo* because only through dialog and self-expression can students and teachers really learn from one another. By sharing our history, culture, *familia*, experiences, and even opinions on controversial issues we give our students a chance to make connections with us as human beings. When students are able to make connections with their teacher, they start to see us as an extension of their *familia* and are more open to following instructions and participating in academic activities in the classroom. Furthermore, it shows students that as teachers we are human beings like them who have hopes, dreams, and struggles in life. If I am willing to put myself out there and express aspects of my identity that are very personal (and can even be embarrassing at times), students know that it is okay for them to do the same. It is important to take the time to build a sense of community and create connections between teachers and students by encouraging and inspiring self-expression and identity development.

These types of self-expression activities can help to foster *carnalismo* in the classroom, and I am certain that it was a major reason for the success that we had in the MARSD in eliminating achievement disparities. *Carnalismo*, however, is essentially about having respect for our students as human beings in ways that go beyond the walls of the classroom or the contents of the textbook. Ultimately, it is simply the recognition of obstacles that our students face and the challenges they overcome every day. Additionally, it is a rejection of the punitive measures often used by teachers and schools to control student behavior and push Xican@ and other minoritized youth out of school. Above all else, it is the cultivation of the assets that Xican@ youth and their families bring to the school and classroom that are often unaddressed by a majority of U.S. schools.

Implementing a Curriculum Based on Chicanismo

Just as important as pedagogy that establishes *carnalismo*, teachers must present a curriculum that is culturally relevant to Mexican American and other students of color. It is especially important for school districts like TUSD, where Mexican American students are almost 65% (over 30,000) of the student population, to implement *Chicanismo* in the curriculum. Xican@ students need to know about their ancestors and the contributions they made to American history. Research supports the fact that when Mexican American and other minoritized students are conscious of their history and culture, they have more academic success. Establishing a curriculum based on *Chicanismo* will empower Mexican American students to take ownership of their education and give them the confidence to survive in an academic setting. The problem is that very few educators know what *Chicanismo* is or how to implement it in the schools they work.

Chicanismo is a term that was coined during the Chicano Youth Liberation Conference in Denver, Colorado, that was organized by Rodolfo "Corky" Gonzales and the Crusade for Justice on March 23, 1969. It was a national gathering of about 1,500 Chicano activists, most of whom were youth, who were discussing and debating plans to create a national Chicano movement. During the conference, activists unified themselves under the banner of *Chicanismo*, which was a philosophy of cultural nationalism based on the term *Chicano*. At the heart of *Chicanismo* was *El Plan Espiritual de Aztlan,* a poem written by Alurista that became the preamble for a 13-part plan for achieving liberation and self-determination in the Xican@ community. This plan became the founding document for MEChA, a national student organization, with chapters in universities, colleges, and high schools across the country. *Chicanismo* has evolved into Xicanismo and even Xicanisma and other variations, but however it is spelled, it is based on the idea that to be Xican@ means to be proud of your Mexican Indigenous roots and committed to the struggle for the liberation of all oppressed people. The following excerpt best captures the spirit of *Chicanismo* expressed in this plan.

> In the spirit of a new people that is conscious not only of its proud historical heritage but also the brutal "gringo" invasion of our territories, we, the Chicano inhabitants and civilizers of the northern land of Aztlan from whence came our forefathers, reclaiming the land of their birth and consecrating the determination of our people of the sun, declare that the call of our blood is our power, our responsibility and our inevitable destiny.
>
> *(Alurista, 1969)*

Ethnic studies opponents claim that the sentiments expressed in historical Xicano documents like this are subversive or divisive, but the spirit of *Chicanismo* is a very positive idea, which has enriched not only the Mexican American community, but also our overall society. Antagonists claim that ethnic studies programs and classes promote hate and racial superiority, but in reality, they are the antithesis of this. In fact, they serve students of *all ethnicities* and are on a mission to eliminate the achievement gap by helping minoritized youth graduate from high school and matriculate into college. At the same time, there is a spirit of resistance, defiance, and rebellion embedded in the concept of *Chicanismo*, which is why it has the habit of creating political adversaries like in the case of MARSD in TUSD. Dr. Roberto "Cintli" Rodriguez explains what was at the heart of the term *Chicano* in his piece, *The X in La Raza*:

> Chicano ... Resistance ... Defiance. It was more than understanding our bloodlines ... it was more than understanding our history ... the savagery of Spanish and Yanqui imperialism ... Chicano was to rebel. To be Chicano was to take a stand ... NO COMPROMISE–NO ACCOMMODATION. To be Chicano was to say "WE ARE NOT THE FOREIGNERS!"
>
> *(Rodriguez, 1996)*

Stated another way, adopting the term *Chicano* rejects conformity to the system or dominant culture (e.g., Hispanic). When we use the term Xicano, which emphasizes an Indigenous identity, we are saying that we belong in this territory because it is our ancestral land. We are saying that we are part of a movement of people struggling for the liberation of oppressed peoples. Inside the classroom, it promotes critical thinking and analysis of history and literature; outside of the classroom, it encourages activism and participation in the political system. This is why MARSD teachers were not surprised when the attack to dismantle MARSD in TUSD occurred. An examination of history shows that programs that challenge White supremacy are often the target of negative attention and are presented with misconstrued information on the part of conservative politicians.

In fact, the argument that *Chicanismo* is anti-White is ridiculous because it is a concept that transcends race. Xican@s are a racially diverse group of people that can trace ancestral lineage to all the races of the world, so racial superiority is irrelevant to this cultural identity. There is another aspect to *Chicanismo*, which is based on the development of an identity that unfolds in and between multiple worlds (i.e., Mexico and the United States, Spanish and English, Spanish and Nahuatl, the country and the city, etc.). Within these multiple worlds, the Xican@ is not only able to exist but thrive because we are able to easily adapt to different cultural settings and people. Tucson writer, Mario Suarez, referred to Xican@s who lived in Barrio El Hoyo (the historic neighborhood that was demolished to build the Tucson Convention Center) as a *capirotada* (a Mexican desert that incorporates many different types of ingredients).

> Perhaps El Hoyo, its inhabitants, and its essence can best be explained by telling you about a dish called *capirotada*. Its origin is uncertain. But it is made of old, new, stale, and hard bread. It is sprinkled with water and then it is cooked with raisins, olives, onions, tomatoes, peanuts, cheese, and general leftovers, that of which are good and bad. It is seasoned with salt, sugar, pepper, and sometimes chili or tomato sauce. It is fired with tequila or sherry wine. It is served hot, cold or just "on the weather" as they say in El Hoyo. The Garcias like it one way, the Quevedos another, the Trilos another, and the Ortegas still another. While in general appearance it does not differ much from one home to another, it tastes different everywhere. Nevertheless, it is still *capirotada*. And so it is with El Hoyo's *Chicanos*. While many seem to the undiscerning eye to be alike, it is only because collectively they are referred to as *Chicanos*. But like *capirotada*, fixed in a thousand ways and served on a thousand tables, which can only be evaluated by individual taste, the *Chicanos* must be so distinguished.
>
> *(Suarez, 1992)*

It can be argued that this is true of the Xicano people or La Raza in general because of the vast array of cultural, social, and political differences that we have depending on the region we live in or the way in which we were raised. So, to truly embrace the concept of *Chicanismo* means to be able to adapt to and thrive in different worlds. In this sense, *Chicanismo* is about being able to speak in Spanish with one group of people, English with another, and even *Caló* (the Chicano dialect) with yet another. It means enjoying and appreciating hip hop and rock one moment and *norteñas, rancheras*, and *cumbias* another, while at the same time being able to understand the deeper meanings in each type of music. It is the cultural competency to survive in a *pueblito* (little town) in Zacatecas, a farm town in Colorado, a huge metropolis like Mexico City, Los Angeles, or Chicago, or even overseas in Ireland, Italy, Japan, or China. To be Xican@ means to be willing and able to adjust to the social and cultural traditions, customs, and languages that exist in any setting. In the following excerpt of the song "Pocho," Ramón "Chunky" Sanchez breaks down the spirit of Chicanismo in which he describes the term *pocho*, which was a term used in Mexico to describe Mexican Americans.

> Pocho, a name I was called as a kid with the intention of degrading and humiliating me … it promoted self hatred and confusion of who I was and what I was doing here. Pocho I wasn't like here I wasn't like there … I knew I was Mexican, I look Mexican but why did I have trouble speaking Spanish … my name was Ramón when I started kindergarten but by the third grade everyone called me Raymond … all the confusion produced a curiosity in me. I began to question the implications of the word pocho … I began to realize that I had absorbed the strengths of two cultures and lifestyles. Is that good or bad? Good que no? I have an innovative way of expressing myself that relates to both sides of the border … What will it be today? Tacos or hamburgers? Pedro Infante or the Rolling Stones? Tequila or whiskey? … Pocho, I'm beginning to think that there's a pride in the word, a pride that was incarcerated by shame and stereotypes … You know what? I'm a proud Pocho, proud because I have survived cultural denials and attacks on my soul …
>
> *(Sanchez, 2014)*

This is why it is so important that educators push forth curriculum based on *Chicanismo*: because Xican@ students in the United States need to know that their identity, culture, and experiences are an asset to their education and life. In the classroom, this simply means using materials that highlight the Mexican American experience in U.S. History and literature. *Chicanismo* in the classroom means flipping the narrative by focusing on historical episodes in which Mexican Americans had an impact on the fight for social justice in the U.S. Dynamic events in history like the Mexican Revolution, the Treaty of Guadalupe Hidalgo, The Repatriation Act, The Mexican American Generation, The Sailor Riots (aka the Zoot Suit Riots), The Chicano Movement, the Xicano/a Indigenous movement and many others that document the impact that Mexican people had on U.S. history and society. It also means introducing students to great literary works by Xicano and Xicana authors like *I Am Joaquin* by Rodolofo "Corky" Gonzales, *Occupied America* by Rodolfo Acuña, *Borderlands* by Gloria Anzaldua, *Always Running* by Luis Rodriguez, *House on Mango Street* by Sandra Cisneros, *Bless Me Ultima* by Rudolfo Anaya, *The Devil's Highway* by Luis Alberto Urea and countless others. To implement *Chicanismo* at the highest level, though, a teacher has to go beyond the contents of the book and walls of the classroom by sponsoring and supporting student activities and organizations like MEChA (at the elementary, middle, and high school level) that promote civic engagement and activism in the community.

Carnalismo and Chicanismo Must Begin with the Teacher

All things considered, to fully implement the spirit of *Chicanismo* and *carnalismo* in the classroom, schools must start by recruiting and retaining teachers that exhibit these cultural assets. That is, school districts must recruit teachers that have a knowledge and appreciation of Mexican culture and history and the impact it has had on U.S. society. This must be followed by building a critical mass of teachers who are not only conscious of the historical oppression that Mexican people have overcome in the U.S., but also committed to systematically transforming the pedagogy, curriculum, and instruction of their school and district. There are two things that schools and districts must do if they aim to eliminate the achievement gap like educators in the MARSD were able to accomplish. First, schools need to utilize materials that reflect Mexican and Mexican American history and culture with an emphasis on social justice. Second, teachers need to incorporate classroom procedures and activities that create a classroom environment that is an extension of the students' *familia* based on mutual love and respect for one another.

If we as educators ever expect to eliminate the achievement gap like the MARSD, then schools and districts must organize groups of critically conscious teachers who are given the authority to make direct and systematic changes to the overall pedagogy and curriculum. The size and scope of these groups can vary, but there must be a focus on creating academic safe spaces for Xicano/Raza students based on curriculum that is culturally relevant and pedagogy that is culturally responsive. TUSD's MARSD students proved that the achievement gap can be eliminated when students are taught to embrace their culture and history and utilize it as an asset in their lives. They graduated from high school and matriculated into college at higher rates because of an asset-based pedagogy and curriculum that were centered on the empowering concepts of *Chicanismo* and *carnalismo*. These concepts have historical roots that continue to be relevant in *barrios* across *Aztlan* and they must be tapped into if we ever expect Xican@ youth to have academic achievement. These concepts represent undying values that are organic to the Xicano community and, regardless of any legislation created by the state of Arizona or any other legislative body, they continue to live on. They can eliminate programs like MARSD, but they will never eliminate the spirit of *Chicanismo* and *carnalismo* because these concepts belong to *el pueblo* (the people) and will never die. I will conclude with a memory of *el 16 de Septiembre* during my Senior year in high school when I joined about 2,000 Xican@ youth in a walkout of Denver Public Schools, demanding the implementation of Chicano Studies. The words of Corky Gonzales (the father of *Chicanismo*) from the steps of the capital building that day expressed a spirit of endurance that continues to live on in our community, "People say the Chicano movement is dead but as long as long as there is one Chicano, one Chicana, one viejito and one viejita we will be alive" (Escamilla, 1994).

Notes

1 By Rodolfo Gonzalez, published in 1967 https://www.goodreads.com/book/show/2817254-i-am-joaquin.
2 Clapping begins slowly and disharmoniously, and crescendos into a unified, harmonious, collective clap.

References

Alurista. (1997). El Plan Espiritual de Aztlan. In R. A. Anaya, F. A. Lomelí, & E. R. Lamadrid (Eds.), *Aztlán: Essays on the Chicano Homeland* (pp. 27–30). Albuquerque, NM: University of New Mexico Press.

Arce, M. S. (2016). Xicana/o epistimologies: Towards a decolonizing and liberatory education for Xicana/o youth. In D. M. Sandoval, A. J. Ratcliff, T. L. Buenavista, & J. R. Marín (Eds.), *'White' washing American education [2 volumes]: The new culture wars in ethnic studies* (pp. 12–40). Santa Barbara: ABC–CLIO, LLC.

Escamilla, A. (1994, September 23). 1500 Protest against unequal education in DPS; Centaurus Latinos join walkout. *The odyssey* [Lafayette, CO.] p. 1.

Escamilla, A. (2011, November). *The Xicano raiders de Aztlan: Transforming the barrio through basketball*. MARSD teacher and student workshop presented at La Cosecha Dual Language Conference. Santa Fé, New Mexico.

Gonzales, R. (2001). I am Joaquin. In A. Esquibel (Ed.), *Message to Aztlán: Selected writings of Rodolfo "Corky" Gonzales* (pp. 16–29). Houston, TX: Arte Público Press.

Rodríguez, R. (1996). *The X in la Raza: An anti-book*. Albuquerque, NM: Imprint by Roberto Rodriguez.

Sanchez, R. (2017, January–July). *Pocho*. Perf. Los Alacranes Mojados. *YouTube*. N.p. Retrieved from https://www.youtube.com/watch?v=7ls9zSWPWIM

Suarez, M. (1992). El Hoyo. In E. Simmen (Ed.), *North of the Rio Grande: The Mexican-American experience in short fiction* (pp. 94–96). New York: Penguin Press.

Valdez, L. (1971). *Early works–Luis Valdez*. Houston, TX: Arte Público Press.

INDEX